The Evolution of Multinationals from Japan and the Asia Pacific

The rise of the Japanese multinational company (JMNC) marked, from the 1980s onwards, an historic change in the structure and in the dynamics of the international economy. For the first time, businesses from a non-Western nation established a competitive global presence, and they did so by bringing their advanced products and management systems to the developed economies of Europe and North America. In the last 30 years, our interpretations of JMNCs have undergone a series of revisions. Korean firms followed JMNCs by investing in foreign markets in the 1990s and the Chinese likewise in the 2000s. A seeming decline in JMNC competitiveness and developments in the structure of the international economy challenged a business model of parental company direction, control and capabilities. Both trends asked questions about how Japanese subsidiaries should operate in global production chains increasingly reliant on contracting out and off-shoring, and how JMNCs might engage more in strategic cooperation and empower subsidiary decision-making. The contributors to this volume consider a wide range of relevant issues: they demonstrate the long-term evolution of JMNCs; they compare the experience of JMNCs with firms from the other two major Asia Pacific economies, Korea and China; they evaluate the applicability of established foreign direct investment (FDI) theory to MNCs from Japan and the Asia Pacific; and they reflect on the internal organization of JMNCs at the global, national and subnational level.

This book was originally published as a special issue of *Asia Pacific Business Review*.

Robert Fitzgerald is located at Royal Holloway, University of London, UK. He specializes in business history, Asia Pacific business, and multinational enterprise, and he has recently published *The Rise of the Global Company: Multinationals and the Making of the Modern World* (Cambridge University Press, 2015).

Chris Rowley is a Visiting Fellow, Kellogg College, Oxford University, UK, Adjunct Professor, Griffith Business School and Griffith Asia Institute, Griffith University, Australia, Visiting Fellow, Institute of Asia and Pacific Studies, Nottingham University, UK, and Professor Emeritus, Cass Business School, City University of London, UK. He is the editor of the *Journal of Chinese HRM* and the book series *Working in Asia, Asian Studies*, and *Asian Business and Management*. He has published widely in the area of human resource management and Asian business and management, with over 500 journal articles, books and chapters and other contributions in practitioner journals, magazines and newsletters, and is also frequently interviewed and quoted in the media globally.

The Evolution of Multinationals from Japan and the Asia Pacific

Comparing International Business Japan, Korean, China, India

Edited by
Robert Fitzgerald and Chris Rowley

LONDON AND NEW YORK

First published 2017 by Routledge

2 Park Square, Milton Park, Abingdon, Oxfordshire OX14 4RN
52 Vanderbilt Avenue, New York, NY 10017

Routledge is an imprint of the Taylor & Francis Group, an informa business

First issued in paperback 2018

Chapters 2–5 © 2017 Taylor & Francis
Chapters 1 & 6 © 2017 Fitzgerald and Rowley

All rights reserved. No part of this book may be reprinted or reproduced or utilised in any form or by any electronic, mechanical, or other means, now known or hereafter invented, including photocopying and recording, or in any information storage or retrieval system, without permission in writing from the publishers.

Notice:
Product or corporate names may be trademarks or registered trademarks, and are used only for identification and explanation without intent to infringe.

British Library Cataloguing in Publication Data
A catalogue record for this book is available from the British Library

ISBN 13: 978-1-138-28986-4 (hbk)
ISBN 13: 978-0-367-13951-3 (pbk)

Typeset in Myriad Pro
by RefineCatch Limited, Bungay, Suffolk

Publisher's Note
The publisher accepts responsibility for any inconsistencies that may have arisen during the conversion of this book from journal articles to book chapters, namely the possible inclusion of journal terminology.

Disclaimer
Every effort has been made to contact copyright holders for their permission to reprint material in this book. The publishers would be grateful to hear from any copyright holder who is not here acknowledged and will undertake to rectify any errors or omissions in future editions of this book.

Contents

Citation Information	vii
Notes on Contributors	ix
Acknowledgement	xi

1. Internationalization patterns and the evolution of multinational companies: comparing Japan, Korea, China and India
   Robert Fitzgerald and Chris Rowley — 1

2. Whose fall and whose rise? Lessons of Japanese MNCs for Chinese and emerging economy MNCs
   Robert Fitzgerald and Huaichuan Rui — 12

3. Is there an East Asian model of MNC internationalization? A comparative analysis of Japanese and Korean firms
   Martin Hemmert and Keith Jackson — 45

4. An empirical investigation into the internationalization patterns of Japanese firms
   Pearlean Chadha and Jenny Berrill — 73

5. Japanese production networks in India: spatial distribution, agglomeration and industry effects
   Sierk A. Horn and Adam R. Cross — 90

6. MNCs from the Asia Pacific in the global economy: examples and lessons from Japan, Korea, China and India
   Robert Fitzgerald and Chris Rowley — 119

Index — 125

Citation Information

The chapters in this book were originally published in the *Asia Pacific Business Review*, volume 22, issue 4 (October 2016). When citing this material, please use the original page numbering for each article, as follows:

Chapter 1
Internationalization patterns and the evolution of multinational companies: comparing Japan, Korea, China and India
Robert Fitzgerald and Chris Rowley
Asia Pacific Business Review, volume 22, issue 4 (October 2016), pp. 523–533

Chapter 2
Whose fall and whose rise? Lessons of Japanese MNCs for Chinese and emerging economy MNCs
Robert Fitzgerald and Huaichuan Rui
Asia Pacific Business Review, volume 22, issue 4 (October 2016), pp. 534–566

Chapter 3
Is there an East Asian model of MNC internationalization? A comparative analysis of Japanese and Korean firms
Martin Hemmert and Keith Jackson
Asia Pacific Business Review, volume 22, issue 4 (October 2016), pp. 567–594

Chapter 4
An empirical investigation into the internationalization patterns of Japanese firms
Pearlean Chadha and Jenny Berrill
Asia Pacific Business Review, volume 22, issue 4 (October 2016), pp. 595–611

Chapter 5
Japanese production networks in India: spatial distribution, agglomeration and industry effects
Sierk A. Horn and Adam R. Cross
Asia Pacific Business Review, volume 22, issue 4 (October 2016), pp. 612–640

Chapter 6
MNCs from the Asia Pacific in the global economy: examples and lessons from Japan, Korea, China and India
Robert Fitzgerald and Chris Rowley
Asia Pacific Business Review, volume 22, issue 4 (October 2016), pp. 641–646

For any permission-related enquiries please visit:
http://www.tandfonline.com/page/help/permissions

Notes on Contributors

Jenny Berrill is Assistant Lecturer at Trinity College Dublin. Her research interests are in the area of multinational companies and their role in the international diversification of portfolios.

Pearlean Chadha is a PhD researcher at Trinity College Dublin. Her research interests concern multinational companies and indirect international portfolio diversification.

Adam R. Cross is Professor of International Business and Associate Dean for Learning and Teaching at the International Business School Suzhou (IBSS), Xi'an Jiaotong-Liverpool University (XJTLU). He has co-edited three books, and has contributed to more than 35 book chapters, and scholarly papers.

Robert Fitzgerald is located at Royal Holloway, University of London, UK. His research interests include business history, comparative business, and MNCs from Japan and the Asia Pacific. He has recently published *The Rise of the Global Company: Multinationals and the Making of the Modern World* (Cambridge University Press, 2015).

Martin Hemmert is Professor of International Business at Korea University. His current research interests focus on technology collaborations and comparative studies of management systems, innovation systems, and entrepreneurship in East Asia.

Sierk A. Horn is Professor of the Economy of Japan, Ludwig Maximilian University. He has published widely in the fields of East Asian business and international management, and, more specifically, focuses on the interplay of language, psychology, and business practices.

Keith Jackson is a tutor and researcher at SOAS, University of London, and Professor of Sustainable Human Resource Management, Doshisha University. He is also book reviews editor for *Asia Pacific Business Review*.

Chris Rowley is a Visiting Fellow, Kellogg College, Oxford University, UK, Adjunct Professor, Griffith Business School and Griffith Asia Institute, Griffith University, Australia, Visiting Fellow, Institute of Asia and Pacific Studies, Nottingham University, UK, and Professor Emeritus, Cass Business School, City University of London, UK. He is the editor of the *Journal of Chinese HRM* and the book series *Working in Asia, Asian Studies*, and *Asian Business and Management*. He has published widely in the area of human resource management and Asian business and management, with over 500 journal articles, books and chapters and other contributions in practitioner journals, magazines and newsletters, and is also frequently interviewed and quoted in the media globally.

Huaichuan Rui is Senior Lecturer in International and Comparative Business, Royal Holloway, University of London, and Director of the China-Africa Research Project, Centre of Development Studies, University of Cambridge. Her research interests include the strategy and impact of Chinese MNCs, especially in Africa.

Acknowledgement

Professor Rowley gratefully acknowledges the kind support of the Korea Foundation in his research.

Internationalization patterns and the evolution of multinational companies: comparing Japan, Korea, China and India

Robert Fitzgerald[a] and Chris Rowley[b,c,d,e]

[a]Royal Holloway, University of London, London, UK; [b]Cass Business School, City University, London, UK; [c]IHCR, Korea University, Seoul, Korea; [d]Institute of Asia and Pacific Studies, Nottingham University, Nottingham, UK; [e]Griffith Business School, Griffith University, Nathan, Australia

ABSTRACT
We consider past and present trends in the internationalization patterns of Japanese multinational companies (JMNCs) and compare them against the experience of Korean and Chinese MNCs. The analysis assesses the relevance of recent changes in the nature of the global economy and multinational business organization, and reviews insights from established theories of international business. We call for a reassessment of the assumed decline of Japanese multinationals and fuller consideration of areas of continuing strength.

Introduction

The rise of the Japanese multinational (JMNC), marked, from the 1980s onwards, an historic change in the structure and in the dynamics of the international economy. For the first time, businesses from a non-Western nation established a competitive global presence, and they did so by bringing their advanced products and management systems to the developed economies of Europe and North America (Fitzgerald 2015). In the last 30 years, moreover, our interpretations of JMNCs have undergone a series of revisions. Korean firms followed JMNCs in the 1990s (Jun and Rowley 2014; Rowley and Bae 1998; Rowley and Paik 2009; and Rowley, Sohn, and Bae 2002) and the Chinese likewise in the 2000s. A seeming decline in JMNC competitiveness and developments in the structure of the international economy challenged a business model of parental company direction, control and capabilities. Both trends asked questions about how Japanese subsidiaries should operate in global production chains increasingly reliant on contracting out and off-shoring, and how JMNCs might engage more in strategic cooperation and empower subsidiary decision-making.

The high preponderance of Asia Pacific firms in the lists of leading emerging economy MNCs, at first sight, hinted at region-wide factors or similarities in patterns of internationalization. The contributors to this volume, as a result, consider a wide range of relevant issues: they demonstrate the long-term evolution of JMNCs; they compare the experience of JMNCs with firms from the other two major Asia Pacific economies, Korea and China; they evaluate the applicability of established foreign direct investment (FDI) theory to MNCs from Japan and the Asia Pacific; and they reflect on the internal organization of JMNCs at the global, national and subnational level.

The international economy and MNC strategy

During the 1980s, and more spectacularly from the 1990s, FDI and trade accelerated rapidly, and ever-larger businesses enhanced their control over the cross-border movement of commodities and manufactures. While the shortest survey of international business would soon dismiss the idea that 'globalization' was historically unprecedented, have there been trends amongst MNCs, their strategies and organization that have particularly distinguished the period since the end of the twentieth century? There were greater examples of MNCs acting more regionally and even globally in their commercial interests, in the sense of becoming less dependent on the revenues of their home nation market. FDI began to move towards the fast growing emerging economies, away from the very richest nations that had so markedly attracted inward investment during the post-war decades. Developing and Transition Economies (DTEs) were hosts to some half of inward FDI flows by 2009, although the bulk gravitated to the most successful countries among them. The developed world's share of inward FDI stock, therefore, fell from about 75 to 65% between 1990 and 2010. The lowering of government restrictions encouraged FDI and, especially, rapid increases in international mergers and acquisitions (M&A). Investors looked to the many opportunities provided by privatizations, in the West, but in the Soviet Union and its East European satellites too, when these former Communist nations had for so long been closed to the international economy. China, likewise, opened its borders, and became for a period the primary magnet for inward FDI. In other words, both the geographical dimensions and the economic scale of the international economy changed. Of great historical significance was the transformation of businesses from emerging economies into the global lists of notable MNCs. International services grew markedly in relation to manufacturing, in a reversal of post-war trends. Multinational subsidiaries became more operationally integrated, and global value chains and vertically divided cross-border production systems evolved in significance and complexity (Fitzgerald 2015).

By 1980, the value of FDI stock remained smaller in proportion to the world GDP than before the First World War. During 1984–1987, global outflows of FDI tripled and then grew by a further 20% in both the years that followed. Five major investing countries – Japan, the United States, Britain, Germany, and France – maintained their 70% share of FDI outflows, and the contribution of developed economies as a group increased to over 81%. Japan, by the end of the 1980s, was the much noticed new entrant, thanks to an appreciating Yen and protectionism in the United States and the European Union compelling its major manufacturers to adapt highly successful export strategies. The expansion of total FDI flows continued during 1992 to 2008, multiplying eightfold overall. Following three years of particularly robust performance, FDI flows peaked at a phenomenal 40% increase for the year 2000 and remained high during the decade that followed. Because of the new scale and advantages of FDI, from 1982 onwards, sales of foreign-owned MNC affiliates grew faster than world exports, and they were throughout the 2000s twice the dollar totals. By 2007, there were an estimated 79,000 MNCs, operating some 790,000 overseas subsidiaries, and employing 82 million people. Outward FDI stock in 1993, as a ratio of world output, finally overtook the pre-1914 level of 11.1 and reached 11.3. The surge in FDI during the 1990s propelled the world GDP ratio of FDI stock by 2000 to 18.7, and the even more dramatic developments of the 2000s would create by 2009 a figure of 34.5 (Fitzgerald 2015).

MNC affiliates – excluding therefore the major contribution of parent companies in their home economies – were responsible for a third of world exports by the 1990s. MNCs – parent and subsidiary alike – had by 2000 some two-thirds of merchandise and service exports, much of it in intra-trade. This intrafirm trade – cross-border activities organized by MNC management between directly owned plants and offices – expanded in importance, from 20% of international commerce to about 40% by 2000. The upward trend in the sales, value added and exports of the foreign affiliates indicates how MNCs became more internationalized and less predominantly home country enterprises with added foreign subsidiaries.

Such impressive measures do not, moreover, include the complex international networks of contracted suppliers and associated businesses increasingly coordinated and determined by MNCs and requiring new strategies and forms of organization. The manufacturing MNCs that had been at the forefront of FDI in the post-war decades had revealed a preference for wholly-owned subsidiaries and frequently green field investments, and they had demonstrated concern for the direct control of their management and therefore the firm's proprietary knowledge. For the post-1980 period, across all sectors, strategies showed a greater inclination towards joint venture and strategic alliances. They reflected, depending on industries or location, the intention to share the costs of R and D, production or marketing; to exploit locational efficiencies and off-shoring in cross-border vertical production chains; or to meet the investment requirements of emerging economy governments, or to obviate the commercial or political risks of investment.

Another crucial trend in the entry-mode strategies of MNCs was the pursuit of international M and A. The lowering of investment barriers, plus a worldwide spate of privatizations, supplied the compelling mix of opportunity and incentive. M and A allowed MNCs to respond to intensifying international competition by enabling rapid and global expansion; it accelerated the international consolidation and restructuring of industries, as well as the capture of technology, cost or infrastructure advantages available in overseas locations. Contrary to strategies of market-seeking through nationally orientated subsidiaries, utilizing capabilities transferred from the parent company, it empowered patterns of asset-seeking and the purchase of capabilities in R and D, production or marketing.

The decline of manufacturing, as a share of all outward FDI assets, was characteristic of the period: the figure of 44% in 1990 fell to some 26% by 2005. Among manufacturing FDI, chemicals and chemical products maintained its role as the lead sector, but electricals and electronics fell back to fifth place, directly supplanted at number two by motor vehicles and transportation. The food, beverages and tobacco, and the metals and metal products sectors maintained their prominent position, as did, further down the rankings, machinery and equipment, and textiles, clothing and leather. As with services and natural resources, there was some shift in the location of manufacturing assets: the percentage found in developing economies increased from nearly 20 to over 24, between 1990 and 2005 (Fitzgerald 2015).

The 1980s was the decade of the JMNCs, when their surging investments in the United States and the European Community sought to defend overseas sales threatened by rising tariffs and stricter import quotas. Japan's outward FDI levels had formerly been low – mainly to secure raw materials or key components – and it took less favourable trade policies in major export markets to provoke a change in international business strategy and the conversion of leading Japanese companies into global multinationals. By 1988, Japan had overtaken the European Community nations and the United States as the largest contributor of outward FDI flows. Businesses such as Toyota, Sony and Panasonic transferred the management and production techniques, which had made them successful exporters, to their new foreign affiliates. This practice produced a stream of literature on Japanese management practices and the so-called 'Japanization' of various industries (Rowley 1996).

In order to enhance market access and to gain experience of the United States, Toyota did for a period found a joint enterprise with General Motors, and similar decisions can be found amongst Japanese firms. Yet the majority or full control of foreign-based subsidiaries became associated with the safeguarding of product and managerial knowledge and the effective transfer of capabilities from the parent company. Largely determined by newly imposed tariffs and import quotas, the strategies of JMNCs differed in important respects from the motivation of the US and European MNCs that had dominated international business. On the other hand, JMNCs were continuing the pattern of transferring ownership advantages to owned or controlled subsidiaries, as established by US MNCs in the post-war period.

The United Nations Conference on Trade and Development (UNCTAD) acknowledged how Japanese MNCs through their rapid 'multinationalization' encouraged the development of regional and global production networks. 'Fit within the global value chain' was a major strategic consideration, and transnational coordination, alongside internal firm-based capabilities such as R and D or production management, formed an increasingly important source of competitive advantage. Some 77% of the sales to Japan made by Japanese-owned plants in Asia were components for a parent company, in 1987, while the figure for sales to Japanese-owned plants in the US and the European Community were over 50% (Farrell 2008; Fitzgerald 2015; Fitzgerald and Rowley 2015).

As has been well attested, MNCs looked increasingly from the 1990s onwards to externalize, contract out or off-shore production, while exerting authority through the setting of technical, quality or delivery standards. They could focus on those parts of the global value chain that secured competitive advantage, value-added or control, most likely involving R and D, product definition, marketing, or branding. JMNCs had established subsidiaries in developed markets in fulfilment of a different approach and had done so with centralized management structures associated with a strong belief in ingrained practices. It was argued that JMNCs were slow to meet changing trends in the nature of international business. They faced growing competition from other producers, often from East Asia, which could exploit efficiency-seeking FDI in low-cost locations and employ asset-seeking strategies that could leap-frog their lack of ownership advantages. Japan's era of low growth became associated with the perceived fall in the competitiveness of JMNCs, and, indeed, leading sectors and companies had to address issues of restructuring and re-location.

As well as needing the faster growth to be found in overseas markets, JMNCs had to consider their management practices, and to foster strategic partners and collaborative arrangements covering R and D, production or marketing or cooperation in host markets. They required subsidiaries that could better customize products and services, employ indigenous decision-makers and cooperate with local producers and investors. Compared to major competitors, Japanese firms continued to internalize a greater number of production stages as well as core functions such as R and D (Farrell 2008; Fitzgerald 2015; Fitzgerald and Rowley 2015).

The contributors to this volume, accordingly, address a number of important questions about the patterns of internationalization followed by JMNCs. What changes in strategy, organization or core capabilities did JMNCs need to make since the late 1990s, and how successfully have they achieved transformation? To what extent has the internationalization of companies from other Asia Pacific nations differed from their Japanese predecessors, and does the record of JMNCs offer any important lessons for competitors? Has, lastly, the control and direction of overseas subsidiaries evolved to meet contemporary demands of managerial localization, global production chains or organizational learning?

Comparisons and patterns of internationalization

We now present a useful overview of the content of this collection. This surveys the main themes, methods, findings and implications and it will give readers a quick grasp of the totality of the pieces. What is quickly apparent are the useful Asian comparisons made, including Korea, China and India. This approach helps counter the narrowness of the dominant US ethnocentricity of too much ahistorical work in business and management studies (Rowley and Oh 2016a, 2016b) (Table 1).

Fitzgerald and Rui begin by considering the rapid rise of Chinese MNCs in the global economy, and ask to what extent their characteristics are unique or reflective of Asia Pacific enterprise more generally. They ask to what extent their expansion has mirrored the internationalization of Japanese enterprises, and, it follows, to what extent their earlier transformation can provide lessons for Chinese and other developing economies. Through a comparative literature review, they identify fundamental factors that influenced the decision-making, growth patterns and competitiveness of JMNCs and Chinese MNCs (CMNCs): they review three firm-specific considerations of strategy, core capabilities and organizational structures, and, in addition, the context of business–state relations. Fitzgerald and Rui apply an historical approach by comparing the evolution of international business since the 1980s, and by analyzing the changing dynamics and needs of strategy, capabilities, organization and government policy. They point out that there are few studies that directly compare FDI from Asian nations, and stress the importance of extending the analysis through case studies. The existing literature, looking separately at Japanese firms (JMNCs) and Chinese firms (CMNCs), seems to indicate that they share important features, such as state-sponsored support and a centralized corporate structure. There exists praise for JMNCs in having demonstrated strategic intent, core competence and unique management systems, but there is a shortage of studies and a range of assumptions about JMNC decline during Japan's low growth era. Others argue, in turn, that CMNCs are lacking in their core competencies and management systems. Fitzgerald and Rui employ a comparative case analysis to reveal that the realities are more nuanced or ill-defined than suggested by available studies and present a wide ranging survey of firms based on original evidence and interviews within a framework that identifies key influences.

On motivation and strategy, and as is well known, the raising of tariffs and import quotas determined the switch of Japanese firms from exporting to Europe and the United States towards FDI. In doing so, Japanese manufacturers revealed strategic intent or purpose in internationalizing rapidly and in developing subsidiaries at scale. These JMNCs leveraged

Table 1. Overview: Content, themes, methods, findings and implications.

	Content	Themes	Methods	Findings	Implications
1	Internationalization patterns and the evolution of MNCs: comparing Japan, Korea, China and India	Comparing phases and patterns of internationalization Re-assessing the JMNC specifically and Asia Pacific MNCs generally	Literature survey	Legacies of JMNCs affect approach to contemporary strategies Relevance of parallels and variations in internationalization patterns of MNCs from Asia Pacific	Need to re-consider declinist analysis of JMNC Assessment of interaction of macro and microeconomic factors influencing strategy, organization and competitiveness of Asia Pacific MNCs
2	Whose fall and whose rise?: Lessons of Japanese MNCs for Chinese and emerging economy MNCs	Comparison of JMNCs and CMNCs	Literature review Case studies Historical analysis	Identifying and examining key factors determining MNC strategies, capabilities and organization	Strategic need of MNCs to consider phases of internationalization Adapting or building core capabilities in different internationalization phases Importance of role of governments Balancing of long and short term strategic goals
3	Is there an East Asian model of MNC internationalization? A comparative analysis of Japanese and Korean firms	Comparison of Japanese and Korean MNCs in China Critical review of FDI theories	Literature review Case studies	Established FDI theories leave key questions about internationalization of Asia Pacific MNCs unanswered	Call for more grounded case study and comparative research into Asia Pacific MNCs Re-evaluation of internationalization by Asia Pacific MNCs should address regional, national and industry factors
4	An empirical investigation into the internationalization patterns of Japanese firms	Internationalization strategies and investments of JMNCs	Longitudinal data analysis	JMNCs increased levels of 'multination-ality' JMNC strategies continue to be global rather than regional	Re-evaluation of assumed failings of the JMNC, despite restructuring of specific sectors
5	Japanese production networks in India: spatial distribution, agglomeration and industry effects	Investigation of JMNC investment behaviour in India	Multivariate data analysis	JMNC investment in India determined by agglomeration patterns at the national and subnational level in interaction with economic, institutional and infrastructure factors	Prior investment and location decisions assist corporate learning and recruitment of trained personnel, and obviate risk Research required into industry versus national effects on investment decisions, and role of JMNC subsidiaries in global production networks
6	MNCs from the Asia Pacific in the global economy: examples and lessons from Japan, Korea, China and India	Evaluating available evidence and research questions on Japanese and Asia Pacific MNCs	Literature review	Assessment of new strategies or organizational forms by Asia Pacific MNCs FDI theories, comparisons of JMNCs with MNCs from China and Korea Lessons of JMNCs for emerging economy MNCs, and operations of subsidiaries in host economies and global production networks	Call for renewed research interest in the JMNC Importance of comparative and historical approaches Need to include and weight global, national, sub-national, industry, parent firm, and subsidiary level factors

their leadership in core capabilities such as technology, production and management through their transfer to host economies, frequently and preferably within wholly owned or controlled subsidiaries, and they revealed a capacity for long-term planning and organizational adaptation. By contrast, CMNCs were more short-termist in their internationalization goals. Despite the financial and administrative support of government, and close influential relationships, the management of JMNCs could decide on their strategic objectives, based on export success, firm-level capabilities, and availability of capital; for CMNCs, at least in the case of state-owned enterprises (SOEs), government policies swayed the decision to internationalize and choice of host markets. Many CMNCs did not possess globally superior technology and management practice, and only a small number followed long-term strategic goals; as a result, internationalization served as a means of acquiring strategic capabilities, leveraging home advantages in low-cost products and services, or targeting emerging economies where they could utilize a comparative advantage or their intuitive understanding of developing markets.

From the late 1990s, as Japan's competitiveness waned, many JMNCs appeared less certain about how to operationalize strategic intent in a global scenario of decentralized cross-border management, joint ventures, alliances, interfirm organizational learning and cross-border capability acquisition. In terms of core capabilities, JMNCs in the electronics sector encountered strong challenges from low-cost producers and struggled to retain leadership in products, brands and technology. In other sectors, such as automobiles, strong internal capabilities and management often fitted uneasily with the deepening of collaborative relationships and organizational learning processes in host economies, and top-down decision-making and centralization acted as brakes on the empowerment of subsidiary management. Lengthy planning horizons and parent firm control, previously advantageous, potentially inhibited organizational renewal and product innovation in established JMNCs.

CMNC competitiveness continues to rest on imitation capability, cost advantage, and a responsive supply chain, rather than on superior technology and best management practice. Frequently going abroad opportunistically, they remained organizational learners when transforming into MNCs, but, as noted, they had ownership advantages relevant to emerging economies. While proving their capacity for quick decision-making and local adaptation in foreign markets, there are only a few notable exceptions among CMNCs to the general lack of competitive capabilities, management and structures that might serve as a foundation for developing leading business systems and technologies in the next stage of their internationalization.

In terms of internal management, both JMNCs and CMNCs share a preference for centralized corporate structures, and localization rates have been relatively low compared with Western MNCs. The benefits for JMNCs, during the early period of Japanese competitive leadership, had lain in transferring home-grown capabilities to newly founded and highly controlled subsidiaries. Yet such practices embedded an approach not necessarily appropriate to a desired subsequent phase of internationalization. JMNCs became associated for a period with the use of expatriate managers, as a mechanism for facilitating capability transfer and control. CMNCs rely more heavily on expatriates than the Japanese historically speaking, and, in addition, firms in oil, mining and construction in developing economies transferred large numbers of labour. Centralization has enabled CMNCs to exploit home-based cost and supply advantages in the expansion of their host economy operations.

However, it may often be less useful in developed markets or restrictive of a competitively more advanced phase in the ownership of technologies and products.

Fitzgerald and Rui emphasize the contribution of firm-level factors, but they do not stand in isolation from external considerations, such as government policy. In addition to the role of the Japanese and then the Chinese state in the industrialization of their home economies, both influenced the outward internationalization of firms. Japan's government evolved into one of the world's most active subsidizers of FDI, and the nature of the financial support met changing policy objectives. The focus shifted from the acquisition of natural resources, vital components, and the relocating of labour intensive or cost sensitive industries; the aim, from the 1980s onwards, was to assist with the costs of building full-scale subsidiary operations in developed markets. In the new century, the encouragement of technology acquiring FDI, cross-border M and A, and international managerial and technological interchange took prominence, and the Japanese government policy in effect acknowledged the new challenges JMNCs were facing in the global marketplace.

Chinese managers in SOEs believed that they were obliged to join their government's 'go global' policy, and many CMNC overseas contracts were associated with Chinese state aid or loans to emerging host economies. On the other hand, government support was viewed as unsystematic and not sustained. Despite notable achievements in numerous host economies, CMNCs lacked strategic intent and long-term planning, as indicated by continued failure to address shortfalls in technology, products or management methods. The cases analysed by Fitzgerald and Rui reveal the important relationship between home and host government policies and stages of economic development, on the one hand, and varying approaches to strategy, the utilization and evolution of core capabilities, and internal organization, on the other. The earlier phase of internationalization by JMNCs provides lessons for CMNCs, while indicating points of difference. The historical and contemporary comparison indicates the dynamic characteristic of FDI operations, in particular the complex challenges MNCs encounter in establishing themselves overseas and in initiating a further phase in their global competitiveness, and the influence of internationalization pathways in facilitating redirection and restructuring.

Hemmert and Jackson emphasize how established theories explaining the strategies and organization of MNCs were predicated on research into Western MNCs. They argue that these approaches can only partially explain the internationalization of the JMNC and KMNC, which they illustrate and compare through a series of case studies. The 'International Product Life Cycle' suggests that the success of MNCs rests initially on product leadership that can be competitively exploited in foreign markets. With rising competition from imitators and falling profit margins, long-term success rests on further phases of innovation that can instigate another product life cycle. As well as prioritizing innovation over the firm as producer or marketer, the theory takes little account of the internal structures and procedures needed to generate product innovation, including recent trends in the internationalization of R and D within MNCs, and it does not consider how the cross-border vertical integration of production or contracting-out affect the uniqueness of a firm's product. FDI decisions, for example, can become disconnected from its innovation management.

The 'Eclectic Paradigm' of the OLI model states that three advantages in Ownership, Localization and Internalization must apply in order to justify foreign investment: an O-advantage in technology, product or management enables a MNC to succeed in a foreign market; an L-advantage such as tariffs, labour skills, or nearness to customers explains the preference for FDI over exporting; and an I-advantage such as knowledge retention or production integration provides reasons for subsidiary control over licensing or contracting-out. In reviewing FDI in China, Hemmert and Jackson doubt if an essentially static framework can explain the speed with which some companies developed commercial activities in China. They note, in part answer, the relevance of political and commercial links or joint ventures with state firms or local producers in controlling institutional and market environments, in leveraging available advantages, or in compensating for competitive weaknesses. The role of Japanese trading firms further highlights the porous nature of firm boundaries and the contribution of external networks in shaping decision-making and organization building. The 'Uppsala School' model, on the other hand, predicts that MNCs, notably during the early phases of their international expansion, will be concentrated in overseas markets that have geographical proximity or cultural and institutional similarity. Hemmert and Jackson note the difficulties of finding evidence from Asia Pacific MNCs that would substantiate the importance of cultural–institutional familiarity over other considerations. They stress the complexities and range of external and internal factors that shape MNC decision-making in investment, products, production and marketing.

Following their analysis of Japanese and Korean cases, the authors call for more grounded research into the Asia Pacific and its MNCs, in order to address questions about the boundaries of firms, their strategies and the sequencing and processes of investments and organization building. Hemmert and Jackson suggest that, while their study has shown similarity in the internationalization patterns of Japanese and Korean firms at an aggregated level, there have been important differences in the strategic behaviour of individual MNCs. As evidenced by their investments in China, Korean firms appear to be more risk taking and flexible in their approaches than the Japanese, and so, despite institutional-cultural similarities, current theoretical perspectives can hide microlevel differences. Their study seems to indicate difficulties in formulating models that might capture and predict the internationalization of East Asian MNCs generally.

Chadha and Berrill investigate the internationalization patterns of JMNCs, and demonstrate, in the era of low or falling economic growth in Japan, that they continued to 'multinationalize' and to establish themselves overseas. The authors conduct a longitudinal analysis of changing levels of 'multinationality' among firms listed on the Nikkei 225 between 1998 and 2013, categorized into 10 industries, and they argue that there is a dearth of such studies on the topic. They measure 'multinationality' through foreign sales percentage, location of sales and location of subsidiaries, and their inclusion of subsidiary data represents a significant expansion on previous analysis. Chadha and Berrill confirm that manufacturing and extractive firms have a greater multinational dimension than service firms, and they discover that the consumer goods, technology, and oil and gas sectors are the most international. Their data indicate that over four-fifths of the firms in their sample have subsidiaries of some type beyond the Asia Pacific region, and point to the continued 'multinationalization' of JMNCs after the peak of their FDI in the 1980s and 1990s. Their results for JMNCs broadly reflect patterns among US and UK MNCs. They counter, moreover, established ideas that only a few MNCs are truly global, and that the vast majority are essentially regional in their investments and sales. Chadha and Berrill argue that most firms listed on the Nikkei 225 from 1998 to 2013 had exposure to North America and Europe as well as Asia, and that the number with a presence in Africa, South America and Oceania increased. In 2013, Japan registered as the second largest contributor to outward FDI, with the United States taking first place, and information on FDI flows and subsidiary numbers shows a switch by JMNCs from Asia to Africa.

Horn and Cross continue the theme of looking at the internationalization patterns of JMNCs. They concentrate on Japanese FDI in India and ask how established subsidiaries can embed themselves more effectively in rapidly emerging economies in furtherance of their internationalization strategies. They consider the wide range of discussions germane to the evolution of JMNCs, including networks and business group membership, the relocation and reconfiguration of production networks across the Asia Pacific region, at a national level the determinants of location choice and cluster and agglomeration effects. Horn and Cross note bias in this literature to the study of developed host economies, the lack of research into location choice at a sub-national level and the exclusion of industry as opposed to national factors. They present, as a result, a study of agglomerative behaviour by JMNCs in India, an increasingly important and open locale for inward FDI. The substantial differences in economic development, institutions and infrastructure between the regions of India make them a useful means of considering the localization behaviour of JMNCs in emerging markets at a subnational level. Horn and Cross argue that geographic concentration and agglomeration effects constitute a prevalent characteristic of JMNC behaviour and that these tendencies are observable in determining subnational investment decisions in India. They begin by envisaging two trends. JMNCs may, in the first instance, evolve from their initial investments to greater engagement with the host economy business community and the building of localized production networks, as a key part of their international production base. They may, in the second instance, be inclined to move away from long-term geographic clustering at a subnational level and towards more flexible interfirm arrangements and off-shore networks based on cost considerations and the vertical fine-slicing of operations, as witnessed in recent patterns of global business.

Horn and Cross employ firm and state-level data to investigate the behaviour of JMNCs in India, and to draw conclusions about their strategic intent and localization levels. They identify, for JMNCs, six determinants of FDI location: market size, market growth, human capital, infrastructure, agglomeration and manufacturing density. Studies highlight the influence of agglomeration on the international strategies and operational location of JMNCs. The geographical clustering of economic activity may be the outcome of locales progressively facilitating the procurement of human resources or intermediate products, and agglomeration induces spillover effects through information-sharing and experience. Through their home economy traditions of vertically fragmented manufacturing, risk reduction, subcontracting, information sharing and business networks, JMNCs may be particularly responsive to agglomeration and geographical concentration. Horn and Cross indicate that Japanese FDI in India is at an early phase and asks questions about how their subsidiaries can develop. As well as following other Japanese investors, they anticipate a preference for regions with traditions of manufacturing, since JMNCs in India are largely found in transportation, electronics, machinery, chemicals and IT. The empirical analysis indicates the iterative interaction of several factors, namely the economic (levels of development, market access, labour quality), institutional (regional openness, economic zones) and infrastructure, and the prominence of agglomeration behaviour to date and for the future. India's position within Japanese global production networks is problematic, given cultural differences and geographic distance between India and Japan, and the high risks associated with the policy and regulatory environment.

Conclusion: Japanese multinationals past and present

The authors in the volume review influential concepts in the theory of multinational business and introduce a wide range of new data and case evidence. In doing so, they suggest questions about the legacies of JMNCs and their contemporary challenges in the global economy. As well as comparing past and present trends, the contributors compare the internationalization patterns of Japanese, Korean and Chinese MNCs, asking what lessons can be derived for each nation and for Asia Pacific business generally. They provide a useful opportunity to assess claims about the decline of the JMNC and to consider more precisely what constitutes the macro and microeconomic challenges they are encountering. Their research and analysis enables us, too, to evaluate and compare more fully areas of continuing strength in management, organization and core competencies.

Acknowledgement

The support of the Korea Foundation is noted.

References

Farrell, R. 2008. *Japanese Investment in the World Economy*. Cheltenham: Edward Elgar.
Fitzgerald, R. 2015. *The Rise of the Global Company*. Cambridge: Cambridge University Press.
Fitzgerald, R., and C. Rowley, eds. 2015. *Multinationals from Japan: Capabilities, Competitiveness, and Challenges*. London: Routledge.
Jun, W., and C. Rowley. 2014. "Change and Continuity in Management Systems and Corporate Performance: Human Resource Management, Corporate Culture, Risk Management and Corporate Strategy in South Korea." *Business History* 56 (3): 485–508.
Rowley, C. 1996. "Are We Turning Japanese?." *Asia Pacific Business Review* 3 (1): 73–80.
Rowley, C., and J. Bae, eds. 1998. *Korean Businesses: Internal and External Industrialization*. London: Frank Cass.
Rowley, C., and I. Oh. 2016a. "Business Ethics & the Role of Context: Instutionalism, History & Comparisons in the Asia Pacific Region." *Asia Pacific Business Review* 22 (3): 353–365.
Rowley, C., and I. Oh. 2016b. "Relinquishing Business Ethics from a Theoretical Deadlock: The Requirement for Local Grounding & Historical Comparisons in the Asia Pacific Region." *Asia Pacific Business Review* 22 (3): 516–521.
Rowley, C., and Y. Paik, eds. 2009. *The Changing Face of Korean Management*. London: Routledge.
Rowley, C., T.-W. Sohn, and J. Bae, eds. 2002. *Managing Korean Business: Organization, Culture Human Resources and Change*. London: Frank Cass.

Whose fall and whose rise? Lessons of Japanese MNCs for Chinese and emerging economy MNCs

Robert Fitzgerald and Huaichuan Rui

Royal Holloway, University of London

ABSTRACT

There are limited studies evaluating multinational corporations (MNCs) from different countries, and a comparison of the leading Asia Pacific economies, Japan and China, offers useful insights. This contribution considers in turn business strategies, firm-level capabilities, management organization and government policies in determining the patterns and impact of Japanese MNCs and Chinese MNCs in host economies. It reveals the relevance of phases of internationalization on strategic intent, the cross-border transfer of capabilities, and the costs and benefits of parental firm control vs. subsidiary autonomy.

Introduction

The recent interest of researchers in developing economy multinational corporations (MNCs) has been one of the drivers sustaining or revitalizing interest in International Business as a subject of enquiry. As well as being a developing nation, China is of course the world's second largest economy, as measured by exchange rate values, and its foreign direct investment (FDI) has grown noticeably since the early 2000s. We might ask to what extent the activities of its MNCs demonstrate unique characteristics, or, conversely, bear similarities with cross-border enterprise from developing economies more generally or from East Asia in particular. In this analysis, we make direct comparisons with Japan, which still holds the highest levels of outward FDI assets in Asia, and is established as a developed economy. By taking a long-term perspective, and exploring how Japan moved from the position of developing economy to being one of the world's wealthiest, we can test, firstly, if the earlier rise of Japanese MNCs (JMNCs) through their powerful impact on the global economy can proffer lessons for China. We can ask, secondly, how the fall of JMNCs from the peak of their success in the 1980s and early 1990s might provide different but relevant insights into the current characteristics and the potential of Chinese MNCs (CMNCs). New and fiercer competition, most obviously from other East Asian countries, supply only a partial answer to the difficulties faced by JMNCs since the 1990s, and the analysis concentrates on contributory factors such as the strategy, capabilities and organizational structures of JMNCs and business-government relations for direct comparison with their Chinese counterparts.

There is a glib assumption that JMNCs have lost their place in the world economy to CMNCs, but the nature of Japan's fall and China's rise is more nuanced. Given the difficulties confronting Japan since the decades of the 'economic miracle' and international leadership in business methods, there is a tendency to speak of dramatic decline. From 1991 to 2012, its economy grew at a barely detectable 0.2% – although much is explainable through a declining population and deflation – and its share of global GDP fell from 19.9% in 1995 to 8.8 by 2010. On the other hand, the Japanese continue to enjoy one of the world's highest standards of living. Japan retains comparatively significant levels of productive foreign assets, including, for 2014, $1193.1 billion in outward FDI stock. It continues to be the notable Asian exporter of technology, and, unlike other regional rivals, with Korea as an exception, its MNCs retain a prominent presence in the developed markets of North America and Europe. Japan is the world's third largest economy, by exchange values; and the eighth largest holder of outward FDI stock (UNCTAD 2015; Pilling 2014), significantly ahead of its major Asian competitors, China included. Since the 1990s, Japan's corporations have been shifting production overseas and, with some revealing high levels of 'multinationalization', their interests have gradually diverged from the circumstances of the low or no-growth Japanese economy. If we look at the list of the largest 100 MNCs, for 2012, we can discover that Japanese automobile MNCs obtained the majority of their sales from overseas subsidiaries: 64% in the case of Toyota, 81% for Honda, and 78% for Nissan. Sony achieved 67%. Yet, while the trading company Sumitomo Corporation achieved a figure of 47% of total sales being generated from overseas subsidiaries, the three rivals of Mitsubishi Corporation, Marubeni and Itochu were far behind in the range of 20–30% (UNCTAD 2012). China, when it became the second largest economy, put Japan into third position, and it is the 11th largest holder of outward FDI stock, equal to US729.6 bn, in 2014 (UNCTAD, 2015). Although China has exceeded Japan in terms of OFDI annual flows and the number of MNCs listed among the *Fortune 500*, perhaps only one company, Huawei Technology, can claim that more than 50% of its revenue is generated overseas. While numerous Japanese companies such as Toyota, Honda, Sony, Toshiba, Panasonic, and Nintendo are well known to global consumers, only a few Chinese MNCs can claim wide company or brand recognition.

If acknowledged competitive JMNCs could fall so quickly, we wonder what might happen to CMNCs. Existing literature suggests that Japanese and Chinese MNCs share many common features such as government support and a centralized corporate structure. In contrast, there is praise for JMNCs in possessing strategic intent (Prahalad and Hamel 1990), core competence (Hamel and Prahalad 1989), and unique management systems, while there is criticism for CMNCs due to their lack of core competence and the nature of their management systems (Rugman and Li 2007). There are few studies that directly compare FDI from Asian nations, and Yang et al. is unusual in considering CMNCs in relation to the Japanese experience (Yang et al. 2009). This contribution considers a greater range of case studies and explores the relationship between strategic motivation, core capabilities, organization and government policy. It poses and seeks to answer two key questions:

(1) Why, from the perspective of strategic management, did JMNCs fall from their once high level of success, and to what extent have they adequately adjusted their strategies since the 1990s?

(2) How does our assessment of JMNCs and their changing fortunes provide useful long-term lessons for developing economy MNCs such as those from China?

Moreover, in order to answer these two questions, we will analyse how corporate strategy, capability and structure as well as government support brought in turn the rise and fall of JMNCs, and then consider how these factors contributed to the current rise of the CMNCs and the circumstances in which that rise might be sustained or falter. While some CMNCs have already realized the potential risks that have accompanied their rapid growth, most have not considered the issue and its consequences.

Literature review

Rise of Japanese MNCs

The literature on Japanese business has overall focused on its unique, national or culturally-determined characteristics. In fact, the history of Japanese firms shows extended international and foreign MNC influence. Before the First World War, in the very first phase of industrialization, Japanese trading and shipping firms increasingly established themselves overseas, frequently through government support, strategic alliances and organizational learning from foreign multinationals. The Mitsubishi *zaibatsu* and especially its trading entity (the modern Mitsubishi Corporation) expanded rapidly in this period (Kawabe 1987, 1989; Fitzgerald 2015). Mitsui Bussan (now Mitsui and Co.) was another example, and it founded cotton spinning enterprises and flour millers in Shanghai, in addition to representative offices across the world (Allen and Donnithorne 1954; Fitzgerald 2015). Inward FDI allowed the transfer of technology and production methods, as when Western Electric invested in Nippon Electric Company (NEC), and when General Electric of America became a major shareholder in the Tokyo Electric Company (Tokyo Denki) and the Shibaura Engineering Works (which would evolve into Toshiba). From the outbreak of the First World War in 1914 until 1937, the Japanese industrial base broadened, and instances of FDI by foreign firms in Japan increased. The government used import licensing, tariffs and quotas to foster domestic manufacturing, and especially encouraged international joint ventures to facilitate technology and management transfer: Fuji Denki Seizo (ultimately Fuji Electric) in partnership with Siemens, Mitsubishi Electric through the involvement of Westinghouse, and General Motors and Ford with Toyota and Nissan were prominent cases. With the invasion of Manchuria, in 1931, an increasingly nationalist-militarist government reduced the influence of foreign firms, and, following the invasion of China in 1937, and then the attack on Pearl Harbour in 1941, overseas capital was sequestrated and industry came under state direction (Mason 1987, 1990; Udagawa 1990; Fitzgerald 2015).

After defeat in the Second World War and US occupation, Japan developed through a combination of active industrial policy, the exclusion of foreign investment and ownership, and, thanks largely to US support during the period of the Cold War, international technology and management acquisition. As has been well documented, during the 'economic miracle' of the 1950s and 1960s, Japan established a range of manufacturing enterprises with competitive capabilities in production management, employment practices, business organization, products and eventually technology. With the participation and encouragement of government and technical associations, Japanese revealed a capacity for organizational learning and subsequently a capacity for adaptation and innovation (Dore 1973; Vogel 1979;

Thurow 1993). Strategic alliances and technology cooperation were instrumental to the growth of steel making, the automobile industry and the electronic, silicon chip and computer sector (Cusumano 1985; Fransman 1995; Fitzgerald 2015). From 1961, IBM was an unusual case for being allowed to establish a subsidiary, but it had to provide technical assistance to the development of computing at Fujitsu, which received in addition support and large orders from the government and Nippon Telegraph and Telephone (or NTT). Japanese manufacturers preferred to exploit their advantages through exports, and outward FDI, not substantial in relation to GDP, was largely concerned with securing raw materials or the need of the textile sector for Asia's cheaper labour (Fitzgerald 2015).

Capital and exchange controls had been formally lifted for some time in Japan before its key manufacturers became committed MNCs in the 1980s. Their main motive was to overcome the imposition of tariffs and import quotas in the developed markets of the US and Western Europe, that is to protect the large export trade they had created. The rising value of the Yen was an additional reason. Post-war FDI followed the development of the wider economy, and so JMNCs built an international presence in heavy industrial goods, complex machinery, consumer durables and automobiles. Before the take-off in Japanese outward FDI during the 1980s, some 66% of the total could be found in developing countries (Kojima 1978). By 1970, outward Japanese FDI was substantial in mining, timber, pulp and textiles only, and by 1975 three general trading firms accounted for 40 per cent of outward FDI stocks (Ozawa 1979). In 1977, Japan provided approximately 6% of total global FDI flow. In 1980, some 34% of FDI flows from Japan went to North America, 12% to Europe and 25% to Asia; by 1989, the figures were 50, 22 and 12% respectively, witnessing the new determination of Japanese MNCs to invest in North America and Europe and less in Asia. Japanese outward FDI flows reached their peak in 1989, when they supplied some 30 per cent of the world total. Japan was home to eight of the top 50 non-financial MNCs, as ranked by assets, in 1992, seven in manufacturing, one in trading; it could claim eight manufacturers and six trading companies in the top 100 by 1998 (UNCTAD 1994, 1998).

Strategic intent was first termed by Hamel and Prahalad (1989) to describe the dramatic post-war ascent of Japanese companies. They relentlessly pursued a long-term strategic objective, which in most cases was to become global leaders, although in the West such an objective was considered highly unrealistic in view of Japanese resources and capabilities. Leading Japanese manufacturers emerged from the 1980s as MNCs with substantial investments in North America and Western Europe (Trevor 1983; Strange 1993; Campbell and Burton 1994; Sachwald 1995; Ando 2004; Farrell 2008). In these developed markets, JMNCs became associated with the exercise of strong control by the parent enterprise over subsidiaries and by their strategic intent to transfer management methods and technologies (Sekiguchi 1979). To assist in the maintenance of MNC parent control and in the overseas installation of home country practices, Japanese companies relied extensively on the sending of expatriate engineers and managers to their subsidiaries. The centralization of power within the headquarters of JMNCs can be seen as a strategy or a hierarchical management process for the international extension of domestic business models (Westney 1993; Hatch and Yamamura 1996; Seki 1997). In the case of JMNCs, Harzing (2002) associates parent control and headquarters-driven coordination with the sending of expatriates, bureaucratic rules and standardization, management by results, or acculturation and common values. Groot and Merchant (2000) distinguish between types of control mechanisms to be used in either joint ventures or wholly owned subsidiaries. In the former, in which there is a greater likelihood of hybrid systems, management strategy has to align partner motivations and organizational strengths. In the latter, the MNC does not require local partners in order to overcome the disadvantage of operating in a foreign market. Alternatively, it has proprietary knowledge it wishes to safeguard from potential rivals, or management and technological capabilities that necessitate its direct control. There is evidence that joint ventures formed a more common form of entry mode in developing markets, due to government policies and the perception of risks, and indications that parental control was less pronounced than in developed economies (Lu 2002; Belderbos 2003; Delios and Henisz 2003; Makino, Beamish, and Zhao 2004).

US and European businesses attempted, from the 1980s, to upgrade their failing competitiveness by imitating Japanese management methods. The term 'Japanization' implied that a global competitive standard had been set and that it was highly transferrable to different national contexts (Turnbull 1986; Stewart 1998; Taylor 1999, 2001; Saka 2003; Florian 2009). Some authors noted the particular superiority of Japanese lean production (Womack, Jones, and Roos 1990; Florida and Kenney 1991; Oliver and Wilkinson 1992; Alder 1993; Kenney and Florida 1993; Abo 1994). Kenney and Florida (1995) argue that Japanese firms adapted their processes in each subsidiary but retained the substance of their methods. In their interpretation, the strategic intent of the parent company remains paramount to the effective transfer of capabilities and their incorporation within subsidiaries. Critics have questioned the assumption of superior or global practice and emphasized the locational factors that temper the transfer of capabilities to a host country (Alder 1993; Florian 2009). Another strand of the Japanization literature, concerned with employment systems, puts greater stress on the impact of contextual factors on international system transfer, even if extensive 'multinationalization' of practices is feasible (Trevor 1983; Morris 1988; Bratton 1990; Oliver and Wilkinson 1992). Nonetheless, some researchers questioned whether the international diffusion of Japanese work systems to subsidiaries occurred in any meaningful sense (Turnbull 1986; Ackroyd et al. 1988; Elger and Smith 1994).

By the end of the 1990s, JMNCs had to consider how to maintain or expand the place they had established in foreign national or regional markets. Subsidiary-level decision-making in product development, research or employment policies and the evolution of local capabilities would have to replace centralized, cross-border control. The top-down parent-subsidiary relationship did not, moreover, assist the ability to absorb lessons in managerial practices from overseas markets. Slow or negative growth rates in Japan emphasized the need for growth in overseas markets and underlined the case for subsidiaries having an enhanced role in relation to the parent business. From the 1990s, JMNCs had to give greater consideration to FDI strategies of efficiency seeking (through overseas RandD networks, or through access to lower production or labour costs) and asset seeking (acquiring foreign firms and attempting to utilize their capabilities). As with MNCs from other nations, they joined the vast flows of FDI to China, establishing low-cost factories with which to supply world markets, and securing a place in that country's large domestic market. As opportunities in Asia and emerging economies grew, JMNCs required a revision of global investment and production policies (Hasegawa and Hook 1998; Encarnation 1999; Horaguchi and Shimokawa 2002; Cross and Horn 2007). Given changes at home in the post-bubble period, and changes in developed and emerging markets, a fundamental issue for JMNCs was how different their strategies and organization had to be from those on which they had built their previous achievements.

Rise of Chinese MNCs

The rise of Chinese MNCs was a direct outcome of China's economic reform and open door policy since late 1970s. Although economic reform has been pursued for more than three decades, significant Chinese outward foreign direct investment (FDI) began in the 2000s. The average annual growth rate of the outward FDI flow between 2002 and 2014 was 37.5%, and OFDI flow reached $123 billion in 2014. The value of stock accumulated between 1978 and 2002 was $30 billion. By 2014, it accounted for 3.4% of the world total (from 0.4% in 2002). There were 18,500 Chinese investment entities, and they had established 30,000 overseas firms in 186 countries and regions (MOC 2014). Regarding the entry mode of non-trade Chinese firms, early research (e.g. Deng 2004) suggested that they had a preference for joint ventures (JVs) with local firms, rather than for wholly owned subsidiaries. Equity shares of 40–70% were the most popular choice, except for banking and trade-supporting investments, which were almost all Chinese ventures with 100% ownership. Further on this, Zhang and Edwards (2007) found that Chinese firms in the 1990s made green field investments in developed countries, such as the UK, strategically to acquire managerial knowledge. In the six large state-owned Chinese firms operating in London, they without exception heavily relied on local expertise and management systems to survive. Even so, they largely failed after several years' operation in the host country, due to their lack of expertise and experience. Research on Chinese firms in the 2000s argues that Chinese firms increasingly used cross-border acquisitions to achieve their goals, gaining and leveraging strategic capabilities and location advantage to offset competitive disadvantages, while making use of institutional incentives and minimizing institutional constraints. At an early stage of their development, CMNCs were weak in both corporate capability and government financial support, and, as a result, they had to rely on local expertise (e.g. Buckley et al. 2007; Rui and Yip 2008). Since the late 2000s, Chinese firms were able to acquire Western firms by using profits earned in their domestic market or funding from policy banks pro-actively to acquire foreign firms at lower prices amid or post the 2008 financial crisis. Many of them targeted technology and managerial knowhow in acquired firms in order to compensate for their inherited weakness in these areas: the wave of Chinese equipment firms buying machine tool firms in Germany and the USA, automobile firms taking ownership of MG Rover and Volvo, resource firms with mixed outcomes targeting oil businesses, and petrochemical firms gaining oil, gas and mining firms in US, Canada and Australia were all examples. However, most Chinese firms' internationalization was considered opportunistic and without a clear strategic intent (Cai 1999; Deng 2004; Child and Rodrigues 2005; Luo, Rui, and Maksimov 2013). They were found to go overseas in order to avoid fierce competition, high tax or the inefficient institutional environment in China. In state-owned CMNCs especially, managers pursued individual benefits or pursued inter-firm rivalry and short term strategies (Luo, Rui, and Maksimov 2013).

In terms of capability, measured by either owned proprietary knowledge, revenue and profit-generated overseas, market share in host countries or brand awareness in global markets, Chinese MNCs arguably do not hold the distinctive capabilities associated with developed country MNCs (Child and Rodrigues 2005; Rugman and Li 2007). Regarding business performance, except for the earlier investment in the resource sector and later in telecommunications and construction, many Chinese overseas affiliates were not very profitable (Quan 2001; Deng 2004; Zhang and Edwards 2007; Rui and Yip 2008; Rui 2010). There are several reasons to account for such losses, the most important being inexperience and the fact that enterprises are often humbled by their own miscalculations (Deng 2004). Apart from that, state ownership and inappropriate government policies arguably contributed to the losses as well (Zhang and Edwards 2007). For example, state-owned CMNCs were criticized for lacking core competence and relying on government support and soft loans from state-owned banks. For the handful of successful CMNCs, which obtained substantial market share in host countries or brands recognition, they shared common characteristics: they thrived by creatively combining the open resources or generic capabilities available to them, resulting in the enhanced speed and price/value ratio that are well suited to large numbers of mid- and low-income consumers in emerging markets (Luo and Rui 2009; Luo and Sun 2014).

In terms of corporate structure, currently, there is no significant research investigating this subject except for a few (e.g. Rui 2010) who argue that most CMNCs favour centralized and top-down structures, allowing prompt intervention by the headquarters, but resulting in lower levels of localization compared to other MNCs. There is relatively more research on the Chinese government's role in supporting or hindering CMNCs' overseas expansion. There is a wide range of literature accounting for how the Chinese government made great efforts since the 1980s in order to attract FDI and to facilitate domestic firms in learning advanced technology and management capabilities from developed country MNCs (e.g. Nolan 2001), while pushing them further to go international (Luo, Xue, and Han 2010). China implemented industrial policies by forming and prioritizing 120 large corporate groups to enhance their competitiveness, mainly from the 1990s onwards. It then actively encouraged domestic firms to 'go out', from the latter part of that decade onwards. These were important steps in nurturing Chinese firms to evolve and become international. For those Chinese firms that went international, the government provided strong support in many ways, including firstly and in particular the acquisition of strategic assets from overseas, and secondly assistance from diplomatic to financial resources. For instance, China Development Bank and the China Export and Import Bank, together with other state-owned banks, are committed to providing the best possible service to help firms to invest overseas. The government thirdly gave access to state-supported scientific and technical research (Cai 1999; Deng 2004; Child and Rodrigues 2005; Rui and Yip 2008; Luo, Xue, and Han 2010). Such a supportive institutional environment, together with the nation's huge foreign exchange reserves and domestic savings, certainly provides Chinese firms with the most important foundation for their internationalization (Hitt et al. 2004).

However, Chinese government industrial policy was criticized for not being consistent and well designed (Nolan 2001). The government's major policy of enabling domestic firms to learn from MNCs – the so called 'exchanging technology with [giving up] the market' – was widely considered a failure, as domestic firms were unable to learn the best technology and management practice. The automobile industry is the best example. Almost all the major Chinese automobile firms have joint venture partners. However, after decades of forming JVs, none of these domestic partners own independent intellectual property and brands, and they are therefore handicapped in entering the international market (Nolan 2001). While the central government aimed for 'importation, digestion and absorption' of foreign technology, Chinese automobile firms as executors fell into the cycle of 'importation, outdating, and new importation', because they were unable to create new knowledge by combining existing knowledge and absorbed foreign knowledge (Wu 2012). Moreover, for decades, the Chinese government failed to establish a long-term and well-organized R and D system at national, industrial and firm level, as well as lacking effective policy to protect intellectual property rights (Boisot 2004), which frequently discourages firms to maximize their effort in R and D. When going overseas, Chinese firms often launch a 'price war' and compete at lower cost, which further undermines their profitability and reputation (Luo, Rui, and Maksimov 2013).

Methodology

Taking JMNCs and CMNCs as examples, we use case study and interview data to explore two questions. The data were collected from one project on JMNCs and another on CMNCs respectively during the past decade. Overall, we conducted detailed examination of more than 50 JMNCs and CMNCs, and we have conducted over 300 interviews in more than 20 countries. For assessing and comparing the overall competitiveness of the MNCs from the two countries, we paid particular attention to cases from industries in which the JMNCs or CMNCs operated most actively and influentially in global markets. The Japanese cases are mainly from automobile, electric and electronic, engineering and trading industries, while CMNCs are mainly from oil and gas, electric and electronics, telecommunications and construction. Each case includes an examination of its internationalization history, corporate strategy, capabilities, structure, levels of government support, and other potential contributing factors linked to the cycle of an MNC's rise or fall.

Semistructured interview questions were designed for each case to obtain more detailed information. Our interviewees consisted of managers and employees in the headquarters and subsidiaries of the MNCs, their suppliers and competitors, government officials and scholars who had good knowledge of MNCs. While interview questions for each interviewee are tailored, there were some headline questions including the introduction of the internationalization of the case study company (motivation, entry mode, key stages and outcomes), plus the analysis of the core resources and capabilities, strategy, structure and government relations. In addition, open questions such as 'What are the key features and determinants of the rise or fall of your company?' were designed.

We used the case study methodology described in Yin (2008) and Eisenhardt (1989) to understand and analyze the rise and fall of JMNCs and CMNCs. We analyzed the archival data to understand the origin and evolution of the MNCs' internationalization. We then analyzed interview data by means of data reduction techniques. Next, we focused our efforts on the factors that appear to have greatest relevance to the MNCs' strategy, capabilities, structure and government support. We then compared and contrasted the factors in each case and mapped out their commonalities and differences. We also compared and contrasted the case study with existing theoretical arguments, gaining an understanding of the findings, and improving validity. Finally, the data have been analysed inductively to work out what lessons from the JMNCs might be useful for CMNCs.

Japanese MNCs' internationalization

Motivation and strategy

The Japanese automobile industry became internationally competitive through lean production, rapid product development, product quality, and high skill levels. Toyota established its first overseas manufacturing operation, in 1958, an assembly plant in Brazil, and it followed with two more in South Africa in 1964 and Ghana in 1969. In these investment cases, government pressure, tariffs and content regulations were the principal motivation. The imposition of import quotas and tariffs in the UK from 1977, the US from 1981, and in the European Union from 1986 led Toyota and other Japanese manufacturers to switch to FDI as a means of securing export markets, although the growing value of the Yen was influential too. Toyota, which sought greater market access, and General Motors, which sought to learn production methods, founded in 1984 a joint venture, New United Motor Manufacturing Incorporated (NUMMI). Nonetheless, in developed markets, and in the leading automobile and electronics industries, Japanese MNCs showed an increasing bias towards wholly owned overseas operations. They similarly preferred 'green field' developments that were free of financial, employment or management legacies. Ownership or, more exactly, control facilitated the transfer of management methods and protected proprietary knowledge and technology. The failure of licensing strategies, as evidenced by Toyota's agreement with Volkswagen, or Nissan's with Alfa Romeo and Motor Iberica, reinforced the preference (Interview, Production Director, Toyota Europe, 19 February 2010; General Manager, Toyota UK, 17 January 2013). From 1990, the company began to view Europe operationally as a single market, and, as other manufacturers did, it adopted a policy of regionalization in an effort to obtain production synergies and vertical integration. By 1995, Toyota owned four plants outright in North America, and two in Britain. Government regulation of the automobile industry in China, where Toyota began manufacturing during 1996, compelled joint ventures. In attempting to exploit its capabilities in production, products and price, Toyota's international strategy moved from protecting its export trade to market-seeking FDI. Toyota, from 2002 onwards, began to produce from various locations in Eastern Europe, with its lower costs and skilled labour. The company aspired to 'true globalization' in the sense of cross-border production and managerial interconnectivity, the elimination of duplication and cost minimization (Interview, Production Director, Toyota Europe; 18 February 2010; General Manager, Toyota UK, 17 January 2013).

Suzuki Motors offers different lessons to Toyota. It founded its first overseas assembly plant, making motorcycles, in Thailand, during 1967; a car components joint venture in Indonesia in 1974 and a car assembly partnership in Pakistan in 1975 followed. However, in order to further internationalization, and to share the capital risks, Suzuki required partners, and it consistently adopted joint ventures as an entry strategy. General Motors took a stake in Suzuki during 1981, and, in the US, Canada, Argentina and elsewhere, the two firms worked in alliance or the US giant manufactured Japanese cars under licence. Suzuki's competitive products were motorcycles and small cars, and its core strengths were in their design, production and pricing. The company, as a result, fared well in developing economies, and FDI occurred through joint ventures in India (1983), Korea (1991), Hungary (1992) and Vietnam (1996). From 2006, GM began to withdraw its investment in Suzuki Motors, and American Suzuki, its small cheap cars not being suited to the US market, filed for bankruptcy in 2012. On the other hand, Suzuki has progressively acquired a majority share in its Indian joint venture, and Maruti Suzuki achieved by 2015 both a higher capitalization than its parent multinational and top place as the largest auto manufacturer by volume in India (Interview, Deputy General Manager, Suzuki Changhe, 10 December 2006; Vice-Minister, Business Planning, Suzuki Changhe, 25 April 2015).

By 1995, Suzuki had founded three joint ventures manufacturing motorcycles in China, and, in addition, two automobile plants in partnership with Chang'an Motors, in Chongqing, and Changhe Motors, in Jingdezhen. Suzuki sought sales in fast-growing developing markets due to long-term low growth in Japan, and because its products and capabilities were less suited to developed nations. As well as China revealing at the time a high demand for lightweight cars, it offered Suzuki a low-cost production base, while the SOE partners required capital and technology support. Although, as in Thailand, Pakistan, India and Vietnam, the Chinese government insisted on joint ventures in all cases of automobile FDI, as a device for management and technology transfer, it was an entry mode that coincidentally suited Suzuki's international strategy. Suzuki needed to localize production in China in order to maximize cost advantage, but it abandoned attempts to establish supply chains of component manufacturers in China for the faster and more practical policy of building in-house capacity (Interview, Deputy General Manager, Suzuki Changhe, 10 December 2006; Vice-Minister, Business Planning, Suzuki Changhe, 25 April 2015).

Japanese electronics firms, as is well recognized, won a reputation for innovation, quality and price. Sony was particularly known as an innovator, and, inspired by Philips from The Netherlands, it set a target of exports equalling 50% of total sales. To exploit its ownership advantages, having chosen a Western-friendly company name, Sony was an early Japanese investor in developed markets, opening its first US plant in 1971, and another in the UK by 1974 (Fitzgerald 2015). The company established foreign plants at an increasing rate in the 1980s, including Germany and France, and its most famous acquisition, achieving product and geographical diversification, was Columbia Pictures in 1989. When Sony suffered a loss of $1 biilion in 2003, it announced job cuts of 20,000 worldwide and a reduction in its product range, but also, under its Transformation 60 plan, $4.5billion of investment in new lines. Sanyo aspired to compete as a general electronics business, and it sought at home and overseas to match its great rival Matsushita-Panasonic, similarly headquartered in Osaka. The company founded its first assembly operation in Hong Kong, in 1961, and launched production in the developed markets of Europe and the US from 1988 onwards. By 2003, it had established over 150 foreign affiliates, over 85 or so of them in manufacturing (Interview, Deputy General Manager, Shanghai Suoguang Electronics, 12 December 2006). Sanyo Europe made televisions in Britain and Spain, air conditioning and heating equipment in Italy, and electronic components in the Czech Republic, with production and marketing being organized on a Europeanwide basis. Sanyo experienced a financial and organizational crisis in 2005, and looked to cost reductions, a narrow range of world leading products, and the creation of innovative, high margin products through R&D programmes. The company sought particular identification with green technologies and opened solar energy plants in Hungary and California. Despite its restructuring and R&D investments, Sony encountered further problems in its profitability from 2008 onwards and it renewed attempts at cost-cutting and organizational reform. Sanyo's attempt to reduce its diverse range of often low margin products to a portfolio of lines in which it had an identifiable global leadership did not succeed commercially. Under pressure from the Japanese government, Sanyo agreed to acquisition by Panasonic in 2009 (Interview, Vice CEO, Sanyo Rongshida, 9 February 2007; General Manager, Sanyo Europe, 19 February 2009; Deputy R&D Manager, Sanyo Rongshida, 8 February 2007). Hitachi grew as a general engineering and electrical business, with a diverse product portfolio. In recent decades, it has focused on heavy engineering in power plant and transportation, spent on R&D and emphasized its technological and project management skills. As a result, it renewed investment in manufacturing plants in Europe, but never matched the profitability of its chief rival, Siemens

(Interview, Chairman, Hitachi Technologies Europe, 8 March 2012; Corporate Affairs Director, Hitachi Technologies Europe, 12 March 2015).

After being broken up as a company by the US occupying forces after the Second World War, Mitsubishi Shoji was almost fully re-united by 1954. It was one of Japan's largest *sogoshosha*, the general trading companies that dominated the country's export and import trade. These enterprises obtained the raw materials and components that Japan required to industrialize during the 'miracle' decades of the 1950s and 1960s, and organized the exporting of manufactured goods. In a developing economy, in which other businesses lacked international experience, trading firms with knowledge of overseas markets and in command of cross-border supply and sales networks undertook a fundamental role. Working for multiple clients, the *sogoshosha* operated through economies of scale and scope. They could advise in addition on currency and other international transactions, and provide trade finance and credit terms. Their investments in natural resources throughout Asia constituted the earliest examples of outward FDI by Japan. Mitsubishi Shoji worked on LNG production in Brunei, from 1968, its first major overseas investment, and it developed forestry, plantation, food production, and mining interests worldwide. It anglicised its name into Mitsubishi Corporation, in 1971, a statement of its intention to be more global. After 1990, in Japan's low growth era, the *sogoshosha* needed to find growth opportunities in foreign markets, and, in parallel, their importance to Japan's international trade and domestic distribution fell (Interview, Operations Director, Mitsubishi Corporation Europe, 20 February 2014; General Manager, 19 February 2015). Enterprises, such as the Mitsubishi Corporation, Mitsui and Co., and Sumitomo Corporation, are among the largest multinationals in the world, appearing in the Top 100 non-financial TNCs compiled by UNCTAD (UNCTAD, World Investment Report 1998, 2012).

Banks had historically evolved within Japan's highly regulated and uncompetitive financial market. In the 1980s, Sanwa Bank declared its intention to be the world's top bank, and Mitsubishi Bank and Dai-ichi Kangyo Bank entered the US as full-service firms. By 1980, Japanese banks had 290 overseas branches; by 1990, there were 1035, frequently the result of following manufacturers that had begun large-scale FDI in developed markets. When the Japanese economic bubble burst, the Japanese banks' capital melted away, and they retreated internationally. Tokyo's own 'Big Bang', in 1994–1997, was an attempt to mend its declining influence as a global financial hub: it implemented de-regulation, broke down competitive barriers between financial services, and ended key exchange controls. The policy change initiated a series of mergers leading to the rise of 'mega-banks' better able in theory to compete globally, and it created amongst others the Mizuho Group (in 2002) and Mitsubishi UFJ Financial Group (2005) (Fitzgerald 2015). Securities and investment firms were among the most highly internationalized of Japanese banks, yet over 90% of trading by Daiwa Securities occurred within Japan by 2009. Overall, Japanese banks had substantial capital resources, but they lacked capabilities in products, personnel and networks to be major MNCs (Interview, Daiwa Securities, Research Director, 8 March 2012).

Capabilities

Toyota linked their preferred entry strategy of directly controlled, green field subsidiaries to their ownership of highly competitive management and production methods, and it aimed, with adaptations, to transfer these methods to its subsidiaries. The company believed that its subsidiaries should follow the 'Toyota Way', promoted as a concept from 2001 and that the essentials were its production management, customer service mentality and high skills philosophy. As well as ensuring strong direction from the production departments of the main company, Toyota relied on expatriates for the success of its policy. Yet a global firm could not depend on the pool of managers available from Japan, and, ultimately, Japan-centric decision-making inhibited the development of foreign markets. The Toyota Institute was founded, in 2002, to provide training for executives and managers from all over the world. The company acknowledged that employment and working practices would inevitably vary according to local laws and labour markets, but held to its production management being in its essential principles transferable. While there is evidence of degrees of hybrid practice in subsidiaries, executives claimed that Toyota encountered few problems in achieving its core production objectives. Following the 2008–2009 economic crisis, Toyota suffered the first financial loss in its history (although the total was small compared to US rivals). It faced criticism of faulty automobiles and falling quality standards due, it was claimed, to rapid global expansion and growing reliance on international component suppliers. Nonetheless, as well as being Japan's biggest corporate spender on R&D, Toyota maintained competitive leadership in production management and cross-border supply chains (Interview, Production Director, Toyota Europe; 18 February 2010; General Manager, Toyota UK, 17 January 2013).

Although Suzuki was prepared to form international joint ventures, it preferred to be the majority owner. In China, it was forced to accept a 49% share in both of its automobile enterprises, but, according to the Chinese managers at Changhe Suzuki, it exercised a majority control in practice. It was Suzuki that owned the technological know-how and management expertise. Its Chinese partners were responsible for managing human resources, marketing, sales, public relations and government relationships, while Suzuki concentrated on production and product development. Formal operational procedures and regulations, originally drawn up in Japan, were adapted to fit local conditions, laws and regulations. As the deputy general manager at Changhe stated: 'We don't want to fully copy and imitate Japanese work practices. We selected what we thought might be helpful in improving productivity and the quality of our current products. The most important thing is learning by doing and gaining experience.' Suzuki accepted a lower quality requirement in the short-term, but it negotiated for years with Beijing to allow conversion of its joint ventures into wholly owned enterprises. Suzuki did introduce three models with advanced technology and design at Suzuki Chang'an, because its green field operation eased the transfer of Japanese management practices. At Suzuki Changhe, a brown field site with entrenched SOE traditions, only the Suzulight model began production. Since the joint venture arrangements with SOEs continued, Suzuki did not found a substantive R&D development centre in China, despite the low cost of designers and technicians, and it retained product copy and adaptation departments instead. For Changhe, the failure to transfer designs, products and technology soured its relationship with Suzuki, and, for the Japanese, the refusal to consider a WOE forced a reconsideration of its long-term commitment to the venture. When Chang'an Motors entered into another joint venture with Ford, Suzuki reduced its stake in the business. After 2008, Beijing Auto replaced Changhe as the joint venture partner. Suzuki withdrew all its expatriate managers and technical staff and sold out most of its investment. An inability to amend official policy in China and the differing strategic ambitions of SOE partners affected Suzuki's propensity to transfer capabilities. But the company successfully exploited its specific capabilities in the design and production of small cars in what it perceived as the more favourable policy and corporate context of India (Interview, Deputy General Manager, Suzuki Changhe, 10 December 2006; Vice Minister, Business Planning, Suzuki Changhe, 25 April 2015).

Sony continues to be one of Japan's largest multinationals. It built a strong R&D capability and founded a range of innovative lines. In pursuit of a market seeking strategy, it sought to transfer its products and management methods to its US and Western European subsidiaries during the 1970s and 1980s. Japanese electronics firms had succeeded through their ability to manage large-scale plants that manufactured high-quality goods at relatively low prices, and through possessing superior management techniques and processes. Falling profits from consumer electronics, cameras and semiconductors increased the importance of Sony America, whose entertainment interests in film, television and music were the result of asset-seeking. By 2003, the US accounted for 32% of Sony's sales, and, with only 21% coming from Japan, the company could claim to be highly internationalized (Interview, Deputy General Manager, Shanghai Suoguang Electronics, 12 December 2006). Some 47% of Matsushita-Panasonic's sales derived from Japan. Sanyo's core capabilities were established through innovations in batteries and stored energy from the 1960s, and, by 1981, through breakthroughs in colour LED. The plants Sanyo had founded in the US and Europe relied heavily on transfers of technology and management-know, and on the posting of expatriates. The multinational did establish a design and new model capability at its Hungarian factory to coordinate with Osaka and to plan for demand throughout Europe (Interview, Vice CEO, Sanyo Rongshida, 9 February 2007; General Manager, Sanyo Europe, 19 February 2009; Deputy R&D Manager, Sanyo Rongshida, 8 February 2007).

Sanyo began a series of joint ventures in China from 1984 onwards, but the pace and scale of investment accelerated after 1992, and the Sanyo Rongshida joint venture was founded in 1994. The Japanese company's strategy in China was long-term, overlooking initial losses, and investing in equipment, products and skills. With its ownership of technology and management know how, Sanyo exercised operational control at its joint venture, despite becoming the minority shareholder. The Chinese management cooperated in order to facilitate the transfer of capabilities, and to utilize the high levels of expatriates employed. From the Rongshida parent firm, and among Chinese workers, there was a tendency to prioritize results rather than processes and product quality. Yet Japanese managers found Chinese employees willing to adapt, and, to achieve the transformation needed, Sanyo abandoned its Japanese manufacturing traditions in favour of top-down planning and the tight monitoring of procedures at its subsidiary. Omron's strategic motivation in creating the Shanghai Omron joint venture with a Chinese SOE in 1993 was efficiency-seeking. Unlike the case of Sanyo Rongshida, the bulk of the output was intended for export markets. Given the joint venture arrangements, Omron Japan was cautious about the transfer of its core technology, and the localization of R&D in China was minimized (Interview, Strategic Planning Manager, Omron Shanghai, 28 July 2007; Deputy R&D Manager, Omron Shanghai, 20 February 2008). It secured the conversion of Omron Shanghai into a WOE from 2005 before agreeing to the further transfer of know-how. It created an R&D centre, but its function was to customize products for the local market, indicating a continued ingrained caution about the loss of proprietorial knowledge (Interview, Vice CEO, Sanyo Rongshida, 9 February 2007; General Manager, Sanyo Europe, 19 February 2009; Deputy R&D Manager, Sanyo Rongshida, 8 February 2007).

In the post-war decades, as large Japanese enterprises, the *sogoshosha* had capabilities or resources in large-scale operations management, worldwide logistics, commercial intelligence, networks and capital, and they were involved in every stage of the commodity chain. From 1990, the *sogoshosha* encountered major challenges and began the search for a new business model. Japanese manufacturers gained the experience and size overseas to handle their own exports, and new lower cost competitors, usually Asian, challenged the *sogoshosha* for their bulk merchandise trade. With little scope for growth at home, the traders needed to foster business overseas, and Mitsubishi Corporation abandoned policies of sales maximization and providing a fully comprehensive service for, instead, the profit-testing of every commercial activity. It became more involved in business solutions, consultancy, project management, IT, communications, venture capital, investments and technology acquisition, as well as supply chain management. Mitsubishi Corporation stressed its unique global combination of market knowledge, international logistics, capital and marketing (Interview, Operations Director, Mitsubishi Corporation Europe, 20 February 2014; General Manager, 19 February 2015).

Corporate organization

Toyota's internationalization strategy rested on high levels of managerial centralization, heavy use of expatriate staff and reliance on the main business's know-how, technologies and senior personnel. One development was the founding of Toyota Motor Europe, incorporated at Brussels in 1990, to secure regional oversight of European national companies and to promote vertical production integration. The organizational rationale was the re-balancing of power between Europe and the parent firm, replacing expatriates with local executives, and improving commercial responsiveness to European markets. The Yaris constituted the first example of a Toyota car designed for the European market, and, in 2000, the company opened a design centre in France. From October 2005, the manufacturing and marketing divisions within Toyota Motor Europe were merged, in order to improve region-wide coordination between the two functions. The '2010 Global Vision' programme looked for a growth in sales, volume and profit by reinforcing and integrating management and systems worldwide. Despite programmes of devolving decision-making, encouraging the development of local management, and investing in R&D centres overseas, Toyota remained dependent on the management and resources of the parent business (Interview, General Manager, Toyota UK, 17 January 2013). Suzuki, in October 2001, established the Suzuki Investment (China) Company in Beijing as its China headquarters, with responsibility for managing and providing services more efficiently to its two automobile ventures (Interview, Changhe Suzuki, 23 July 2007). A China headquarters formed a starting point for Suzuki's strategy of convincing the government to allow Changhe and Chang'an to convert to wholly owned subsidiaries. Suzuki China could in addition take a more direct role in marketing and distribution. As we have seen, Changhe and Chang'an were reliant on Suzuki's product designs, technology and production methods, and on the use of expatriate managers. After 2006, Suzuki began to reduce its commitments in capital and in design and capability transfer, and to withdraw its personnel, while its Chinese partners looked for other strategic partner options (Interview, Deputy General Manager, Suzuki Changhe, 10 December 2006; Vice-Minister, Business Planning, Suzuki Changhe, 25 April 2015).

From the early 2000s, Sony sought to allow greater operational freedom in its overseas subsidiaries, and most obviously achieved its ambition in the US. International recession from 2008 highlighted continuing problems of bureaucracy and centralized management, plus remaining difficulties over profitability and the reinvigoration of the product-range. Overseas subsidiaries had to coordinate with a complex matrix structure in Japan that integrated responsibility for products, production, marketing and support functions departments (Interview, Deputy General Manager, Shanghai Suoguang Electronics, 12 December 2006). Sanyo Europe, based in London, acknowledged that Europe was not a true single market, and allowed measures of marketing and distribution freedom at the national level, albeit with varying commercial success. Japan, Europe and North America continued to be the competitive locale for the production and sale of automobiles, but, in consumer electronics, production for sale around the globe shifted markedly to China and Asia. Japanese consumer electronics firms as a result lost advantages in price and production management, and Sanyo Europe was forced to focus on the cutting of personnel and costs. Factories in China became a growing source of components for Sanyo's European operations and of products for sale in Europe. Sanyo Rongshida evolved as a special case for a partly foreign-owned enterprise in China: pressured by its SOE partner and by the Anhui and Hefei governments, Sanyo agreed in 2004 to the subsidiary being listed on the Shanghai stock market and, as a result, to Rongshida and local investors having a majority of the ownership. The government approach to Sanyo Rongshida is seen as supportive rather than restrictive. Whereas tighter supervision in automobiles led Suzuki to restrict its technology and systems transfer, Sanyo Electric has increased its control over the subsidiary's production system, sales, and marketing, and invested in measures of R&D, despite its reduced shareholding (Interview, Deputy General Manager, Suzuki Changhe, 10 December 2006; Vice Minister, Business Planning, Suzuki Changhe, 25 April 2015). The formation of Omron Shanghai as a wholly-owned subsidiary in 2005 coincided with Omron's adoption of its global factory policy. China was appointed as the low-cost production centre manufacturing for world markets and the policy was based on the inculcation of international, as opposed to strictly Japanese, 'best practice'. To expand production capacity and to optimize product quality, the MNC sought to enhance the role of local management and subsidiary capability, while integrating the Chinese operation more fully with its international networks. Strong parental control, technology and product transfer, enhanced subsidiary capabilities and the formation of global supply networks, far from being contradictory, proved complementary. Omron's 'global factory' strategy increased the central role of the parent firm within the MNC in key functions (Interview, Strategic Planning Manager, Omron Shanghai, 28 July 2007; Corporate Communications Manager, Omron China, 12 December 2014). Sanyo and Omron's policies in China differed over investment, output, capability transfer, and management control.

Strategic plans in 2000 and 2003 consolidated Mitsubishi Corporation into six profit-orientated business groups and granted its regional headquarters overseas greater autonomy over business decisions and the employment of local talent. By 2005, trading brought only 14% of the company's income and investments a significant 74%. Among a highly diverse portfolio, by 2011, there were convenience stores, fisheries, forestry, agriculture, food manufacturing, consultancy, financing, transport, mining, and oil. As at Mitsui and Co. or the Sumitomo Corporation, there was an attempt to reform the centralized and hierarchical management associated with Japanese enterprises with long histories. Such structures had emerged when the sogoshosha were Japan-centric commodity traders, and they were less suited to diverse service providers requiring a global perspective and responsiveness to regional and national markets (Interview, Operations Director, Mitsubishi Corporation Europe, 20 February 2014; General Manager, 19 February 2015). Since most of their business remained domestic, the overseas branches of banks remained dominated by the parent business and by Japanese management (Interview, Daiwa Securities, Research Director, 8 March 2012).

Government support

The Japanese government after the Second World War implemented an intricate system of policies to promote industrial development in cooperation with large firms. The approach was termed one of administrative guidance (*gyosei shido*), and public officials had oversight of loans, subsidies, licences, tax concessions, government contracts, import permits, foreign exchange, technology assistance and regulatory exemptions with which to guide strategies and management practice. The Japanese state sought to develop selected manufacturing sectors and to encourage high productivity industries. Alongside the Ministry of International Trade and Industry, the Ministry of Finance regulated a sector that provided cheap finance for selected lead manufacturing industries, and the house bank system and cross-ownership favoured long-term approaches to investment in skills, technology and production systems. As a result, major manufacturers evolved, at home, competitive capabilities that fulfilled the policy of export orientated industrialization. Under the capital and exchange controls introduced from 1949 to 1950 onwards, outward FDI was small in scale and the government-granted permission only where overseas investments secured raw materials or components or reduced costs in labour intensive industries such as textiles provided the justification. If we compare China in 2002–2012 with Japan in the late 1960s and 1970s, when per capita GDP were equivalent, it is revealing that Japan's outward FDI reached 0.08% of GDP, while China's was four times larger at 0.31%. Once, in 1971, overseas investment controls had been relaxed, Japanese outward FDI in 12 months exceeded the total for two decades. As capital flows grew, so did the support of state-sponsored finance as a ratio of FDI flows. Whereas, in the first phase from 1953, OFDI lending focused on support for accessing raw materials, a second phase from 1965 saw a greater emphasis on outsourcing declining, labour-intensive industries such as textiles. A third phase, beginning about 1985, matched the surge in Japanese 'multinationalization' in developed economies, with lending going almost entirely to the vehicle, electronics, chemicals and metals industries. Japanese manufacturers were offered substantial incentives and guarantees to undertake tariff-hopping and market-seeking investments. From 1999, greater attention was given to technology-seeking, and mergers and acquisition received preference over licensing. Japan evolved into the world's most active state in financing OFDI (Solis 2004, 2005; Farrell 2008). Overseas investment loans in 1955 represented a mere 1% of government overseas lending, the remaining 99% being dedicated to export loans; they grew to 13% of total loans by 1970, 21% by 1985, 43% by 2000, and then 76% by 2013 (Japan Bank for International Cooperation, Role and Function, 2014). Companies investing and operating abroad could count, in addition, on advice and information from the Japan External Trade Organization (JETRO) with its extensive international network of offices (Interview, Director General, JETRO, Europe, 29 January 2015).

The government-owned Japan Export-Import Bank (JEXIM), founded in 1953, had oversight of OFDI lending until 1999, when it was superseded by the Japan Bank for International Cooperation (JBIC). The institution states that it offers OFDI loans to support private sector finance and operations and to secure policy objectives such as accessing raw materials, improving the competitiveness of SMEs and Japanese industries, and preventing international financial disorder. Its brief is to assist in particular in developing economies, but it provides funds for sectors such as railways, nuclear power plants, and telecommunications and for M&A activities in developed markets. By 2013, maintaining and improving the competitiveness of Japanese industry explained over two-thirds of JBIC's loan and equity commitments (JBIC, Role and Function, document, 2014). Within developing economies, there are guarantees and risk insurance and funding by the Overseas Development Administration is frequently trade-related (Schaede and Grimes 2003). The continued proactive support for Japanese business overseas contrasts with the abandonment of post-war administrative guidance and industrial policy at home. MITI, during 2001, transformed into the Ministry of the Economy, Trade and Industry (METI), which became identified with deregulation. From 2006, a 'new economic growth strategy' sought to improve competitiveness and identified industries with strong growth potential but lacked the direct instruments to promote them specifically. Priorities were focused on the development of SMEs and on innovation, and large firms expressed a preference for making their own strategic decisions. JETRO, while retaining its support for businesses in foreign markets, has the task of attracting inward FDI as a means of introducing capital and global best practice to the domestic economy (Interview, Director General, JETRO, Europe, 29 January 2015). Japanese business leaders generally express their appreciation of government officials and their activities, while being more sceptical of domestic politics. They perceive their international success as largely dependent on the strategies and capabilities of their firms but recognize the backing they receive from government. OFDI lending has supported rather than determined the policies of private sector business, although participation in projects such as the Sakhalin oil pipeline by Mitsubishi Corporation and Mitsui and Co. rested on financial assistance and guarantees. Bridging and start-up loans, furthermore, can rebalance calculations of profit and loss for investments (Interview, Director General, JETRO, Europe, 29 January 2015; General Manager, Sanyo Europe, 19 February 2009; Chairman, Hitachi Technologies Europe, 8 March 2012; Operations Director, Mitsubishi Corporation Europe, 20 February 2014).

Chinese MNCs' internationalization

Motivation and strategy

Chinese firms' internationalization began soon after the government launched the economic reform and open door policy in 1978. Their internationalization motives and strategies varied across industries, locations and stages. At the early stage of China's reform in the 1980s, the motivation for many firms to internationalize was to deal with surplus capacity at home, resulting in restructuring and productivity improvements. CSCEC (China State Construction and Engineering Corporation) is the largest construction company in China. It signed the first international contract project in 1979. As the deputy CEO (Interview, Deputy CEO, CSCEE, 24 June 2011) recalled: 'The construction industry was among the earliest industries liberalized during the Chinese economic reform since 1978. Large state-owned construction firms were separated from government and requested to be responsible for their own profit or loss. The liberalization resulted in more competition in the domestic market, but also more decision-making autonomy for the company, which contributed to higher productivity and then surplus labour force and capability in the domestic market. The government began to encourage us to go overseas. With such requests but without any support from the government, we felt like an unwanted child'. The deputy CEO was among the earliest expatriates to fly to Kuwait in 1982 and afterwards to Iraq. He added: 'As early as 1982 and 1983, our company invited a famous law professor to hold seminars on FIDIC regulations so that our staff received proper training on the basic knowledge of international project management. We were the earliest construction firm in China going overseas for international contract projects after proper training'. CSCEC established wholly or partially owned overseas subsidiaries, across both emerging and developed countries. It ranks 100 in the Fortune Global 500 companies of 2012. Unlike other large SOEs in China, CSCEC did not receive government protection from competition, since the construction industry was among the first to be liberalized. It has never formed large international joint ventures (IJVs) or acquired foreign firms. In other words, CSCEC upgrades its capabilities and has becomes a leading multinational mainly through learning-by-doing. According to the same interviewee, in the early 1980s, many construction and service firms were encouraged to go overseas in order to earn the foreign reserves that China needed.

Since the 1990s, a small proportion of CMNCs had the motivation to learn advanced technology and best management practice. We have found that, between 1991 and 1999, CMNCs set up 18 international R&D centres around the world. The total number of global R&D centres increased to 100 by 2013. Shanghai Fuhua was a software company that set up the joint venture China-Japan Software Inc. in Tokyo, in 1991, in order to learn from its Japanese partner. Lenovo had its R&D centre in Silicon Valley, in 1992, to detect frontier technology. Telecommunication companies, such as Huawei and ZTE, have set up dozens of global R&D centres since 1990s, not only in developed countries, but also in developing countries such as India and Russia. They seek to recruit local talent and gauge technological direction, ultimately to reinforce the parent firm's R&D. By 2015, Huawei Technologies India had more than 2200 local engineers and managers but only about 20 Chinese expatriates. This is because the parent firm expected this subsidiary to benefit from India's IT expertise and to recruit more locals (Interview, Director of Corporate Affairs, Huawei Technologies India, 3 July 2015).

Resource firms also began their international expansion in the 1990s, and, since then, China's foreign direct investment rose quickly. CNPC is China's largest oil and gas company. It started its foreign expansion in 1993 and has acquired large stakes in Kazakhstan, Sudan and Venezuela. Many believe that CNPC simply followed government M&Ate, which is not entirely true. In 1991, the former oil minister Wang Tao stated that China's oil firms needed to go out as a matter of urgency and announced a policy of 'open the door and operate internationally' (Tong 2015). This vision underpinned CNPC's motivation, and, by 2015, it was the fourth largest international oil firm in the world. CNPC came to Sudan in 1995 after an invitation from the Sudanese government, as a consequence of Chevron's withdrawal (in 1981) in order to avoid the civil war and US sanctions. CNPC was subsequently granted the right to operate in the designated 'Block 6'. According to the Chinese Commercial Counselor in Sudan (Interview, 25 April 2008), 'this reflected that the Sudanese did not trust the Chinese initially and gave them one of the smallest oilfields with heavy oil reserves, which required special technology to extract and refine. The Chinese were not offended by this but simply accepted it in order to wait for better opportunities'. In 1996, the Sudanese government called for bids to operate in 'Block 1/2/4'. On 29 November 1996, the four partners from Canada, China, Malaysia and Sudan signed with the government of the Sudan a draft exploration and production sharing agreement. In 1997, the Greater Nile Petroleum Operating Company (GNPOC) was established as a consortium, formed by CNPC, Petronas, Talisman Energy (which sold its share to the Indian state-owned company, Oil and Natural Gas Corporation Limited, or ONGC, in 2003), and Sudapet (representative of the host government). They held 40, 30, 25 and 5% shares, respectively, and CNPC became the operating company for GNPOC. By 2008, CNPC had invested in seven projects in the Sudan, including four in oil exploration and development projects, one pipeline, one refinery, and one petrochemical plant, worth an estimated $5 billion. Sudan evolved into one of CNPC's three major oil sourcing countries, providing eight per cent of China's oil imports (Interview, Official at the Ministry of Energy and Mining, 2008). Critics pointed out that state owned oil firms took advantage of government support and wasted national funds. This accusation might be correct in the sense that CNPC invested in many politically and economically risky countries such as Sudan, Kazakhstan and Iraq. When Sudan was divided into two and civil conflict followed, almost all of the oilfields operated in Southern Sudan had to stop production. On the other hand, many interviewees emphasized that the risks were worth taking, as the investments not only helped China's oil shortage but also improved the technological and managerial capabilities of the company. One typical example was that CNPC had its first PSA (production share agreement) contract with the Sudanese government by copying and pasting an available PSA agreement written by a western MNC (Interview, Geologist, CNPC, 30 June 2010). It also obtained HSE (health, safety and environment) knowledge from collaboration with western MNCs such as Shell (Interview, CEO, 13 December 2010).

Since the 1990s, more and more Chinese firms have adopted a market seeking strategy, sending expatriates to explore global markets. Electric and electronic firms such as Haier and Gree had all built up strong positions in the domestic market and started their exploration of opportunities overseas. In 1999, Huawei held an unprecedented farewell ceremony to see off hundreds of expatriates in the company's conference hall, each with the role and duty to open a new market in different countries. They listened to the CEO's ambitious corporate strategy of becoming a global player, sang inspiring songs, and promised to work to their limit for the company's international expansion. This was the signal that Chinese firms had grown to a point that they were able to sell their products or services to global markets (Interview, Head, Huawei Cameroon, 10 May 2009). Huawei was established in 1987, when China's telecom equipment market was dominated by nine foreign firms and their imported products. In such a high-tech sector with fierce competition, Mr Ren, the founder and CEO of Huawei, has always been ambitions, stating the following when Huawei was a small unknown firm: 'If you are unable to reach top three, you are dead'. Establishing leadership in the large Chinese rural market that foreign MNCs were unable to access, and making considerable R&D investments, Huawei evolved into the top domestic firm in less than a decade. In 1996, Huawei captured its first international contract via bidding in Hong Kong. Since then, Huawei's business has developed rapidly throughout the world except for disappointments in the USA market. In contrast to most Chinese firms, Huawei has never followed joint venture or acquisition as its main internationalization strategy. Instead, it has focused on independent research and going global in order to market its cost-effective products and services. For example, Huawei started its research on wireless communication in 1995. Despite severe criticism, Ren consistently spent billions of dollars in 3G without return for a decade. According to the vice president of Huawei, focusing on 3G was a 'must'. As a latecomer, Huawei had missed out on the 2G market and also the first wave of 3G. Ren was determined not to miss the second wave of the 3G market, and, to that end, Huawei had to 'persist and be competitive'. By 2005, Huawei had become one of the few telecom equipment makers in the world to provide comprehensive 3G systems and products (Interviews, Huawei subsidiary heads in various countries). It has subsequently become the world leader in wireless research. At the 5G World Summit 2015, held in Amsterdam, Huawei was awarded 'Biggest Contribution to 5G Development' for its continuous innovation and industry role (Huawei 2015).

With innovative technology and products, such as those in 3G products, Huawei was able to enter and win a substantive market share in more than 100 countries, becoming the supplier to 46 out of the top 50 international telecommunication carriers around the world. In Europe, Huawei obtained significant market share by providing leading technology and products, and, in developing countries, Huawei dominated by offering customized products to fit the demand and conditions of the 'bottom of the pyramid' (BOP) lower income customers. The company's Ethiopia representative noted: 'Nokia-Siemens operated here. They did not maintain network stations. They considered Ethiopia was not their 'valuable market'. But, for us, we do whatever to access the market' (Head, Huawei Ethiopia, 10 July 2014). Huawei took BOP countries as its core market, even though it owned advanced technology and had broken into developed country markets. It demonstrated the effectiveness of its organizational knowledge to low-income hosts and persuaded them of its usefulness. Relevant knowledge transfer was not always an initial goal of CMNCs in Africa, but latecomer internationalization strategies and their host countries' requirements made the adjustment necessary. Turning necessity into virtue, CMNCs have learnt to use relevant knowledge as a distinctive capability for winning business and attaining competitive advantage in low-income markets. Firms like Huawei maintained a long-term strategy of winning global markets, while CNPC held both a government M&Ate and a corporate interest in securing natural resources. However, among our case study, CMNCs, most firms were impelled to go out and adopt a 'follow-the-leader' approach. For those in the construction sector, for example, they internationalized without any specific strategic intent. Not owning unique products and distinctive capabilities, many CMNCs made huge losses, while others imitated a rival's strategy where it had proved successful. The result was substantial competition among the CMNCs in host countries or region was reinforced.

Capabilities

In line with existing research, we find that most of our case study CMNCs could not provide products or services based on their own technology or management practice. They were, however, able to compete in global markets with the capability of providing products and services with a competitive price and quality combination. Our research finds that CMNCs were particularly capable of reconfiguring existing knowledge successfully in a new context, which in most cases was applying existing advanced technology in developing economies, and often involved simplifying the technology to allow lower costs and to meet particular demands within the host country. At the core of the CMNCs' capability is the use of applied technology and managerial know-how when operating in developing countries. Applied technology is applied or improved from existing invented technology, in order to meet customers' needs. It is usually acquired from developed economy MNCs and modified in the less-developed country context. Huawei's CEO claimed that his company, though a top player in the industry, 'has not had one single original product invention' and achieved its competitive advantages by 'improving and integrating the functions and features of products invented by Western companies' (Ren 2006). The key feature of applied technology is that it adds features demanded locally and avoids incorporating all the available features in order to maximize output quality and labour productivity. But, in so doing, it becomes easier or less expensive for developing countries to install and use. Huawei customized its telecoms network stations to use locally available sonar power resources and to reduce operating costs (Interview, Head, Huawei Ethiopia, 10 July 2014). Another CMNC, China Hydro, redesigned key components of European wind power technology in order to make construction and operations feasible in the Ethiopian context. It was able to offer a package consisting of Chinese domestic suppliers of fan blades from which Ethiopian wind power project owners could select the most appropriate quality and cost from a long list (Interview, Head, HydroChina in Ethiopia, 16 June 2015).

Managerial know-how includes identifying alternative resources and methods to meet the needs of the project, and understanding its adaptation to local conditions. For CMNCs, their success largely depends on CMNC's up-to-date knowledge of international markets and supply chains. The scale of global migration of manufacturing to China has made its firms skilful in applying advanced technology in the less advanced Chinese context in cost-effective ways. It has made China an information centre on the demand and supply of goods and services for emerging markets. The typical CMNC attitude is that, 'whatever is required in this market, I am almost always certain in which location the cheapest or suitable stuff exist. The logistics companies do the rest as long as I place the order' (Interview, Chinese shopkeeper in Dubai, 13 December 2010). Gree is the largest manufacturer of air conditioners in China and their largest exporter in the world. It first entered Brazil in 1998, and became the number one seller in 2004 after dislodging existing MNCs such as LG. The subsidiary head recalled how his business benefited from the full range of the supply chain of major electric goods in China: 'we are able to offer the most complete product range in the market to meet the diverse needs of customers. … Although many of these products are produced in our factory in Manaus, all components, design and R&D are from China. … For example, the costs of compressors account for 70% of the total cost of an air conditioner. In China, there are more than 80 manufactures to supply compressors so we can get the best price and product. But there is only one in Brazil and its offered price is much higher than that in China' (Interview, Head, Gree Brazil, 30 August 2009). He went further to describe how an 'economic, reliable, and fast responsive supply chain' sourced the best possible suppliers and transport to Brazil. A subsidiary head of China Wuyi stated that 'The cost of equipment and facilities for construction companies account for more than one-third of the total project costs. The cost of our equipment and facilities is normally one-third or even one half lower than that of our rivals, which are western MNCs who have been in Kenya's market for decades' (Interview, Head, China Wuyi, Kenya, 21 June 2009).

As exampled earlier, many CMNCs did possess a sourcing and price value capability, earning them a competitive advantage in host countries. However, will they be able to sustain such an advantage? Among the CMNCs we investigated, only a handful of them had conducted R&D. Furthermore, even if CMNCs begin to favour R&D, they have to make correct R&D choices. Our latest interviews with Huawei, an innovative company, highlighted that emphasizing R&D is not sufficient. The company had to pay more attention to basic research: 'pursuing applied technology is fine when we were a follower, but not for a leader. As a leader, you need to sense the direction on your own' (Interview, Huawei Ethiopia, 10 July 2014). Many of our case study CMNCs possess applied technology and know-how, but in recent years, they have realized that they face a great challenge in transforming from an applied technology focus to original technology, or, that is, from imitation to innovation. The Huawei Ethiopia subsidiary head put it in this way: 'In the past, we simply followed the industrial leader, but now we have lost leaders to follow, as we are already in the leading position of the industry. The problem is we tend towards imitating but not innovation. We lack the forward looking vision and strategy as a leader. This is one of the major challenges we are facing'. His view was echoed by many other interviewees at Huawei.

What generally concerned Chinese interviewees, more than an R&D focus, was that many CMNCs lacked core competence and international market experience. CSCEC won a design-build contract in St Petersburg in 2007. After construction had commenced, the management team realized that it was not a simple building project, but technologically challenging. The construction process made the ground sink and neighbouring buildings fall, and the contractor was unable to handle the external and internal wall sculpture decoration. After several months' work, the company appealed to the owner that their bidding price was too low to complete the project. Astonishingly, the owner accepted the appeal, but later CSCEC company found that they were still unable to complete the project at the increased price, and in addition the owner had never approved their design. After lengthy negotiations, the owner took away the design element from the contract. The company subcontracted numerous items to both local and Chinese companies and invited experts from Europe to solve the sinking issue. The building was almost completed by October 2010, but nobody knew by then how much of a loss that project would incur (Interview, Deputy Manager, CSCEC St Petersburg Project, 19 September 2010). The Deputy CEO of CSCEC admitted: 'The unsuccessful project was relevant to many SOE issues, such as lack of responsibility for safeguarding state assets, no thorough pre-investigation before making the bid, and lack of international management experience and also some key technologies. …. We still need time to learn. An aristocrat cannot be born in less than three generations' (Interview, 24 June 2011). Most interviewees emphasized that CMNCs need to address issues of R&D and sustainable competitiveness, while a few optimistic ones predicted that fierce competition would automatically impel strong CMNCs to upgrade their capability and exclude weak firms from competition.

Corporate structure

We discovered that a hierarchical structure is common to CMNCs, in which subsidiary managers were imbued with the values and goals of the parent corporation and highly centralized bureaucratic control was evident. In CMNCs, top-down vertical management lines were clear from the corporate head to the regional subsidiary head and to the country subsidiary head (with variations on precise titles). Based on both formal mechanisms, that is established management systems such as ERP and informal ones such as personal visits, corporate heads tightly monitored subsidiary heads. Key decisions – including overall budgets, R&D direction, production volume, quality control, developing new products and key human resource recruitment – were all made by the parent firm, although the subsidiary's administration, local recruitment, internal budget and sometimes even local marketing were empowered to the subsidiary.

The centralized structure was reflected in the appointment of large numbers of expatriates, another distinctive characteristic of CMNCs. Differing from developed country MNCs, whose expatriates mainly focus on control and knowledge transfer, we discovered that CMNCs' expatriates consist of a systematic combination of all types of roles in control, transfer, coordination, career development and operations. According to medium-level CNPC expatriates in Sudan (Interview, HSE Manager, CNLC, Sudan, 21 April 2008): '[the rival company] Schlumberger has a few expatriates to fill key positions such as technical advisors and marketing officers. We have expatriates at all levels from office chief to construction workers'. Consequently, CMNCs tend to bring the largest number of expatriates, measured by the relative numbers of expatriates in the same industry and host country. Many of our case study, CMNCs had a 20 to 50% expatriate rate, compared to below 10% in developed country MNCs. CMNCs explained the benefits of a centralized structure. They frequently mentioned that it ensured fast decision-making and facilitated market responsiveness. We heard from most interviewees that the heavy use of expatriates, at both managerial and operational level, could considerably reduce costs, speed up projects and transfer knowledge more effectively and efficiently. They believed that Chinese were more hardworking, flexible and obedient than local employees or third country employees. They emphasized that such a capability as fast responsiveness and quick decision making is of paramount importance for hyper-competitive global markets. Huawei's founder Mr Ren holds that Japan's lost competitiveness is closely related to its slow responsiveness from the 1990s onwards. In contrast, Huawei responded to markets, thanks to the centralized structure and a large number of cheap expatriates.

Government support

Our research found that, at the early stages of internationalization, a large number of the contracts that CMNCs secured overseas were related to Chinese government aid or loans to the host countries. On the other hand, many CMNCs suffered from government's unsystematic and discriminate policy and support, meaning that frequently many one-off cases of support were based on requests rather than documented regulations, and support obviously favoured state owned CMNCs. We have two opposite cases to illustrate. Harbin Power Equipment Corporation (HPEC) is one of three dominant state-owned power equipment manufacturers in China. Having carried out small subcontracted projects abroad, starting in 1983, they began outward FDI in the early 1990s. Before going to international market, HPEC had developed a wide range of capabilities through government support, its own R&D and inward internationalization, particularly through international joint ventures and strategic alliances with top global players. Since the 1950s, China had treated the power equipment industry as a priority in order to overcome electricity shortages. When Western MNCs started competing in China in the 1990s, HPEC enjoyed the home government's support, giving it priority in local projects. For example, the government ordered that international consortia for the first phase of the Three Gorges construction must use HPEC's products and transfer technology to HPEC whenever subcontracting occurred. HPEC had thereby acquired some of the most advanced thermal, hydro, and nuclear power equipment and technology. Government support played a part in 'pushing' HPEC to expand globally. In its early stage of internationalization, about 80 per cent of its 'go-global' projects were financed by loans from government-owned banks. With this initial push, HPEC was able to operate overseas. Although its technology was not as advanced as its Western rivals, it was at the level that suited developing markets. Moreover, lower cost and fast delivery facilitated HPEC in winning overseas projects. This position translated into ample opportunities. By 2008, HPEC had undertaken nearly 30 outward FDI projects, all in developing countries (Interview, Head, HPEC Sudan, 1 May 2008). Gradually, through learning by doing overseas, HPEC was able to win international contracts without government assistance. For instance, the ratio of government support related projects fell from 80% in 2008 to 30% in 2011 (Interviews, Senior Managers, HPEC headquarters, 28 March 2012).

However, numerous cases in our research proved that government support was not effective or successful. Nanjing Automobile Corporate (NAC) was a case in point. NAC was one of the oldest Chinese state-owned vehicle manufacturers, and produced the first light-duty truck in China in 1958. NAC was among the earliest Chinese automobile firms to receive FDI. With the direct intervention of automobile ministers, NAC formed 14 IJVs, including two with Iveco and Fiat. The Chinese government induced and supported NAC to form and learn from IJVs. However, the same government, due to its lack of experience at the beginning of China's reform, did not help NAC to secure favourable terms and conditions to impel foreign partners to transfer core technologies. The 50–50 IJV ownership structure created conflicts between the partners. However, the experience of being in IJVs for more than 20 years woke NAC up with a painful fact: they wanted to learn from foreign partners and eventually own independent intellectual property rights, but this ambition never materialized. Through IJVs, NAC was left with numerous arguments, and recognition that it was unable to control its commercial fate for lack of intellectual property (IP). With this realization, NAC was keen to acquire the British firm MG Rover in 2005 and the government (including local governments) strongly supported it. Acquisition of MG Rover was expected by NAC 'to generate pressure on the current two IJVs so as to stimulate the foreign partners to upgrade new technology in time', claimed one of the six negotiators who participated in the MG Rover acquisition (Interview, Head, Foreign Cooperation Department, NAC, 16 June 2006). While NAC aimed for acquisition in order to obtain independent intellectual property, it was its rival SAIC that acquired MG Rover. There had been wide-spread criticism of the unnecessary competition between the two and the government's lack of intervention. The criticism was even stronger after the acquisition, as both sides needed each other, since 'one had purchased the software of MG Rover and the other had purchased the hardware' (Interview, Deputy Head, China Automobile Industry Association, 12 January 2006). Before its acquisition, NAC was already making heavy losses. After gaining Rover, NAC produced its new car and operated an R&D centre in UK in less than two years. Yet it did not have any available funding to further its plans. The government refused its loan request, but forced its integration with SAIC, which was eagerly waiting for NAC's half of MG Rover's capability. NAC was eventually integrated into SAIC in 2007. Throughout NAC's history, since the 1980s, the government did not show a consistent and clear strategy enabling successful internationalization.

Critics have focused on Chinese government policy towards CMNC operations in host countries. Many SOEs have strategic importance to the Chinese economy and enjoy government support at both the central and the local level. One form of support is the 'soft' budget. At the same time, many SOEs' top managers were promoted through support of government. As a result, SOEs are impelled to strengthen their market positions and win contract bids even at very high internal cost. They would take whatever price to win a bid in a host country, so as to boost the company and the manager's performance. However, private CMNCs were unwilling or unable to take a loss. One foreign subsidiary head of a private IT company exclaimed: 'If we expect a project to be unprofitable or generate very little profit, we choose not to bid because the headquarters would not reward us for taking this contract'. In such cases, government support led to unfair competition among CMNCs. When SOEs receive substantial local government support, the rivalry can intensify even between SOEs. For example, the acquisition of MG Rover illustrates the competitive battle between two SOEs with headquarters in different regions in China. According to a senior manager from one of the rival firms, a cooperative solution could have been possible without the intervention of the local governments. Almost all the Chinese commercial counselors we interviewed in host countries admitted that 'Both government and CMNCs were learning by doing in dealing with the firms' internationalization. … It is chaotic as the Chinese government lacked sufficient and clear policies and regulations to guide CMNCs' behaviour in host countries' (e.g. Interview, Chinese Commercial Counselor in Cameroon, 11 May 2009). One of the serious consequences they claimed was that CMNCs were not welcomed by the host country. They urged that the government establish relevant policies as soon as possible, so as to regulate CMNCs overseas.

Comparisons and contrasts

Motivation and strategy

In comparing trends in the internationalization of Japanese and Chinese businesses, a number of factors assume prominence. One very obvious issue concerns timing, with Japanese firms increasingly adopting strategies of multinationalization from the 1980s onwards, and Chinese firms doing so from the early 2000s. As a result, across the two decades, circumstances of international political economy inevitably varied. Levels and flows of world trade and investment, government policies, and commercial relationships between countries would all have influenced opportunities and incentives for FDI. The economic development achieved at these turning-points in multinational-ization conditioned the nature of firm-level capabilities in management and technology in each nation. Furthermore, compared to the previous four decades, world FDI from 1992 witnessed a number of broad trends: accelerating investment flows above rises in world GDP and trade, the increasing importance of service multinationals over manufacturers, the growing use of international M&A and asset-seeking as strategies, the switch in investment to developing and transition nations, and the arrival and expansion of emerging economy multinationals (Fitzgerald 2015). Contexts affected the strategic objectives of aspiring MNCs, choices of host location, entry modes, and the purposes and practices of parent–subsidiary management. Nonetheless, the case studies indicate why we should in addition consider both industry and firm-level factors in determining international strategies and their success. Once Japanese automobile companies such as Toyota or electronics enterprises such as Sanyo had accepted their need to protect and expand their overseas developed economy markets through FDI, they revealed a strategic intent to obtain sustainable success. To fulfil their objectives, major Japanese manufacturers established subsidiary plants at scale. They demonstrated a capacity for rapid internationalization, assisted by core capabilities and experienced managers that were available for cross-border transfer, and a capacity for long-term planning and organizational learning. They had developed their capabilities in management and production within their home economy, to an important extent due to the framework created by government policy. When internationalizing, JMNCs possessed the strategic intent to be leaders in global markets by leveraging their technology, unique management practices, and cost-effective products and services. By contrast, from Haier and Gree in manufacturing to CSCEC in construction and CNPC in oil, CMNCs were more short-termist in their goals. The Japanese government provided important but supplementary financial, administrative and informational support to firms. Yet, in terms of motivation to multinationalize, it was the management of JMNCs that decided strategic objectives, based on export success, firm-level capabilities, and availability of capital. For CMNCs, at least in the case of SOEs, government policies and influence in effect determined the decision to internationalize.

At the point in which JMNCs decided to embrace large-scale FDI in developed markets, they owned brands and products that were already visible in these major host nations; at the later date in which they internationalized, their Chinese counterparts lacked such recognition, and primarily focused on developing economies. CMNCs did not possess globally superior technology and management practice, and only a handful formulated long-term strategic goals. They used internationalization as a means to acquire strategic capabilities or to leverage home advantages in low cost products and services. As well as responding to government encouragement and pressure, Chinese firms acted opportunistically rather than strategically. Furthermore, as confirmed by interviewees mostly located in Africa, CMNCs went international 'to follow others' or 'to follow the trend' of Chinese firms going abroad. They were in the longer term able to utilize and exploit their cost-effective advantages in developing countries and their understanding of emerging market needs. Yet, having internationalized opportunistically, CMNCs had little chance or incentive to attend to the R&D and product differentiation that could offer the sustainable strategic approach advocated by so many Chinese interviewees. JMNC strategy had become associated with rapid internationalization, founded on the transfer and adaptation of home nation capabilities, centralized internal organization, and top-down parent relationships. JMNCs had evolved into established MNCs by the late 1990s onwards, from which point they were beginning for a range of reasons to lose overall international competitive advantages. They required strategies for enhancing or readjusting capabilities, and they needed, potentially, to do so through less centralized and more international horizontal network structures. The growing incidence of off-shoring and efficiency-seeking FDI, notable for example in electronics production, implied less reliance on the capabilities of the headquarters or home nation firm, just as the rising incidence of cross-border M&A and asset-seeking potentially reduced the advantages of transferring capabilities from the parent enterprise to subsidiaries. Many JMNCs appeared less adept at implementing strategic intent in scenarios of decentralized cross-border management, joint ventures, alliances, or inter-firm organizational learning.

Capabilities

JMNCs in manufacturing possessed core competence in production methods, strategic planning and management, and R&D; they had competitive products and brands; and, for a period, they had advantages in price against their major rivals. The Japanese experience was one of competitive 'leaders' that could transfer capabilities from their parent enterprise and home economy; in a sense, they could exploit the advantages of being both Japanese and owners of Japanese management methods. By the end of the 1990s, Japanese companies had matured as established MNCs. Having focused on the transfer of capabilities, served by a dominant parent firm and a centralized structure, they had to evaluate what capabilities and organization they required to retain or improve their international competitiveness. Strong internal capabilities and management did not always suit collaborative relationships and organizational learning in host economies, and centralization hindered the empowerment of subsidiary management or the building of global as opposed to a Japan-dominated MNC. Historically, Japanese firms had a tradition of organizational learning through strategic alliances and licencing, but, as their competitiveness grew, many prominent enterprises had relied on strong internal R&D capabilities. As a result of its financial difficulties, Nissan formed its strategic alliance with Renault in 1999, but then entered a period of rapid recovery due to its strengths in production, technology, and product development; aside from the immediate impact of the 2008–2009 economic crisis, Toyota has enjoyed long-term profitability in addition to global sales growth. Through new rivals and imitation, and the relocation of production to low cost locations, Japanese electronics firms have encountered strong challenges and low-profit returns, as evidenced by Sony and Sanyo. They have lost global advantage in production efficiencies, technology and brands and had to abandon strategies of manufacturing a full range of standardized products. Lengthy planning horizons, extended restructuring and faulty investments have disadvantaged the search for corporate renewal and distinctive products.

Chinese companies remained organizational learners when they transformed into MNCs, although they had reached a capability level that gave them ownership advantages in emerging economies. CMNCs quickly understood the needs of customers in these host countries, in terms of price, basic technology and simplified operations. Centralized structures and sourcing from China enabled them to meet the price and scale demands of customers. CMNCs revealed an ability to adapt their capabilities and a capacity for quick decision-making. But, while CMNCs have exploited their advantages in overseas markets, their competitive capabilities, management and structures are not well suited for the next stage of developing leading business systems and technologies. Comparatively, much fewer Chinese brands are known to the global market, although by 2015 more CMNCs than JMNCs are listed in *Fortune 500*. CMNCs' competitiveness comes from their imitation capability, cost advantage, hardworking culture, and a fast responsive supply chain, rather than superior technology and best management practice in manufacturing practice or product design. Most CMNCs were good at imitation but not innovation, leading to fierce domestic competition due to the lack of differentiation in products or strategy. Furthermore, the cost advantage is being undermined by rising production costs in the home economy, which is a challenge for foreign firms located there but also for CMNCs with international strategies founded on low domestic costs. Indeed, the case studies above cite CMNCs that have moved to Africa or India to access cheap labor and manufacturing in these countries. Large state-owned CMNCs, such as CRC and CSCEC, generated overseas income but frequently made losses. Many large and small private CMNCs create profits overall, although specific subsidiaries may not. Among the cases studied, only a handful of CMNCs have won a significant share of a host market: Gree in Brazil, Huawei and ZTE in several countries, Haier in the USA, CSCEC in Singapore and UAE, and CNPC in Sudan, Angola and Kazakhstan. A small number have made their brands well known around the world, such as Huawei, CNPC, Lenovo and Haier; many are recognized in specific host markets or industries; most are largely unknown and without a reputation based on the quality of their products and services.

Corporate structure

Both JMNCs and CMNCs have favoured a centralized corporate structure, in which the headquarters made the most important decisions and localization rates were relatively low, compared with Western MNCs. JMNCs became heavily reliant on expatriate managers in the 1980s and 1990s. CMNCs have received contemporary criticism for bringing not only managers to host economies but also oil, construction and other workers. Japanese expatriates were needed for the transfer of capabilities to subsidiaries, but, once recognized as a barrier to decentralization and localization, their number was reduced. For CMNCs, Chinese managers understood relative ownership advantages in developing economies, and were well placed to exploit China's cost and supply advantages in the expansion of their host economy operations. While JMNC management sought enhanced competitiveness through measures of regionalization or localization, longstanding centralized structures could work against this ambition and fast decision-making.

Government support

What both the histories of JMNCs and CMNCs reveal is the impossibility of looking in isolation at the motivation of firms that undertake the costs and risks of 'multinationalization'. The contexts of domestic and international political economy exerted a determinant influence in case after case. The role of the Japanese state in fostering industrialization, including associated cross-border knowledge transfers, has long been acknowledged. Until the 1930s, the government encouraged joint ventures and alliances with Western enterprises, in order to gain transfers of technological and managerial knowledge. China followed with this model from the mid-1990s (Fitzgerald 2015). During the 'miracle' post-war decades, the Japanese government coordinated and promoted technology transfer through international licensing arrangements and cooperated with large corporations to fulfil a policy of export-orientated industrialization. As has been recorded a multitude of times, Japanese manufacturers gained capabilities in production, products and technology, with which to make inroads into export markets. The Japanese government sought to retain capital for the development of the home economy. Yet it proved willing to promote FDI that met specific needs in natural resources and components, or FDI that responded to rising domestic labour costs and declining sectors. In the significant new phase beginning with the 1980s, Japanese government financial support was targeted on the wave of manufacturing FDI in the developed economies of Western Europe and the US. From the 2000s onwards, to meet Japan's changing economic needs, there was a switch to technology acquisition FDI and to promoting international mergers and acquisitions as a means of managerial and technological interchange. The Japanese state evolved into one of the world's most active subsidizers of FDI and actively supported trade and multinationals in overseas markets. To date, no extensive research exists looking closely at the support offered by the Japanese and Chinese governments to their respective multinationals. Although a close state–business relationship exists in both countries, Japanese government support was more active and effective, assisting the evolution of core capabilities at home, and subsequently promoting FDI by firms exploiting their core capabilities overseas. The Chinese government attracted foreign firms and encouraged joint ventures and aimed to 'exchange technology by [giving away] the market'. However, it has long been argued that 'the market has been lost, but the technology has not been learnt'. The consequence was that Chinese firms obtained second hand or outdated technology from their joint venture partners, and, unlike Japanese corporations, did not instil an independent R&D capability. Chinese managers in SOEs believed that they had to respond to the government's 'go global' policy, and many CMNC overseas contracts were linked to or underpinned by Chinese state aid or loans to host economies. CMNC managers noted that government support was indiscriminate, unsystematic and sometimes not sustained.

Implications and conclusion

In our survey of JMNCs and CMNCs, as respectively Asian early movers and relative latecomers, we considered the areas of motivation and strategy, capabilities, organizational structure and state-business relationships. What lessons might we take from comparing JMNCs and CMNCs? JMNCs had leading ownership advantages, and government support and subsidies bolstered companies that set their own multinational strategies and decisions. The policy decisions made by the Chinese government were more influential on the decisions made by firms, especially SOEs, and CMNCs frequently required the institutional support of the state as compensation for gaps in ownership advantages. Nonetheless, such support was frequently seen by CMNC managers as inconsistent and un-sustained. Japanese managers accessed government support because it could nurture and further enhance firm specific advantage (FSA). In the example of China, state support has the danger of distracting CMNCs from building and improving FSA, and, certainly, it has had negative effects on large state owned enterprises. The case survey demonstrates that long-term and short-term strategy must be balanced and mutually supportive. Without a long term strategy, MNCs may neglect R&D or fail to sustain their competitiveness; if failing on short-terms targets, MNCs overlook customers in fast-changing markets, and undermine their ability to plan long-term.

JMNCs in the key manufacturing sector underwent a first phase of initial FDI, transferring domestically well-entrenched capabilities. Their strategic intent was clear and long-term strategic planning effective. But, overall, JMNCs found the subsequent stage more problematic, in some cases due to strategic aims being unclear. Long-term planning became associated, over recent decades, with slow responses to broad shifts in the structure of the global economy and in relative firm-level competitive advantage. The highly successful Japanese trading multinationals, on the other hand, had a very different history of international engagement and FDI. Their competitiveness originated from their long historical engagement in cross-border operations, and not, as in manufacturing, from the transfer of domestically nurtured capabilities. Despite their established reliance on Japanese expatriate managers and centralized organization, they have retained their position as leading MNCs. As well as seeking to be more profit-orientated, Japanese trading enterprises have adopted strategies based on developing investment portfolios and business services. CMNCs in many of the cases demonstrate inadequate strategic intent, but in host markets revealed a commendable flexibility and responsiveness to customer needs. In parallel to JMNCs, they might consider the stage that follows from their initial investments and breakthroughs in developing economies. For manufacturing JMNCs, the issues were the localization of decision-making and R&D to assist responsiveness to consumers, and, by contrast, the shifts in production to low cost sites and the deepening integration of global production chains. For CMNCs, generally, there was a need to improve management, technology and product differentiation, and, specifically, a firm such as Huawei offered a role model.

In some respects, centralized management structures and the dominance of the parent business over subsidiaries limited or limits strategic change, the further evolution of capabilities, or the creation of truly 'global' companies. In other respects, core or vertical strengths in management knowledge and advanced technology at the parent business remained a source of competitive advantage within JMNCs, as they strove to develop horizontally with stronger subsidiaries, joint ventures or strategic alliances. Within CMNCs, the home-based parent often provided the basic technologies and low priced supplies sought by host nations. As with JMNCs, CMNCs have to address the complex balance of centralization and decentralization, and the extent to which the ownership or control of subsidiaries is desired. They have to acknowledge the important influences of differences between industry sectors and from varying levels of national economic development. While fast decision-making in each host nation or region is beneficial, the availability of a leveraged central resource or capability may be vital to global competitiveness. The cases imply that JMNCs and CMNCs should give urgent attention to a combination of centralized resources and increased decentralization of decision-making.

References

Abo, T. 1994. *Hybrid Factory: The Japanese Production System in the United States*. New York: Oxford University Press.
Ackroyd, S. S., G. G. Burrell, M. M. Hughes, A. A. Whitaker, and S. Ackroyd. 1988. "The Japanisation of British Industry?" *Industrial Relations Journal* 19 (1): 11–23.
Alder, P. S. 1993. "The Learning Bureaucracy: New United Motors Manufacturing, Inc." In *Research in Organizational Behavior*, edited by B. M. Straw and L. L. Cummings. Greenwich, CT: JAI Press.
Allen, G. C., and A. G. Donnithorne. (1954) 2003. *Western Enterprise in Far Eastern Economic Development*. Reprint, London: Routledge.
Ando, K. 2004. *Japanese Multinationals in Europe*. Cheltenham: Edward Elgar.
Belderbos, R. 2003. "Entry Mode, Organizational Learning, and R&D in Foreign Affiliates: Evidence from Japanese Firms." *Strategic Management Journal* 24: 235–259.
Boisot, M. 2004. *Notes on the Internationalization of Chinese Firms*, Unpublished Paper. Barcelona: Open University of Catalonia.
Bratton, J. 1990. *Japanisation at Work*. Basingstoke: Macmillan.

Buckley, P., J. Clegg, R. A. Cross, X. Liu, H. Voss, and P. Zheng. 2007. "The Determinants of Chinese Outward Foreign Direct Investment." *Journal of International Business Studies* 38: 499–518.

Cai, K. G. 1999. "Outward Foreign Direct Investment: A Novel Dimension of China's Integration into the Regional and Global Economy." *The China Quarterly* 160: 856–880.

Campbell, N., and F. Burton. 1994. *Japanese Multinationals: Strategies and Management in the Global Kaisha*. London: Routledge.

Child, J., and S. B. Rodrigues. 2005. "The Internationalization of Chinese Firms: A Case for Theoretical Extension?" *Management and Organization Review* 1: 381–410.

Cross, A., and S. A. Horn. 2007. *Japanese Multinationals in China*. London: Routledge.

Cusumano, M. A. 1985. *The Japanese Automobile Industry: Technology and Management at Nissan and Toyota*. Cambridge: Harvard University Press.

Delios, A., and W. J. Henisz. 2003. "Political Hazards, Experience, and Sequential Entry Strategies: The International Expansion of Japanese Firms, 1980–1998." *Strategic Management Journal* 24: 1153–1164.

Deng, P. 2004. "Outward Investment by Chinese MNCs: Motivations and Implications." *Business Horizons* 47: 8–16.

Dore, R. 1973. *British Factory-Japanese Factory: The Origins of National Diversity in Industrial Relations*. Oakland, CA: University of California Press.

Eisenhardt, K. M. 1989. "Building Theories from Case Study Research." *Academy of Management Review* 14 (4): 532–550.

Elger, T., and C. Smith. 1994. *Global Japanisation? The Transnational Transformation of the Labour Process*. London: Routledge.

Encarnation, D. J. 1999. *Japanese Multinationals in Asia*. Oxford: Oxford University Press.

Farrell, S. F. 2008. *Japanese Investment in the World Economy*. London: Routledge.

Fitzgerald, R. 2015. *Rise of the Global Company: Multinationals and the Making of the Modern World*. Cambridge: Cambridge University Press.

Florian, A. 2009. *Hybridization of MNE Subsidiaries: The Automotive Sector in India*. London: Palgrave Macmillan.

Florida, R., and M. Kenney. 1991. "Organisation vs. Culture: Japanese Automotive Transplants in the US." *Industrial Relations Journal* 22 (3): 181–196.

Fransman, M. 1995. *Japan's Computer and Communications Industry: The Evolution of Industrial Giants and Global Competitiveness*. Oxford: Oxford University Press.

Groot, L., and K. Merchant. 2000. "Control of International Joint Ventures." *Accounting, Organizations and Society* 25 (6): 579–607.

Hamel, G., and C. K. Prahalad. 1989. "Strategic Intent." *Harvard Business Review* 67 (3): 63–76.

Harzing, A. W. 2002. "Acquisitions vs. Greenfield Investments: International Strategy and Management of Entry Modes." *Strategic Management Journal* 23 (3): 211–227.

Hasegawa, H., and G. D. Hook. 1998. *Japanese Business Management: Restructuring for Low Growth and Globalization*. London: Routledge.

Hatch, W., and K. Yamamura. 1996. *Asia in Japan's Embrace: Building a Regional Production Alliance*. Cambridge: Cambridge University Press.

Hitt, M., D. Ahlstrom, M. Dacin, E. Levitas, and L. Svobodina. 2004. "The Institutional Effects on Strategic Alliance Partner Selection in Transition Economies: China vs. Russia." *Organization Science* 15 (2): 173–185.

Horaguchi, H., and K. Shimokawa, eds. 2002. *Japanese Foreign Direct Investment and the East Asian Industrial System*. New York: Springer.

Huawei. 2015. *Huawei Awarded Biggest Contribution to 5G Development at 5G World Summit 2015*. https://www.theparliamentmagazine.eu

Kawabe, N. 1987. "Development of Overseas Operations by General Trading Companies, 1868–1945." In *Business History of General Trading Companies*, edited by S. Yonekawa and H. Yoshihara, 71–107. Tokyo: Tokyo University Press.

Kawabe, N. 1989. "Japanese Business in the United States before the Second World War: The Case of Mitsui and Mitsubishi." In *Historical Studies in International Corporate Businesss*, edited by A. Teichova, M. Levy-Leboyer and H. Nussbaum, 177–198. Cambridge: Cambridge University Press.

Kenney, M., and R. Florida. 1993. *Beyond Mass Production: The Japanese System and Its Transfer to the US*. New York: Oxford University Press.

Kenney, M., and R. Florida. 1995. "The Transfer of Japanese Management Styles in Two US Transplant Industries: Autos and Electronics." *Journal of Management Studies* 32 (6): 789–802.

Kojima, K. 1978. *Direct Foreign Investment: A Japanese Model of Multinational Business Operations*. London: Croom Helm.

Lu, J. 2002. "Intra- and Inter-organizational Imitative Behavior: Institutional Influences on Japanese Firms' Entry Mode Choice." *Journal of International Business Studies* 33: 19–37.

Luo, Y., and H. Rui. 2009. "An Ambidexterity Perspective toward Multinational Enterprises from Emerging Economies." *Academy of Management Perspective* 23 (4): 49–70.

Luo, Y., and J. Sun. 2014. "An Inquiry on Composition-based View: Its Propellants and Effect on Competitive Advantage." *Management World* 7: 93–106.

Luo, Y., Q. Xue, and B. Han. 2010. "How Emerging Market Governments Promote Outward FDI: Experience from China." *Journal of World Business* 45: 68–79.

Luo, Y., H. Rui, and V. Maksimov. 2013. "Tales of Rivals: Attacks in Chinese International Competition." *Organizational Dynamics* 42 (2): 156–166.

Makino, S., P. W. Beamish, and N. B. Zhao. 2004. "The Characteristics and Performance of Japanese FDI in Less Developed and Developed Countries." *Journal of World Business* 39: 377–392.

Mason, M. 1987. "Foreign Direct Investment and Japanese Economic Development, 1899–1931." *Business and Economic History* 16: 93–107.

Mason, M. 1990. "With Reservations: Pre-war Japan as Host to Western Electric and ITT." In *Foreign Business in Japan before World War II*, edited by T. Yuzawa and M. Udagawa, 176–185. Tokyo: Tokyo University Press.

MOC (Ministry of Commerce and State Statistics Bureau). 2014. *Statistical Bulletin of China's Outward Foreign Direct Investment (Non-finance Part)*. Beijing: Ministry of Commerce.

Morris, J. 1988. "The Who, Why and Where of Japanese Manufacturing Investment in the UK." *Industrial Relations Journal* 19 (1): 31–40.

Nolan, P. 2001. *China and the Global Economy*. Basingstoke: Palgrave.

Oliver, N., and B. Wilkinson. 1992. *The Japanisation of British Industry: Developments in the 1990s*. Oxford: Blackwell.

Ozawa, T. 1979. "International Investment and Industrial Structure: New Theoretical Implications from the Japanese Experience." *Oxford Economic Papers* 31: 72–92.

Pilling, D. 2014. *Bending Adversity: Japan and the Art of Survival*. London: Penguin.

Prahalad, C. K., and G. Hamel. 1990. "The Core Competence of the Corporation." *Harvard Business Review* 66: 79–91.

Quan, Y. 2001. "Access to the WTO and Internationalization Strategy of Chinese Companies." *Enterprise Studies* 8: 12–24.

Ren, Z. F. 2006. "The Practical R&D Direction and Our 20 Years' Endeavour: Speech at a Large Scale Project Demonstrating Conference." *Huawei People*: 182.

Rugman, A. M., and J. Li. 2007. "Will China's Multinationals Succeed Globally or Regionally?" *European Management Journal* 25 (5): 333–343.

Rui, H. 2010. "Developing Country FDI and Development: The Case of the Chinese FDI in the Sudan." *Transnational Corporations* 19 (3): 49–80.

Rui, H., and G. Yip. 2008. "Foreign Acquisitions by Chinese Firms: A Strategic Intent Perspective." *Journal of World Business* 43: 213–226.

Sachwald, F., ed. 1995. *Japanese Firms in Europe*. Reading: Harwood Academic Publishers.

Saka, A. 2003. *Cross-national Appropriation of Work Systems: Japanese Firms in the UK*. Cheltenham: Edward Elgar.

Schaede, U., and W. W. Grimes. 2003. *Japan's Managed Globalization: Adapting to the Twenty-first Century*. New York: M.E.Sharpe.

Seki, M. 1997. *Kudoka o koete: gijutsu to chiiki no saikochiku* [Overcoming Hollowing Out: The Reorganization of Technique and Regions]. Tokyo: Nihon Keizai Shinbunsha.

Sekiguchi, S. 1979. *Japan's Direct Foreign Investment*. Totowa, NJ: Rowan and Allanheld.

Solis, M. 2004. *Banking on Multinationals: Public Credit and the Export of Japanese Sunset Industries.* Stanford: Stanford University Press.

Solis, M. 2005. "From Iron Doors to Paper Screens: The Japanese State and Multinational Investment." In *Japan and China in the World Political Economy*, edited by S. M. Pekaanan and K. S. Tsai, 93–122. London: Routledge.

Stewart, P. 1998. "Out of Chaos Comes Order: From Japanization to Lean Production." *Employee Relations* 20 (3): 213–223.

Strange, R. 1993. *Japanese Manufacturing Investment in Europe.* London: Routledge.

Taylor, B. 1999. "Japanese Management Style in China? Production Practices in Japanese Manufacturing Plants." *New Technology, Work and Employment Journal* 14 (2): 129–142.

Taylor, B. 2001. "The Management of Labour in Japanese Manufacturing Plants in China." *International Journal of Human Resource Management* 12 (4): 601–620.

Thurow, L. C. 1993. *Head to Head: The Coming Economic Battle among Japan, Europe, and America.* New York: Warner Books.

Tong, X. G. 2015. "The Internationalization of the Chinese National Petroleum Corporation." *Oil Observer* January 9. http://oilobserver.com/history/article/1407.

Trevor, M. 1983. *Japan's Reluctant Multinationals: Japanese Management at Home and Abroad.* London: Bloomsbury Academic.

Turnbull, P. 1986. "The 'Japanisation' of Production and Industrial Relations at Lucas Electrical." *Industrial Relations Journal* 17 (3): 193–206.

Udagawa, M. 1990. "Business Management and Foreign-affiliated Companies in Japan before World War II." In *Foreign Business in Japan before World War II*, edited by T. Yuzawa and M. Udagawa, 148–176. Tokyo: Tokyo University Press.

UNCTAD (United Nations Conference on Trade and Development). 1994. *World Investment Report.* Geneva: UNCTAD.

UNCTAD (United Nations Conference on Trade and Development). 1998. *World Investment Report.* Geneva: UNCTAD.

UNCTAD (United Nations Conference on Trade and Development). 2012. *World Investment Report.* Geneva: UNCTAD.

UNCTAD (United Nations Conference on Trade and Development). 2015. *World Investment Report.* Geneva: UNCTAD.

Vogel, E. 1979. *Japan as Number One: Lessons for America.* Cambridge: Harvard University Press.

Westney, D. E. 1993. "Institutionalization Theory and the Multinational Corporation." In *Organization Theory and the Multinational Corporation*, edited by S. Ghoshal and D. E. Westney, 32–57. New York: St. Martin's Press.

Womack, J. P., D. T. Jones, and D. Roos. 1990. *The Machine That Changed the World.* New York: Macmillan.

Wu, W. J. 2012. "It is the Time to Completely Abandon the Idea of "Exchanging Technology with Market"." *Chinese Youth Daily* September 27.

Yang, X., Y. Jiang, R. Kang, and Y. Ke. 2009. "A Comparative Analysis of the Internationalization of Chinese and Japanese Firms." *Asia Pacific Journal of Management* 26: 141–162.

Yin, R. 2008. *Case Study Research: Design and Methods.* London: Sage.

Zhang, M., and C. Edwards. 2007. "Diffusing 'best Practice' in Chinese Multinationals: The Motivation, Facilitation and Limitations." *International Journal of Human Resource Management* 18 (12): 2147–2165.

Is there an East Asian model of MNC internationalization? A comparative analysis of Japanese and Korean firms

Martin Hemmert[a] and Keith Jackson[b]

[a]School of Business, Korea University, Seoul, South Korea; [b]Centre for Financial & Management Studies, School of Oriental and African Studies, University of London, London, UK

ABSTRACT
Research on the internationalization of multinational corporations (MNCs) is mostly built on studies of North American and European firms. East Asian MNCs have been studied less, and commonly with reference to theories developed in Western countries. In this paper, we query the validity of these 'Western' internationalization models for East Asian firms through comparative case studies of representative Japanese and South Korean MNCs' expansion into China. We find that the internationalization processes of leading East Asian MNCs match the predictions made by Western theories only partially. Furthermore, we find considerable differences between the internationalization of Japanese and South Korean firms, indicating both that East Asian MNCs follow diverse patterns of internationalization and that established Western models of internationalization evince limitations or weaknesses when applied to East Asian firms. Overall, the findings of this exploratory study illustrate the need for further, in-depth studies on the internationalization of East Asian MNCs which may result in the extensions of existing theories or even new theoretical frameworks.

Introduction

For much of the twentieth century, North American and European firms and institutions dominated international business activity and foreign direct investment (FDI). Inevitably, early theories of the multinational corporation (MNC) along with models designed to describe, explain and compare the internationalization processes and strategies of MNCs from the 1960s through to the 1990s tend to build on observations of Western firms and, by extension, the research outputs of North American, European and other 'Western' business schools.

To illustrate, Hymer's (1960) theory of monopolistic advantage and Aharoni's (1966) behavioural theory of internationalization are based on an analysis of US firms and Johanson and Vahlne's (1977) so-called 'Uppsala' model – influenced by research into the internationalization activities of US firms – is built on studies of Swedish companies. Buckley and Casson (1976) studied a global sample of predominantly Western MNCs and Rugman (1981) firms in the Canadian banking industry. Generally speaking, the conceptualization, theorizations and thereby definitions of the term 'MNC' have been embedded in Western economic theories (cf. Hood and Young 1979) and, as a consequence, on the strategic investments and other 'multinational' activities of US American firms, corporations or 'enterprises' (cf. Vernon 1966; Ietto-Gillies 2012).

With this paper, we attempt to connect with (in East Asian contexts) well-established and growing streams of more diversified and less 'Westernized' research (Kojima 1978; Peng and Khoury 2009; Ping, Plechero, and Basant 2013; Fitzgerald and Rowley 2015). Specifically, we attempt to query the validity of what we suggest represent markedly 'Western' models of MNC internationalization in a new era of global flows of FDI, increasing amounts of which are sourced in East Asia. Specifically, we re-visit common approaches towards defining the internationalization strategies of MNCs and offer a comparative analysis of the FDI strategies pursued by Japanese and South Korean MNCs in the People's Republic of China, elsewhere referred to as 'PRC' or 'Mainland China' in order to distinguish it from other markets in Greater China such as Hong Kong, Macau, and Taiwan that have been targets for substantial FDI by Japanese and South Korean MNCs over recent years. For fluency of reference, we subsequently identify South Korean MNCs as 'Korean' and the PRC or Mainland China as 'China'.

The overarching aim of this paper is to assess whether there is a case to be made for developing a distinctly 'East Asian' conceptualization of FDI when applied towards describing and comparing the internationalization strategies of East Asian MNCs. By striving towards this aim, this paper contributes to the research of the internationalization of firms through a comparative analysis of Japanese and Korean MNCs' internationalization in recent years across non-domestic markets generally and in China specifically. By implication, this paper also raises broader questions about the validity of models and theories of internationalization when applied in non-Asian contexts.

Specifically, we address the following research questions:

(1) What general features distinguish the internationalization strategies of Japanese and Korean MNCs?
(2) How similar or different are the internationalization strategies of comparable Japanese and Korean MNCs?
(3) To what extent do current internationalization strategies of Japanese and Korean MNCs confirm the predictions of Western-based internationalization theories and models?
(4) Is there sufficient evidence to support the proposal of a new East Asian model for describing current internationalization strategies of East Asian MNCs and predicting how these patterns of internationalization might develop in future?

Towards addressing these questions, we first present a review of previous studies on the internationalization of MNCs generally and on the internationalization of Japanese and Korean companies in particular. We then present an overview of recent export and FDI activities of Japanese and Korean MNCs, followed by a comparative case analysis of the internationalization of leading Japanese and Korean firms in two representative industries: the manufacture of automobiles and of electronics. We discuss the implications of our findings and assess whether there is a case for proposing a distinctly 'East Asian' model of MNC internationalization. We conclude our discussion with recommendations for future research in this field.

Literature review

When researching the internationalization activities of East Asian MNCs we first need to recognize that the term 'MNC' itself is open to various interpretations. To illustrate, Ietto-Gillies (2012) demonstrates how the term 'MNC' is commonly confused with those for Multinational Enterprise and Transnational Corporation (MNE and TNC, respectively), along with more general terms for defining discrete business entities such as *corporation*, *company*, *firm* or *enterprise*. To illustrate further, the United Nations Conference on Trade and Development (UNCTAD) commonly uses the term 'TNC'. When we cite from these data (Table 2), we use the term MNC. In order to promote consistency across this APBR Special Issue, we echo Bartlett and Ghoshal (1991) and subsequently Fitzgerald and Rowley (2015) by defining 'MNCs' as firms that choose to invest substantially and locate large-scale business activities in both 'familiar' and 'less familiar' countries and regions while simultaneously maintaining majority ownership and strategic control of these investments and the returns they are designed to generate.

Comparing 'Western' models and conceptualizations of MNC internationalization

As a key element in our comparative analysis of MNCs headquartered in Japan and Korea, we invoke the International Product Life Cycle Theory (IPLC Theory) popularized by Raymond Vernon (1966, 1979), who led and inspired the *Multinational Enterprises Project* at Harvard Business School – work that further influenced the OECD in their definition and discussion of MNEs (OECD 2008). As suggested earlier, much Western research on MNEs/MNCs has focused on firms competing internationally in manufacturing sectors – a tradition, we maintain in our choice of Japanese and Korean MNCs for comparison: namely Toyota Motor and Hyundai Motor in the automotive sector; Sony Corporation and Samsung Electronics in the consumer electronics sector.

We later explore how far the approaches towards securing strategic control adopted by individual MNCs reflect the international organizational and control structure of the MNC itself: for example, examining why they might choose between entering foreign markets by means of exports, wholly or partially owned subsidiaries, international joint ventures or through franchising and licensing arrangements in the target market (Hollensen 2012). Correspondingly, we attempt to apply the so-called 'Ownership location internalization (OLI) advantages' model developed by John Dunning (Dunning 1977, 1980, 1997, 2000), which is designed to capture motivating factors at both the macro and micro levels of comparative analysis (Ietto-Gillies 2012).

From a generalized 'Western' research perspective, it would appear appropriate to assume that Japanese and Korean MNCs choose to internationalize their activities in Chinese markets from a relatively developed position of 'local knowledge' and perceived 'familiarity' and experienced proximity when compared superficially with 'non-Asian' MNCs seeking to invest in China. In order to challenge such assumptions, we invoke a model designed by economists and management researchers in Sweden: the Uppsala model. This model was developed initially in order to identify and compare longitudinally the internationalization strategies of Swedish firms, including automotive manufacturer Volvo and consumer electronics manufacturer Electrolux, as they moved investment in production and sales from mainly domestic to predominantly international markets (Johanson and Wiedersheim-Paul 1975). Over time, the Uppsala model has come to emphasize two distinct and overlapping patterns of internationalization: firstly, a firm's engagement with a particular nationally or regionally defined foreign market towards creating an 'establishment chain' of investment and control; and secondly, a pattern of investment that might be explained by reference to the actual geographical and 'psychic' distance from the home to the targeted foreign market perceived and calculated by the firm's strategic decision makers (Johanson and Vahlne 1977, 1990). It is worth noting here that the Uppsala model tends to be used by international business (IB) researchers in order to describe and explain relatively early-stage internationalization investments of firms (Ietto-Gillies 2012).

The internationalization of Japanese and Korean MNCs

When Japanese MNCs began to challenge their American and European counterparts in global markets during the early 1980s, research discourse informing models of 'internationalization' shifted to accommodate new dimensions of strategic thinking and behaviour. To illustrate, manufacturing giants such as Toyota entered markets previously dominated by American and European rivals, outstripping these spectacularly through the connected intensity of global supply and distribution channels distinguished by unprecedented degrees of production and distribution efficiency coupled with high product quality (Sekiguchi 1979; Ouchi 1981; Ohmae 1982; Trevor 1983). Terms such as *kaizen*, quality circles, *kanban* and just-in-time (JIT) inventory management became adopted and assimilated in non-Japanese contexts for domestic and international production (Liker 2004).

In recent decades the global business landscape has changed drastically and not least in response to a wave of regional and global 'economic shocks' which MNCs in both their parent and subsidiary locations have been required to weather and (in some cases) barely survive (Das 2013). To illustrate, as Japan's economic stagnation continued into the New Millennium, Korean firms began to appear comparatively better positioned to become more globally competitive on the strength of what they had learned through the so-called IMF crisis of 1997 (Hemmert 2012). East Asian firms have rapidly entered global markets in representative manufacturing industries such as automobiles and electronics. As Porter, Takeuchi, and Sakakibara (2000) argue, maintaining a leading position in global markets requires increasingly smart investment as followers begin to match and even surpass the standards set initially by Japanese brands: we think here of Sony and Panasonic struggling to resist recent incursions by Korean rivals such as Samsung and LG into global markets for consumer electronics.

Nonetheless, many globally prominent Asian MNCs are still headquartered in Japan and, as suggested previously, are now hosted by a relatively 'new kid' on the 'internationalization block' in Korea. Researchers used to talk about how Korean governments invested heavily in human capital and industrial infrastructure in order to catch up with Japan (Rowley and Bae 1998). The observation today concerns the apparent durability of industrial and economic development of the Korean economy and, correspondingly, the rise to global prominence of Korean MNCs. Taken together, most globally prominent East Asian manufacturing MNCs today originate from Japan or Korea. To illustrate, five of the ten largest automobile manufacturers (Statista 2015) and four of the ten largest chipmakers in the world (Ford 2013) are Japanese or Korean. Japan and Korea remain by far the two largest advanced countries in East Asia and home to many of the world's largest and most globally active MNCs (see Tables 3 and 4).

However, and notwithstanding the strong presence of Japanese and Korean firms on global markets, these two countries have attracted only modest attention in internationalization research. Relatively, few scholars studied the internationalization of Japanese firms (Lu 2002; Belderbos 2003; Delios and Henisz 2003) or of Korean firms (Erramilli, Srivastava, and Kim 1999; Guillen 2002, 2003). More recently, comparative studies of the internationalization of Japanese and Chinese firms (cf. Yang et al. 2009a) and of Korean and Chinese firms (Yang et al. 2009b) have been conducted. In contrast, there are few recent dedicated studies on the internationalization strategies of Japanese or Korean MNCs. This is surprising, as most of Japan's and Korea's outward FDI has occurred in the twenty-first century (UNCTAD 2014). In particular, there remains a lack of comparative research on Japanese and Korean MNCs. This is equally surprising in consideration of the fact that these two countries have similar industrial structures yet quite distinct business systems (Hemmert 2014; Witt 2014) which, from a research perspective, become manifest and thereby comparable – an opportunity we seek to exploit later in our case studies.

Western conceptualizations towards researching Japanese and Korean MNCs

Applying Western conceptualizations and theoretical frameworks towards examining the internationalization strategies of Japanese and Korean MNCs markedly reflects an extension of research investigating similar and earlier developments in non-Asian MNCs. One stream of research has focused on the early stage internationalization of MNCs from the two countries. Delios and Henisz (2003) find that the international expansion of Japanese MNCs is broadly in line with the stage model of internationalization proposed by the Uppsala school. However, risk avoidance in response to political uncertainty was identified as an additional driving force of the regional patterns of Japanese firms' internationalization. In a similar vein, a study on international research and development (R&D) by Japanese firms by Belderbos (2003) identifies experience-based organizational learning in a latecomer situation as the overall dominant pattern. Such latecomer or market follower effects were also noted by Lu (2002), who further finds that institutional factors provide a better explanation for Japanese MNCs' international entry mode choices than transaction cost considerations. Specifically, Japanese firms appear to be influenced by isomorphic pressure from Japanese peer companies, resulting in mimetic internationalization behaviour (Lu 2002; Sako and Kotosaka 2012). This mimetic propensity might arise through the mediating and standardizing influence and international market embeddedness of Japanese trading companies providing local knowledge and feeding internalized internationalization experience to individual Japanese MNCs across a range of industries and business sectors.

Examining the early-stage internationalization of Korean MNCs, Erramilli, Srivastava, and Kim (1999) and Guillén (2003) find that the internationalization behaviour of Korean firms was strongly influenced by the physical distance to host countries and is thus well aligned with the stage model of internationalization and driven by the accumulation of experience. However, Erramilli, Srivastava, and Kim (1999) also note that some Korean firms appeared to 'leapfrog' into physically distant markets with full ownership when they perceived a strong market potential. Echoing Lu (2002), Guillen (2002, 2003) identifies isomorphic peer pressure as a major explanation in the mimetic early internationalization of Korean MNCs.

More recent studies focus on specific aspects of Japanese and Korean MNCs' internationalization. Delios and Beamish (2005) identify different types of Japanese MNCs in terms of their geographic expansion and find that a majority of the firms do not expand their business beyond locations perceived historically as 'neighbouring' (East and Southeast Asia). Moreover, Jung, Beamish, and Goerzen (2008) find that Japanese firms demonstrate a higher propensity to engage in international joint ventures than their US counterparts. Zeng et al. (2013) study the link between international experience, cultural (psychic) distance and the mortality of Korean firms' international subsidiaries and find that local experience may trigger the closure of MNC subsidiaries in culturally distant locations. The authors offer MNCs' erroneous inferences from early expansion into host countries with strongly different cultures as an explanation for their observations.

The different patterns of expansion of Japanese and Korean MNCs into developed and emerging host countries have also been studied. Makino, Beamish, and Zhao (2004) find that whereas Japanese investment in developed countries has been relatively stable over time and was accompanied by strong control, Japanese MNCs' expansion into emerging countries has been more rapidly expanding in recent years and was accompanied by lower ownership positions and weaker control structures. Typically for Japanese MNCs, such strategic internationalization concerns are shared with giant general trading companies (*sogo shosha*) holding positions across developed and emerging markets (cf. Goerzen and Makino 2007). Park, Lee, and Hong (2011) find broadly similar regional expansion patterns for Korean MNCs; however, they also note that Korean firms not affiliated to business groups (*chaebols*) show a partially different behaviour and invest more aggressively and riskily into emerging countries with high ownership positions: the independent yet supporting role of international trading companies appears much less pronounced in the Korean case (cf. Tolentino 2001).

Interim conclusions

Overall, this brief review of studies on the internationalization of Japanese and Korean MNCs reveals some interesting similarities between firms from the two countries. First, it seems that the internationalization of Japanese and Korean MNCs has often been a stage-based process driven by incremental experience and isomorphic pressure which is broadly in line with predictions made by behavioural models of internationalization (e.g. Aharoni 1966; Johanson and Vahlne 1977), more so than those made by economic internationalization models. Second, many Japanese and Korean firms appear to concentrate their international activities on geographically and culturally proximate countries.

At the same time, the literature review also hints at partial differences between the internationalization of Japanese and Korean firms. Specifically, when combining observations from different studies, the impression emerges that Korean firms may tend to be more risk taking in their international expansion than their Japanese counterparts by investing more rapidly in emerging countries.

However, this review also illustrates limitations in our knowledge on the internationalization of Japanese and Korean MNCs. In particular, (1) most studies are built on data from the early stages of Japanese and Korean firms' internationalization and thus do not reflect more recent time periods when most Japanese and Korean outward FDI occurred, (2) findings are difficult to combine, as the studies use mostly different theoretical frameworks and data and (3) there are no comparative studies on Japanese and Korean MNCs' internationalization. Therefore, it is extremely difficult to judge the extent to which the internationalization strategies adopted by Korean and Japanese MNCs have been markedly similar or dissimilar, and why. Recognizing this relative lack of current research insight prompted us to embark on this exploratory study.

Research methodology

Given the largely unprecedented structure of economic, technological and political change currently sweeping across national and regional systems for business and management in East Asia (Jackson 2013), and in view of the relative paucity of current research in our chosen context, the following discussion and analysis should be recognized as *exploratory* – a methodological choice that aims 'to find out what is happening, particularly in little-understood situations' and 'seek new insights' by assessing phenomena 'in a new light' (Robson 2002, 59).

Challenging Western research bias

The first of our four research questions led us to conduct a literature review in order to identify distinctive features of the internationalization strategies employed by Korean and Japanese MNCs. The review suggests some degree of bias in non-Asian research into the internationalization of East Asian MNCs. One manifestation of this bias appears to be a rather path-dependent tradition maintained by non-Asian academics in routinely applying Western-based theories on them, invoking concepts and theories such as 'strategic contingency' or 'sequential internationalization' (cf. Jackson and Debroux 2009). Simultaneously, we recognize that although this might express a general observation, such bias of perspective is not unique to Western contexts for IB research: during the heydays of Japanese MNCs expansion, Asian academics could be observed invoking similar bias (cf. Kojima 1978; Ozawa 1979).

Challenging Western research propensities

Over recent years, there appears to have been a loss of Western academic interest in understanding Japanese firms 'from the inside' – an attitude perhaps indirectly encouraged by the relative paucity of research published in English by Japanese scholars (Miles Fletcher and von Staden 2012; Jackson, forthcoming). Another reason might be the relative lack of Western academic understanding about how Korean MNCs actually 'work' – or are managed – in terms of domestic structures and global strategies, whether in comparison to or as distinct from their Japanese and other nationally defined counterparts (cf. Rowley and Benson 2002; Rowley and Paik 2009; Hemmert 2012; Jackson 2013; Rowley and Warner 2015).

This insight led us to formulate a second research question asking about the extent to which similarities or differences are evident in the internationalization strategies of comparable Japanese and Korean MNCs. In order to address this question, we adopt a two-step process. First, we examine country-level statistical data to assess and compare the overall internationalization of Japanese and Korean firms. Second, we apply a case study approach whereby we make an 'empirical investigation of a particular contemporary phenomenon within a real-life context', drawing on 'multiple sources of evidence' (Saunders, Lewis, and

Thornhill 2012, 666). The 'real-life phenomenon' that we observe and describe is represented by the flows of FDI from comparable Japanese and Korean MNCs; we draw on evidence from government statistics, trade associations, along with industry- and firm-specific data. For purposes of comparison, we subsequently discuss data for each MNC systematically within established theoretical frameworks or models for describing flows of FDI as manifestations of an MNC's internationalization strategy. Taking this approach enables us to address the third and fourth research questions.

Country-level overview analysis

Table 1 shows summary information on the development of exports from Japan and Korea since 1990. Overall, exports from both countries have greatly increased over the last two and a half decades. However, there is a clear difference in the pace of export increase between the two countries. Whereas Japan's exports have increased by approximately two and a half times, Korea's exports have scaled up by more than ten times over the same period. Moreover, the ratio of exports to GDP for Korea has increased from less than 25% in 1990 to more than 50% in 2013. In contrast, Japan's export-to-GDP ratio, while also increasing, has remained below 20% over the same period of time.

Additionally, the composition of Japan's and Korea's recent merchandise exports, which account for approximately 80% of the two countries' overall exports (WTO 2015), is shown in Figures 1 and 2 by product categories and regions. Both in Japan and Korea, approximately, 60% of all merchandise exports fall to assembly products, including transport equipment, electronics and machinery. At the same time, there are differences between the two countries in the weight of specific product categories. In Japan, the largest category is transport equipment, which mainly consists of automobiles, whereas in Korea, it is electronics, including microelectronics.

The regional distribution shows that a majority of both Japan's and Korea's merchandise exports is being shipped to Asia. The concentration on the Asian region is particularly strong for Korea, where exports to China alone exceed those to North America and Europe combined (Figures 1 and 2).

Information on the development of the two countries' outward FDI stock since 1990 is summarized in Table 2. The stock of outward FDI of the two countries has increased even

Table 1. Development of Japanese and Korean exports.

		1990	2000	2013
Japan	Exports (billion US-$)	319.7	515.7	797.0
	Exports/GDP (%)	10.3	10.9	16.2
Korea	Exports (billion US-$)	70.1	196.6	703.2
	Exports/GDP (%)	24.6	35.0	53.9

Source: World Bank (2015).

Table 2. Development of Japanese and Korean outward FDI stock.

		1990	2000	2013
Japan	Outward FDI stock (billion US-$)	201.4	278.4	992.9
	Outward FDI stock/GDP (%)	6.5	5.9	20.1
Korea	Outward FDI stock (billion US-$)	2.3	21.5	219.1
	Outward FDI stock/GDP (%)	0.9	4.0	17.9

Source: UNCTAD (2015).

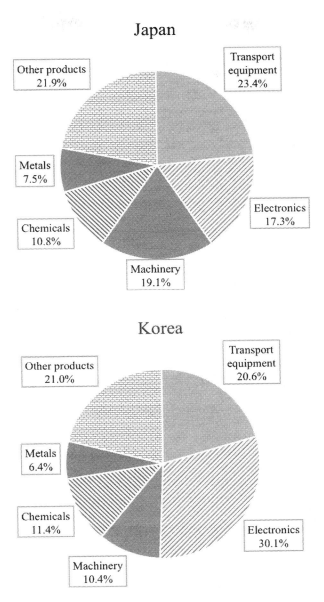

Figure 1. Composition of Japan's and Korea's merchandise exports by product category, 2013. Source: Statistics Bureau, MIAC (2015); KIET (2014).

more steeply than their exports. At the same time, a clear difference in can be observed again in the speed of expansion between Japan and Korea. Whereas Japan's FDI stock has expanded by approximately five times between 1990 and 2013, an increase by almost 100 times has occurred in the Korean outward FDI stock over the same period of time. Notwithstanding Korea's much faster rate of increase, however, its total outward FDI stock still amounted only to approximately one fifth of Japan's in 2013. This remaining gap in the FDI stock of the two countries can be mostly attributed to the different size of their economies – as Japan's economy is bigger than Korea's, so is its outward FDI stock. When set in

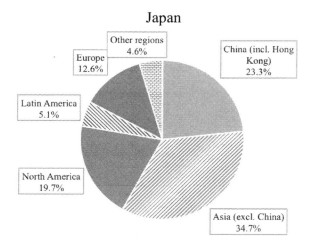

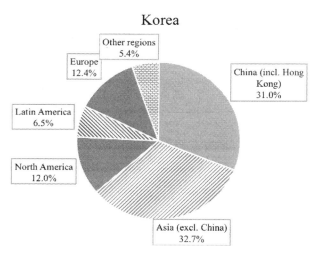

Figure 2. Composition of Japan's and Korea's merchandise exports by region, 2013. Source: Statistics Bureau, MIAC (2015); KITA (2015).

relation to GDP, Korea's outward FDI stock, which was much lower than Japan's also by this measure 1990, has reached a similar level by 2013.

Summary information on the distribution of the outward FDI stock of the two countries across industries and regions is given in Figures 3 and 4. From a sectoral perspective, the FDI stocks of Japan and Korea show various similarities. In manufacturing, the largest amount of FDI carried out by Japanese and Korean firms falls to transport equipment and in non-manufacturing to finance. Both in Japan and in Korea, the manufacturing sector is overall much less dominant in FDI than in exports. Moreover, both countries hold notable outward FDI positions in the mining industry.

From a regional perspective, however, clear differences in the composition of the outward FDI stocks of the two countries can be observed. Whereas the largest FDI destination for

Table 3. Japan's largest MNCs, 2013.

Name of company	Industry	Sales (millions US$)
Toyota Motor	Motor vehicles	256,381
Honda Motor	Motor vehicles	118,176
Nissan Motor	Motor vehicles	104,606
Sony	Electrical and electronic equipment	77,510
Mitsubishi Corporation	Wholesale trade	75,734

Source: UNCTAD (2015).

Table 4. Korea's largest MNCs, 2012.

Name of company	Industry	Sales (millions US$)
Samsung Electronics	Electrical and electronic equipment	179,060
Hyundai Motor	Motor vehicles	75,211
POSCO	Metal and metal products	56,632
LG Electronics	Electrical and electronic equipment	49,080
Doosan Corporation	Construction	21,683

Source: UNCTAD (2015).

Japanese firms is North America, more than half of Korea's outward FDI falls to Asia, with China holding a share of more than 30% alone (Figures 3 and 4).

Finally, the ranking of the two countries' five largest MNCs is shown in Tables 3 and 4. In the manufacturing sector, automobile and electronics firms dominate the top ranks in both countries, with one company in each country which clearly outsizes all others: Toyota Motor (Japan) and Samsung Electronics (Korea). Moreover, it can be observed that there is only one non-manufacturing company among the top five firms in each country: Mitsubishi Corporation (Japan) and Doosan Corporation (Korea).

Case studies

For our case analysis, we chose four leading Japanese and Korean MNCs that have invested heavily in China. As the following case studies illustrate, these MNCs are globally prominent and compete in manufacturing industries that feature prominently in the outward internationalization of Japanese and Korean firms in general. The case studies selected for comparison are: Toyota Motor (Japan) and Hyundai Motor (Korea), each competing in the automotive manufacturing sector; Samsung Electronics (Korea) and Sony Corporation (Japan) competing in the manufacture of consumer electronics, including entertainment media and digital communications. We outline details of their respective internationalization strategies, focusing on the patterns of their investments into China.

Toyota Motor

Toyota Motor Corporation was founded in 1937 by Kiichiro Toyoda. Its headquarters is located near the city of Nagoya and that now has developed to become Toyota City. The current CEO is Akio Toyoda, who thereby maintains a family line of share ownership combined with executive stewardship. Toyota is currently the world's leading automobile manufacturer by volume, recording worldwide sales of 8971,864 units in Fiscal 2014–2015, with 2153,694

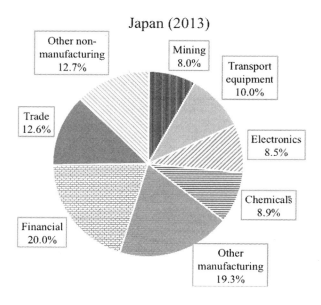

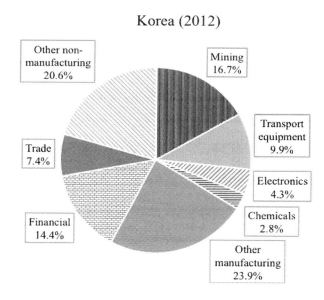

Figure 3. Composition of Japan's and Korea's FDI stock by industry. Source: OECD (2015).

units being sold in Japan (Toyota 2015). Toyota also produces commercial vehicles and trucks under the Hino brand, mainly targeting domestic markets. Toyota has approximately 340,000 employees worldwide and, according to Forbes (2015), currently has the world's eighth most valuable brand.

Toyota introduced the *Lexus* luxury brand in the United States in 1989. Although remaining to this day a leading luxury brand in North America, sales of the brand in China since have been relatively modest, reaching 75,000 in 2014, a figure far below sales for rival Audi, BMW and Mercedes vehicles. One reason for this shortfall might

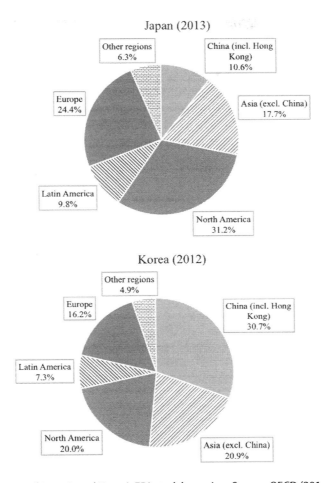

Figure 4. Composition of Japan's and Korea's FDI stock by region. Source: OECD (2015).

lie in the relative maturity of the North American and European markets compared to China (Bloomberg 2011). Another suggestion concerns recent political and diplomatic tensions between the current Chinese and Japanese governments (Reuters 2014).

Toyota began exporting vehicles to China already in the 1930s, and although Toyota has hitherto resisted transferring any *Lexus* production to China (Bloomberg 2011), the firm has already two well-established joint ventures in China supporting the production, distribution and sale of more mid-range vehicles. In 2002, a comprehensive manufacturing, distribution and sales relationship was formed with China FAW Group Corp, a Chinese state-owned enterprise (SOE). Drawing on the success of this initial venture, Toyota subsequently formed a joint venture in 2004 with the much smaller GAC Group, primarily to assemble and supply engines for the *Camry* label targeting middle-income consumers in China (Toyota 2015). Listed now as GAC Toyota Motor Co., Ltd., GAC and Toyota each hold 50% share ownership. In sum, China remains one of Toyota's main markets for sales: 1.03 million units in 2014, up 12.5% from 2013 (Reuters 2015a).

Toyota recently announced a ¥150 trillion (ca. US$ 1.3 million) investment in new plant in the southern city of Guangzhou, scheduled annually to produce 100,000 units of the mid-range Toyota *Yaris* (in China, *Vitz*) from 2018 (Japan Times 2015). Despite such headline investments, Toyota in China faces a number of enduring and emerging challenges. Firstly, Toyota's status as the world's largest automotive manufacturer by production volume continues to appear overshadowed by the fact that, in China, Toyota ranks only sixth among global automakers and sells less than one-third as many vehicles as its two main rivals, Volkswagen and General Motors. Secondly, and as the Chinese market becomes increasingly mature and 'globally savvy', the image of MNCs such as Toyota are vulnerable to immediate negative association by (for example) the recall of millions of vehicles worldwide after faults had been found in brake installations and passenger air bags – components manufactured by trusted Toyota suppliers but nonetheless ultimately associated with the Toyota brand in China as elsewhere. An emerging challenge is likely to arise as shareholders in Japan become increasingly active in their demands for return on investment (Financial Times 2011). To illustrate, the return to Toyota shareholders on current investments in China equates to a multiple of 4.52 as compared to an industry five-year average of 18.57 (Reuters 2015b).

Hyundai Motor

Hyundai Motor, founded in 1967, is Korea's leading car manufacturer and has become one of the largest automobile producers in the world. In 2014, Hyundai Motor, together with its wholly owned subsidiary Kia Motors, sold eight million automobiles, out of which 1.77 million units (22.1%) were sold in China (Hankook Kyungjae 2015). Thereby, China is Hyundai's globally largest market.

Following a small-scale contract with a local Chinese company for knock-down assembly of minibuses in Wuhan in 1994, Hyundai made a full-fledged market entry in China only in 2002, after previously focusing on Western countries in its global business and setting up full-scale overseas production facilities in Canada (subsequently closed due to a lack of demand), Turkey and India. Hyundai thereby entered China much later than most major Western and Japanese automobile firms (Oh 2013). However, Hyundai's market entry into China was prepared with a lead time of six to seven years by developing a pool of expatriate managers for its future operations who learned Chinese and established relationships with local stakeholders (Chang and Park 2012).

Shortly, after China's WTO accession and following the Chinese government's requirements for inward FDI in the automobile industry, Hyundai entered a 50:50 joint venture with the local SOE Beijing Automobile Industry Holding Company in April 2002 (Oh 2013) and soon thereafter started producing and selling its mainstream car models in China. It became the second largest market automobile company in China by market share as soon as 2005 and thereafter further increased its production by setting up two additional factories. Hyundai also quickly localized its supply chain in China by working with Korean suppliers, who rapidly built manufacturing facilities in nearby locations, and to a somewhat lesser extent, with Chinese suppliers. A high satisfaction by Chinese customers in terms of value, functionality and service further enhanced Hyundai's local business development. Hyundai is currently building another two additional factories in China and plans to increase its annual production capacity in the country to 2.7 million units by 2018 (ChosunBiz 2015).

Hyundai's initial fast growth in China was supported by its insider status (Chang and Park 2012; Oh 2013). As various Hyundai managers were preparing for the market entry, they had built networks with important local stakeholders, including government officials. The local government in Beijing, empowered by the factual decentralization of administrative power after China's WTO entry, was keen to develop the local economy by increasing automobile production through a joint venture of its local automobile SOE (Beijing Automobile Industry Holding Company) with a foreign partner. After a meeting of Hyundai Chairman Chung Mong-koo with a high-ranking local Chinese government official in 2001, Hyundai was not only selected as joint venture partner, but the Chinese side also supported the business by expediting administrative procedures and providing assistance in land purchase, infrastructure development and staff recruitment (Oh 2013).

Samsung Electronics

Samsung Electronics, founded in 1969, recorded sales of US$208.9 billion in 2014, which made it not only Korea's, but also the world's largest IT company by business volume (Fortune 2015). The company has four large business segments: consumer electronics, mobile devices, semiconductors and digital displays (Samsung Electronics 2014b). In geographical terms, Samsung's most important business regions are Asia, North America and Europe. In 2012, 14% of its global sales and 19% of its global employees fell to China, which whereby is one of the most important countries for Samsung's business.

Samsung Electronics entered China at a later stage than Western and Japanese electronics companies. Whereas the North American and Western European markets were entered by Samsung since the 1980s, the company began doing business in China only around 1992, when full diplomatic relations between Korea and China were established. Samsung's aim was producing for the local Chinese market, and the company rapidly invested into the establishment of integrated manufacturing sites both in Northern China (Tianjin) and Southern China (Guangdong province) (Samsung Chairman Secretariat Office 1998; Lee and He 2009). Specifically, Samsung Electronics set up a joint venture with a Chinese SOE with a 50:50 equity share in Tianjin in January 1993 for the production of video cassette recorders and components. Another joint venture with the same partner for the production of monitors followed in 1994, in which Samsung increased its equity share to 80% by 1998. In parallel, other Samsung group companies functioning as suppliers for Samsung Electronics, including Samsung Electro-Mechanics, Samsung SDI and Samsung Corning, also set up joint ventures or wholly owned subsidiaries in the Tianjin area throughout the 1990s.

A similar approach was taken in Guangdong Province (Lee and He 2009). A Samsung affiliate with 90% ownership was established in late 1992 in Huizhou for the production of audiovideo products. Whereas the core components were initially imported from Korea, they were soon substituted by local production when Samsung group suppliers set up wholly owned subsidiaries or joint ventures and began producing in nearby locations in Guangdong Province. At the same time, stable business relations with local suppliers were sought additionally in order to establish a robust local supply chain (Gamble, Morris, and Wilkinson 2003).

As a result, the scale and scope of Samsung's business in China rapidly increased. The company established a regional headquarter in China no later than in January 1995, thereby giving the country the status of one of its most important global business locations (Samsung Chairman Secretariat Office 1998).

Samsung faced various challenges when establishing its business in China (Lee and He 2009). As the company entered China later than its main competitors, it struggled to find competent local partners, as the strongest Chinese electronics companies were already tied up with other MNCs. Moreover, Samsung met initially not a very strong success in the Chinese market, as it introduced relatively cheap products based on outdated technology which failed to differentiate from products made by local competitors. Later on, however, Samsung changed its approach and focused on producing and selling high-end products in China. This rapid switch to technologically advanced products such as flat displays and large screen displays was enabled by the full localization of production based on vertical integration with its technologically advanced group-internal suppliers. Whereas Taiwanese, Japanese and European competitors struggled to respond to shifts in the market conditions in China, Samsung could reliably produce the high-end products popular with Chinese customers, and thereby rapidly increase its market share (Lee and He 2009).

As of 2013, Samsung Electronics (excluding its group-internal suppliers) had 17 local subsidiaries in China, including 13 manufacturing subsidiaries, two sales subsidiaries and two regional headquarters in Shanghai and Beijing (Samsung Electronics 2014a).

Sony Corporation

Sony Corporation is the electronics business unit of the larger Sony Group, a Japanese MNC with investments in electronics (including mobile phone handsets, digital communications, computers, gaming consoles), entertainment media (including film studios and distribution channels), and financial services, including life insurance.

The founders of Sony were two entrepreneurs, Akito Morita and Masaru Ibuka, who in 1946 opened an electronics store in Tokyo specializing in recycling components of radios and other electronic equipment discarded by the American military. From these inauspicious beginnings, Sony has become one of the most recognized Japanese brand names, appearing consistently adaptive and innovative by designing, developing and introducing miniaturized high-quality products such as the TR63 radio, the Sony Walkman, the Sony Discman and today's PlayStation.

Sony (China) Limited was established in 1996 as a wholly owned subsidiary of Sony Corp. As with the Tokyo headquarters, the Beijing office also acts as a museum, showroom, and drop-in multimedia entertainments centre. Sony (China) has been headed since its inception by Japanese CEOs. Consequently, Sony Corp's appointment of a non-Japanese CEO (Sir Howard Stringer) in 2005 appeared to herald a new era of corporate governance in Japanese MNCs (Japan Times 2005). However, an alliance between Sony and Swedish Ericsson with the purpose of becoming more globally competitive in the manufacture of mobile phone handsets did not help either company resist the incursion of Korean rivals such as Samsung and LG. To illustrate: since 2013, Samsung has been market leader in the Chinese market for smartphone sales with a market share of 26.6% in 2015, while Sony's market share in China has fallen from 4.1% (ranked 6th) in 2013 to 3.1% (ranked 10th) in 2015 (Trendforce 2015). Meanwhile, Apple has maintained second position in the Chinese market, with a share consistently around 16.5%.

Since 2014, leading business commentators in Asia were suggesting the reasons for Sony's decline in the manufacturing of handsets digital could be found, conversely, in the reasons for Apple's spectacular success in similar global markets (Forbes 2015). Increasingly, business researchers are asking whether Sony's exposure to the Chinese market has contributed towards their loss of global market share in PC manufacture to a 'next generation' of Chinese MNCs such as Lenovo (Nguyen, Okrend, and Tan 2013). In China as elsewhere, Sony's attempts to strategically refocus and restructure can appear cumbersome. For example, the decision to sell off its VAIO PC line to Lenovo will generate a net loss of over 100 billion Yen (Bloomberg 2015). This dramatic divestment should facilitate increased investment into the rapidly expanding gaming market, a move prompted by the Chinese government's lifting of a ban on non-domestic games consoles in 2014 (Technobuffalo 2015). To facilitate a more immediate launch of its PS4 console in January 2015 while simultaneously challenging rival Microsoft's XBOX, Sony entered a 49:51 share joint venture with Shanghai Oriental Pearl. However, the much-heralded January 2015 launch was delayed for undisclosed reasons, among which was probably Sony's need to re-assess the existing 'black' and 'grey' markets for gaming software in China (Bloomberg 2015).

Discussion

Similarities and differences between Japanese and Korean firms

Our first two research questions focused on the features of Japanese and Korean firms' internationalization strategies, and their similarities or differences. The country-level analysis has shown broadly similar patterns in outward internationalization of firms from the two countries with an initial focus on exports, followed by a steep increase in outward FDI, in particular after the turn of the Millennium. Compared to Japan, Korea was a latecomer in internationalization but currently has surpassed Japan's export intensity and caught up with its FDI intensity.

The case studies comparing individual Japanese and Korean firms' approaches in penetrating the Chinese market revealed strong differences among them, however. The two Korean firms entered China later, but much more forcefully than their Japanese counterparts. As a result, Hyundai's and Samsung's business volume in China is now much larger than Toyota's and Sony's respectively. The large-scale investment by the two Korean firms from an almost zero base indicates a higher extent of risk-taking than the relatively incremental approach of the Japanese firms. This finding is in line with earlier studies, which described Japanese firms' strategies as relatively conservative (Delios and Henisz 2003) and Korean firms' strategies as comparatively more aggressive (Hemmert 2012).

Another notable difference between the Japanese and Korean firms as regards their business strategies in China is their different degree of flexibility. Since investing on a significant scale, Toyota and Sony do not appear to have made many changes or adjustments in their approaches towards customers and other stakeholders in China; Sony's recent restructuring is exceptional in this regard. In contrast, the Korean firms appear more inclined to change their approaches in response to customer needs. This tendency is particularly visible in Samsung's case: after having achieved only modest results with selling low-end products in China, the company changed its approach and focused more strongly on high-end products, with evident success.

Taken together, and while the country-level analysis indicates broad similarities in the internationalization patterns of Japanese and Korean firms, the case studies of four leading Japanese and Korean MNCs suggest strong differences in their strategic behaviour on the

Chinese market. In order to ascertain how and why this might be, the following discussion is structured with specific reference to the three conceptual frameworks derived from the literature review: IPLC theory (Vernon 1979); the OLI advantages paradigm (Dunning 1977, 2000); and the Uppsala model (Johanson and Vahlne 1977, 1990).

IPLC theory

IPLC theory – along with the common linear depictions of its application – is predicated on the assumption that where a manufacturer identifies and fills a 'technology gap', market advantages will accrue (Posner 1961). It assumes that a strategy of 'technology push' will be met by a 'market pull' from a sufficiently large and potentially growing market segment of consumers whose attitudes and behaviours are influenced by observed confluences in local macro- and microeconomic conditions: for example, across China and in rapidly developing urban conglomerations and powerful regional economies such as Shanghai where increasingly affluent socioeconomic segments aspire to lifestyles distinctly different to their fellow citizens in less developed regions of China (cf. Griffiths 2012). From the foreign MNC perspective, managing changes in the firm's internal structure is vital: for example, sustained investment in foresighted innovation and patent protection combined with staffing and training strategies adjusted to local human resource availability and consumer expectations (Fitzgerald and Rowley 2015).

Location decisions by MNCs are key towards how quickly and sustainably they might continue to exploit these advantages (Vernon 1979). For example, recent market data illustrates how the innovation lead advantage once enjoyed across global markets by Sony in the manufacture of mobile phone handsets has been eroded by Apple, Samsung and LG along with new entrants such as China's Huawei and Lenovo. Apple appears to be marketing 'lifestyle'; Samsung appears to be marketing technological finesse combined with global brand recognition; Huawei appears to be marketing utility. With their museums and mega-entertainment centres concentrated in major conurbations – Beijing, New York, London, Tokyo – what is it that Sony is marketing, and to whom? Indeed, the Sony example illustrates one of the major criticisms of IPLC theory: namely, the research emphasis given to product as opposed to the firm as producer of the product (Ietto-Gillies 2012). Applying IPLC to the Sony–Samsung comparison does not appear to predict the effect that internationalization in relation to FDI decisions became sporadically and only weakly supported by effective internationalization of Sony's organizational structure for managing innovation and consequently for targeting FDI.

Another factor appearing to undermine the predictive power of IPLC theory is the reliability of data used to describe, for example, a 'product' unique to the firm. The theory helps little towards mapping the international vertically integrated patterns of production whereby, for example, Toyota components are transported between assembly sites in Japan, China and other markets in order to produce a Toyota-labelled 'product' for sale in China or for 're-importation' to Japan (Yamashita 2010). Already in the mid-1990s, up to one third of world trade was conducted on a cross-boundary 'inter-firm' basis (UNCTAD 1996).

The weak explanatory power of IPLC theory for the internationalization strategies of the companies we have studied is further illustrated by the Samsung case. Samsung initially entered the supposedly 'emerging' Chinese market with mature products based on outdated technology, following the IPLC paradigm. However, this approach did not resonate well with

Chinese customers. Samsung only became successful in China when it introduced high-end products – an approach that challenges common interpretations of IPLC theory.

The OLI paradigm

The OLI paradigm offers a dynamic and triangulated framework within which to analyse and predict how MNCs locate and time their international investments. It adopts a systems view applied within nationally defined economies as targets for a firm's FDI and the returns it expects to accrue from these investments. According to Ietto-Gillies (2012, 103), 'ownership' advantages describe distinctive features of individual firms: for example, their technological capabilities, their human resources, their knowledge and experience learnt through succeeding – or failing – in a variety of markets. Relevant to this current discussion, Zhang (2013) compares how MNCs can appear to adopt very differing strategies towards recruiting and retaining human resources with relevant 'local' (China) knowledge into their foreign investments. Correspondingly, and for both FDI and international 'talent' recruitment purposes, the 'location' element of the OLI paradigm should help predict likely outcomes when competing Korean or Japanese MNCs invest in 'neighbouring' Chinese markets, where managing supply chains effectively should appear equally challenging for both rivals.

The 'internalization' element in the paradigm refers to advantages generated by the structures specific to each firm such that actual and potential negative market and other business environmental influences might be ameliorated by the firm's own efforts: for example, using accrued 'local knowledge' and nurturing local networks in China towards securing sufficient national and regional political influence such that transaction costs might be reliably planned and controlled for. Specifically, forming joint ventures with powerful Chinese SOEs automatically creates opportunities for non-Chinese MNCs to internalize political, legal, technological and economic returns from their investments in China; and here, we can recognize internalization as a two-way process, as Chinese partner firms potentially and over time accrue similar benefits. This latter case illustrates one of the core assumptions of the OLI paradigm; namely, that individual MNCs are more likely than non-MNCs to achieve OLI advantages on the strength of their relative size, history, strategic resource base and brand recognition among influential actors in both developed and emerging markets (Dunning 1977).

To illustrate from our case studies, in automobile manufacture Hyundai is no longer playing 'catch up' in technological or global marketing terms with Toyota. In such a highly structured and globally imitative industry, what can Toyota managers achieve when predicting the development of OLI elements in their investment strategies for China that Hyundai managers cannot achieve? What can they learn in relation to controlling transaction costs, now evening out after Hyundai's possible advantage as a late entrant, and further towards forming joint ventures with Chinese SOEs in order to secure and sustain ownership, locational and internalization advantages? More sustainable progress might be made towards securing OLI advantages through investments in international marketing rather than in international production. To illustrate, although Toyota continues to dominate the market for taxi vehicles across Japan and (until recently) in major cities in the Philippines, the firm needs to ask itself why Hyundai dominates taxi vehicle sales in Beijing, why Volkswagen continues to dominate in Shanghai, and why taxi drivers in The Philippines are switching to Korean-made vehicles.

Dunning realized that his original conceptualization of potential OLI advantages might become reduced to a 'shopping list of variables' used descriptively by IB researchers comparing the internationalization strategies of MNCs (Ietto-Gillies 2012, 105). His later conceptualizations were modelled more dynamically and with increased emphasis on operational in tandem with strategic decisions made by MNC managers (Dunning 2000). To illustrate, the existing internal hierarchies of Toyota in Japan are likely to come under unprecedented strain as shareholders begin openly to challenge senior executives they hold responsible for the relatively poor return on investments in the firm's operations in China, especially as China can no longer be considered a source of low-cost labour. Correspondingly, applying OLI analysis to describe and (retrospectively) predict Hyundai's FDI to China appears almost mechanistic, given that the firm's investment rapidly increased form near zero to substantial during 2002. It is not plausible that the company suddenly acquired ownership, location and internalization advantages in such a short period and – as in the Toyota case – against determined local and international rivals.

The Uppsala model

A major strength of the Uppsala model is that it guides researchers towards identifying and comparing patterns of FDI by individual MNCs and eliciting the perceptions, experiences and expectations that drive senior managers in these MNCs to make the decisions that form these observable FDI-related behaviours. In other words, rather than relying predominantly on the analysis business, market and firm-specific data towards describing and predicting flows of FDI, researchers are encouraged to bring the light of critical enquiry into the 'black box' of the firm in order to analyse its decision-making process in a specific field, such as sales in foreign markets (Ietto-Gillies 2012, 112).

The model conceptualizes two distinct yet overlapping patterns of decision-making, and hence of FDI (Johanson and Wiedersheim-Paul 1975; Johanson and Vahlne 1990). The first describes the firm's strategic and operational engagement in a target market: a process of decision-making leading to the formation of an 'establishment chain' that becomes manifest in terms of (for example) volume of investments through the agency of local representatives leading to the establishment of a sales or distribution subsidiary and eventually to the creating of a production subsidiary. An analogous pattern of investment would be to invest in more markets perceived as familiar or operationally accessible markets first before later diversifying to other more 'psychically distant' and less readily accessible markets (Johanson and Vahlne 1990). To illustrate, in our case study, we saw how managers at Samsung had to wait until diplomat relations between Korea and the PRC became normalized in 1992. Immediately, Samsung managers appeared to use their 'late entrant' advantage in the China market and draw on their experience of investing in other 'Chinese' markets such as Taiwan and Hong Kong to first invest in production facilities designed to serve local markets (1992) before entering a 50:50 joint venture with a Chinese SOE (1993) followed by another in 1994 that in 1998 became an 80:20 owned investment as the Chinese government relaxed laws on the ownership rights of non-Chinese firms.

The Uppsala model remains a durable model and, from a researcher perspective, suggests an enduring predictive appeal. For example, the type of data sources we used in developing our case studies to trace and compare patterns of original and incremental investment – and, as in the Sony case, sudden divestment help define the 'state' element of the Uppsala model.

Such data can be readily correlated across various incremental MNC investments towards explaining how prior investments made by each comparable MNC might prompt subsequent investments in the same location by the same or competing firms. Similarly, by comparing the business performance over time of selected East Asian MNCs, we can identify some of the 'change' aspects included as key variables in the Uppsala model.

Applying the Uppsala model in order to gain insights into other variables relevant towards identifying 'change' outcomes of management decision-making such as market specific-knowledge, we can infer from public announcements of apparent strategic failure: for example, Sony's abortive PS4 launch in January 2015. However, we would need to infer heavily in order to offer reliable insights into these firm-specific decision-making processes and the patterns of FDI that emerged from East Asian MNCs in particular (Ando and Zing 2012). In short, further to examining 'culture' as an element in the context of interpreting the formulation and implementation of firm-level FDI strategies, we might need to consider the culture(s) that give rise and meaning to models that researchers choose to apply (cf. Jackson 2011). Add to this complexity the major shifts that have occurred in terms of currency fluctuations within and across national boundaries – for example, as now when the Beijing government advances its policies towards making the RMB a more convertible yet still strictly 'managed' currency for foreign exchange – we recognize how threatening an over-reliance of publicly available business data can be to measures of research reliability and validity (Aliber 1971; Ietto-Gillies 2012).

Implications

As regards our first two research questions addressing specific features of and similarities and differences between the internationalization strategies chosen by Japanese and Korean MNCs, our study has shown that while the internationalization patterns demonstrated by Japanese and Korean firms might appear relatively similar on an aggregated level, there are strong differences in their strategic behaviour at the level of the individual MNC as a business entity. For example, the Korean firms we have studied appear to be clearly more risk-taking and more flexible in their approaches towards the Chinese market than their Japanese counterparts. Such observable discrepancies suggest that neither theorists nor MNC managers should assume that the internationalization strategies of East Asian MNCs from countries with institutional and cultural similarities, such as Japan and Korea, are highly similar, as macro-level similarities are masking micro-level differences. In other words: we should not expect Japanese and Korean MNCs to behave 'more or less the similarly' in overseas markets (Lechevalier 2014).

As regards our third research question on the applicability of Western-based internationalization theories in East Asia, we have seen how the theories and models that gave structure to our discussion appear limited when applied specifically to East Asian MNCs. For example, Western-based models appear oriented towards defining the markets targeted by MNCs for FDI as 'national', invoking a broader context of 'globalization', however defined. In the case of China, the political influence of 'national' government in Beijing impacts on FDI decisions of all MNCs in China, and not least MNCs headquartered in Korea and Japan. This insight supports a compelling argument that one economic impact of 'globalization' appears to prompt greater 'regionalization' in East Asian contexts, thus challenging established assumptions among Western researchers (Boyer 2014). Consequently, IPLC theory and the OLI paradigm as theoretical frameworks imbued (we suggest) with Western bias appear not to work particularly well towards predicting the internationalization of East Asian MNCs in an East Asian target market, whereas the Uppsala model with its behavioural emphasis appears to have relatively stronger explanatory power.

Furthermore, as we illustrated in relation to predictive applications of IPLC theory and inter-form trade and investment flows, fundamental problems arise from selective a priori definition in relation to the MNC as a 'firm'. It is convenient to define firms as discrete socio-economic and techno-legal entities. However, to what extent should we take account of the role played by giant Japanese trading companies (*sogo shosha*) such as Marubeni and Mitsui towards gathering and channelling (internalizing) 'market-specific knowledge' and 'internationalization experience' into the firm? Where should the boundaries for this strategic interaction be drawn, how, and why? Whose 'local knowledge' influences the final market entry decision? From a research perspective, to what extent might the role of such mediating firms or agencies impact on measures of 'psychic distance'? To what extent can the boundaries for FDI decision-making in Japanese MNCs drawing on *sogo shosha* and other 'external' agency support be compared reliably with similar boundaries in Korean MNCs who rely on more easily inferred internalized resources to make decisions about FDI?

Taken together, our exploratory study has revealed and, in effect, confirmed various limitations and weaknesses of Western internationalization theories towards explaining the internationalization behaviour and FDI strategies of East Asian MNCs. In this respect, we connect with existing streams of IB research observation and investigation (cf. Malhotra, Agarwal, and Ulgado 2003; Rugman 2010). By invoking and specifying an East Asian context for IB research, we believe that this current paper contributes towards raising a fresh series of critical questions about the explanatory and predictive power of existing internationalization models.

Correspondingly, the final research question driving this paper asks whether sufficient evidence might already exist to support proposals for a new 'East Asian model' for describing internationalization strategies of East Asian MNCs. The findings from our case studies indicate that the strategic behaviour of firms from two East Asian countries with partially common institutional and cultural roots (Japan and Korea), while not being well-aligned with most Western-based internationalization theories, is highly diverse. This suggests that any new 'East Asian' internationalization model might need to look beyond focusing only on MNCs' manifest business activities and instead guide researchers towards digging deeper into the underlying forces that might or might not drive the behaviour of East Asian MNCs. In doing so, theorists will need to consider the high diversity in the East Asian economic and institutional landscape, which clearly reached beyond the behavioural diversity of Japanese and Korean MNCs. To illustrate, Chinese MNCs are rapidly becoming influential players in determining current and future flows of global FDI, leading Chinese researchers to examine whether there is sufficient evidence already to propose a distinctly 'Chinese' conceptualizations of global supply chains and FDI (cf. Song 2013). This suggestion might cause original designers of the Uppsala model to reflect on China's Zhejiang Geely Holding Group's acquisition of Volvo's automobile manufacture from Ford in 2012: if we can speculate already about a 'Chinese' model for internationalization, why not expand this scope towards exploring the validity of both 'Japanese' in contrast to 'Korean' models? Indeed, the current rise to global prominence of Chinese-sourced FDI causes us to question how reliable and valid existing 'Western' models of MNC internationalization are; both in terms of explaining how long-established market rivalries between the type of Korean and Japanese MNCs we discuss in this paper; and predictively in respect of the extent to which Chinese MNCs do or might seek to emulate FDI patterns of their Asian and non-Asian rivals.

Analogous to the staged patterns of FDI described by the 'establishment chain' concept central to the Uppsala model, the development of a differentiated model for identifying and comparing the internationalization strategies of East Asian MNCs might by increasing our critical involvement with the 'markets' that already exist for established models and theories. As we suggested from the beginning of this discussion, as researchers we have an opportunity – and, perhaps, a responsibility – to challenge the 'Western bias' in existing models: critically re-examine the boundaries for definition and analysis they set; travel back along the path dependencies they appear to express; invite more local perspectives towards assessing the research efficacy of such models.

Correspondingly, our findings suggest that other relevant areas for further critical enquiry include a re-examination of the role of institutional embeddedness in the home context for MNCs competing for positions in emerging markets – a more dynamic and reliable 'country of origin' factor than over-generalized and, in conceptual terms, markedly 'static' references to 'national culture' (Boyer 2014; Lechevalier 2014). A further challenge to Western bias in analyses of FDI sourced in East Asia comes when comparing how Japanese and Korean MNCs now appear to 'play catch-up' to Chinese MNCs investing in newly emerging markets such as those across Africa. Are established models of internationalization sufficiently valid to predict how such evolving scenarios for IB might play out?

Such questions, we believe, support our stated objective with this paper to explore whether there is sufficient evidence to support the proposal of a new 'East Asian' model for describing, explaining and predicting the internationalization of MNCs. They further suggest that we should be working to identify key elements of differentiation in the internationalization strategies of MNCs from across Asia and, as we have done in this paper, use these to question the extent to which existing and long-established 'Western' models remain valid - or even credible - in their research application.

In this context, it should also be noted that this study has some clear limitations due to its exploratory nature. Specifically, we have studied the internationalization strategies of only four leading East Asian MNCs from Japan and Korea in the largest East Asian market: China. Clearly, there is scope to identify and compare the investments made by a broader range of East Asian MNCs into more countries and regions in order to uncover the underlying driving forces of their strategic behaviour. Our reliance on secondary data sources is another limitation: future research in this field ideally would build on information directly obtained from the firms' managers in order to deepen and enrich our understanding of their respective and particular internationalization strategies.

Taken together, the results of our explorative study of the internationalization of Japanese and Korean MNCs suggest a need for further research on how the internationalization of firms from the East Asian region unfolds. Given our findings which indicate that Japanese and Korean firms only partially follow the predictions made by Western internationalization models, an unbiased approach in the tradition of grounded research is recommended in order to identify potential new explanations for the strategic behaviour of firms from this region which may result in extensions of existing theories or even in new models of MNC internationalization.

Conclusion

This study set out to explore whether current internationalization activities by Japanese and Korean MNCs might suggest an opportunity to expand on existing conceptualizations and theories of internationalization relevant to describing and explaining the strategic activities of leading East Asian MNCs. In drawing these comparisons, we asked whether there is an opportunity or even a need to visualize and design new internationalization models that might capture and predict the internationalization activities of MNCs headquartered in Japan or Korea and, by extension, across East Asia generally. As the internationalization strategies of Japanese and Korean MNCs appear only partially to follow predictions generated by established theories and models, and given that we can observe marked differences in the behaviour of selected rival firms, we can conclude that further research into the internationalization of East Asian MNCs is more than warranted. Such in-depth studies might reveal whether the internationalization strategies of firms from this region as a whole and from regions within the whole might be explained through adaptations or extensions of established theories. Alternatively, researchers might ask questions designed to develop and test new theoretical frameworks and test these in an attempt towards creating a distinctly 'East Asian' model of MNC internationalization, an endeavour we encourage with this paper.

References

Aharoni, Y. 1966. *The Foreign Investment Decision Process*. Boston, MA: Graduate School of Business Administration, Harvard University.

Aliber, R. Z. 1971. "The Multinational Enterprise in a Multiple Currency World." In *The Multinational Enterprise*, edited by J. H. Dunning, 49–60. London: Allen and Unwin.

Ando, N., and D. Z. Zing. 2012. "An Integrative Institutional Approach to MNC Performance in China." *Asia Pacific Business Review* 20 (4): 541–557.

Bartlett, C. A., and S. Ghoshal. 1991. *Managing across Borders: The Transnational Solution*. Boston, MA: Harvard Business School Press.

Belderbos, R. 2003. "Entry Mode, Organizational Learning, and R&D in Foreign Affiliates: Evidence from Japanese Firms." *Strategic Management Journal* 24 (3): 235–259.

Bloomberg. 2011. "Why Lexus Doesn't Lead the Pack in China". Accessed May 14, 2015. http://www.bloomberg.com/bw/magazine/content/11_14/b4222032202135.htm

Bloomberg. 2015. "China's Video-Game Smugglers Are Helping Sony's PS4." Accessed June 4, 2015. http://www.bloomberg.com/news/articles/2015-04-27/china-s-video-game-smugglers-are-helping-sony-s-ps4

Boyer, R. 2014. "Foreword: From 'Japanophilia' to Indifference? Three Decades of Research on Contemporary Japan." In *The Great Transformation of Japanese Capitalism*, edited by Sébastien Lechevalier, xiii–xxv. Abingdon: Routledge.

Buckley, P. J., and M. Casson. 1976. *The Future of the Multinational Enterprise*. London: Palgrave Macmillan.

Chang, S.-J., and S. H. Park. 2012. "Winning Strategies in China: Competitive Dynamics between MNCs and Local Firms." *Long Range Planning* 45 (1): 1–15.

ChosunBiz. 2015. "Hyundai Motor to Target the Inland Market by Building Its 5th Factory in China. Engaging in Lead Competition with Volkswagen and GM." *ChosunBiz.com*, June 23. Accessed January 18, 2016. http://biz.chosun.com/site/data/html_dir/2015/06/23/2015062301945.html

Das, D. K. 2013. "How Did the Asian Economy Cope with the Global Financial Crisis and Recession? A Revaluation and Review." *Asia Pacific Business Review* 18 (1): 7–25.

Delios, A., and P. W. Beamish. 2005. "Regional and Global Strategies of Japanese Firms." *Management International Review* 45 (1): 19–36.

Delios, A., and W. J. Henisz. 2003. "Political Hazards, Experience, and Sequential Entry Strategies: The International Expansion of Japanese Firms, 1980–1998." *Strategic Management Journal* 24 (11): 1153–1164.

Dunning, J. H. 1977. "Trade, Location of Economic Activity and the MNDE: A Search for an Eclectic Approach". In *The International Allocation of Economic Activity*, edited by B. Ohlin, P. O. Hesselborn, and P.M. Wijkman, 395–418. London: Macmillan.

Dunning, J. H. 1980. "Explaining Changing Patterns of International Production: In Defense of the Eclectic Theory." *Oxford Bulletin of Economics and Statistics* 41 (4): 269–295.

Dunning, J. H. 1997. *Alliance Capitalism and Global Business*. London: Routledge.

Dunning, J. H. 2000. "The Eclectic Paradigm as an Envelope for Economic and Business Theories of MNE Activity." *International Business Review* 9 (2): 163–190.

Erramilli, M. K., R. Srivastava, and S.-S. Kim. 1999. "Internationalization Theory and Korean Multinationals." *Asia Pacific Journal of Management* 16 (1): 29–45.

Financial Times. 2011. "China Ends Ban on Foreign Game Consoles". Accessed July 2, 2015. http://www.ft.com/intl/cms/s/0/1ffe5fac-7779-11e3-807e00144feabdc0.html#axzz3eXIFYzaw

Fitzgerald, R., and C. Rowley. 2015. "Japanese Multinationals in the Post-Bubble Era: New Challenges and Evolving Capabilities." *Asia Pacific Business Review* 21 (3): 279–294.

Forbes. 2015. "5 Reasons Apple Looks like the Next Sony". Accessed June 10, 2015. http://www.forbes.com/sites/kylesmith/2014/03/25/5-reasons-apple-looks-like-the-next-sony

Ford, D. 2013. "Semiconductor Sales Recover in 2013; Micron Surges to Fourth Place in Global Chip Market." IHS Technology Press Release, December 3. Accessed January 18, 2016. https://technology.ihs.com/467553/

Fortune. 2015. "Fortune Global 500 2014." Accessed January 18, 2016. http://fortune.com/global500/samsung-electronics-13/

Gamble, J., J. Morris, and B. Wilkinson. 2003. "Japanese and Korean Multinationals: The Replication and Integration of Their National Business Systems in China." *Asian Business and Management* 2 (3): 347–369.

Goerzen, A., and S. Makino. 2007. "Multinational Corporation Internationalization in the Service Sector: A Study of Japanese Trading Companies." *Journal of International Business Studies* 38 (7): 1149–1169.

Griffiths, M. B. 2012. *Consumers and Individuals in China: Standing out, Fitting in*. New York: Routledge.

Guillén, M. F. 2002. "Structural Inertia, Imitation, and Foreign Expansion: South Korean Firms and Business Groups in China, 1997–95." *Academy of Management Journal* 45 (3): 509–525.

Guillén, M. F. 2003. "Experience, Imitation, and the Sequence of Foreign Entry: Wholly Owned and Joint-Venture Manufacturing by South Korean Firms and Business Groups in China, 1987–1995." *Journal of International Business Studies* 34 (2): 185–198.

Hankook Kyungjae. 2015. "Now Ahead Everywhere except for the US, Japan and South-East Asia: Hyundai Motor Dashing to Chase Toyota." March 13, 2015 (in Korean).

Hemmert, M. 2012. *Tiger Management: Korean Companies on World Markets*. London: Routledge.

Hemmert, M. 2014. "The Business System of Korea." In *Asian Business and Management: Theory, Practice and Perspectives* 2nd Ed. edited by H. Hasegawa, and C. Noronha, 219–238. Houndmills: Palgrave Macmillan.

Hollensen, S. 2012. *Essentials of Global Marketing*. Harlow: Pearson.

Hood, N., and S. Young. 1979. *The Economics of Multinational Enterprises*. Basingstoke: Macmillan.

Hymer, S. H. 1960. *The International Operations of National Firms: A Study of Direct Foreign Investment*. Cambridge, MA: MIT Press.

Ietto-Gillies, G. 2012. *Transnational Corporations and International Production: Concepts, Theories and Effects*. 2nd Ed. Cheltenham: Edward Elgar.

Jackson, K., P. Debroux, eds. 2009. *Innovation in Japan: Emerging Patterns, Enduring Myths*. London: Routledge.

Jackson, K. 2011. "Models of HRM." In *Human Resource Management: The Key Concepts*, edited by Chris Rowley, and Keith Jackson, 140–145. Abingdon: Routledge.

Jackson, K. 2013. "East Asian Management: An Overview." In *Managing across Diverse Cultures: Issues and Challenges in a Changing Globalized World*, edited by Malcolm Warner, 49–63. Abingdon: Routledge.

Jackson, K. Forthcoming. "Japanese Management Style". *The Encyclopedia of Social Theory*. New York: John Wiley.

Japan Times. 2015. "Toyota to Build New Plants in China, Mexico". Accessed June 16, 2015. http://www.japantimes.co.jp/news/2015/04/03/business/corporate-business/toyota-build-new-plants-china-mexico/#.VZDF_XqD75Y

Japan Times. 2005. "Foreign CEO Signifies a More Globalized Japan". Accessed May 20, 2015. http://www.japantimes.co.jp/news/2005/03/10/business/foreign-ceo-signifies-a-more-globalized-japan/#.VaYjd3qD79B

Johanson, J., and J. E. Vahlne. 1990. "The Mechanism of Internationalization." *International Marketing Review* 7 (4): 11–24.

Johanson, J., and J. E. Vahlne. 1977. "The Internationalization Process of the Firm: A Model of Knowledge Development and Increasing Foreign Market Commitments." *Journal of International Business Studies* 8 (1): 23–32.

Johanson, J., and F. Wiedersheim-Paul. 1975. "The internationalization of the firm: four Swedish cases." *Journal of Management Studies* 12 (3): 305–323.

Jung, J. C., P. W. Beamish, and A. Goerzen. 2008. "FDI Ownership Strategy: A Japanese-US MNE Comparison." *Management International Review* 48 (5): 491–524.

KIET (Korea Institute for Industrial Economics and Trade). 2014. *Key Indicators for Major Industries. 2014.12*. Sejong: KIET.

KITA (Korea International Trade Association). 2015. "K-Stat (Korean Trade Statistics)." Accessed January 18, 2016. http://stat.kita.net/stat/kts/ktsMain.screen

Kojima, K. 1978. *Direct Foreign Investment: A Japanese Model of Multinational Business Operations*. London: Croom Helm.

Lechevalier, S., ed. 2014. *The Great Transformation of Japanese Capitalism*. Abingdon: Routledge.

Lee, K., and X. He. 2009. "The Capability of the Samsung Group in Project Execution and Vertical Integration: Created in Korea, Replicated in China." *Asian Business and Management* 8 (3): 277–299.

Liker, J. K. 2004. *The Toyota Way*. New York: McGraw-Hill.

Lu, J. 2002. "Intra- and Inter-Organizational Imitative Behavior: Institutional Influences on Japanese Firms' Entry Mode Choice." *Journal of International Business Studies* 33 (1): 19–37.

Makino, S., P. W. Beamish, and N. B. Zhao. 2004. "The Characteristics and Performance of Japanese FDI in Less Developed and Developed Countries." *Journal of World Business* 39 (4): 377–392.

Malhotra, N. K., J. Agarwal, and F. M. Ulgado. 2003. "Internationalization and Entry Modes: A Multitheoretical Framework and Research Propositions." *Journal of International Marketing* 11 (4): 1–31.

Miles Fletcher, W. III, and P. W. von Staden. 2012. "Epilogue: Retrospect and Prospects: The Significance of the 'Lost Decades' in Japan". *Asia Pacific Business Review* 18 (2): 275–279.

Nguyen, K., M. Okrend, and L. Tan. 2013. "Are Chinese Companies the Next Generation of Multinational Companies? Lenovo versus Sony in the Global PC Industry." *American International Journal of Contemporary Research* 3 (2): 1–10.

OECD (Organisation for Economic Co-operation and Development). 2008. *Benchmark Definition of Foreign Direct Investment*. 4th ed. Paris: OECD.

OECD (Organisation for Economic Co-operation and Development). 2015. "*OECD Statistics*." Accessed January 18, 2016. http://stats.oecd.org/

Oh, S.-Y. 2013. "Fragmented Liberalization in the Chinese Automotive Industry: The Political Logic behind Beijing Hyundai's Success in the Chinese Market." *The China Quarterly* 216: 920–945.

Ohmae, K. 1982. *The Mind of the Strategist: The Art of Japanese Business*. New York: McGraw-Hill.

Ouchi, W. G. 1981. *Theory Z: How American Management Can Meet the Japanese Challenge*. Reading, MA: Addison Wesley.

Ozawa, T. 1979. *Multinationalism, Japanese Style*. Princeton, NJ: Princeton University Press.

Park, Y. R., J. Y. Lee, and S. Hong. 2011. "Location Decision of Korean Manufacturing FDI: A Comparison between Korean Chaebols and Non-Chaebols." *Global Economic Review* 40 (1): 123–138.

Peng, M. W., and T. A. Khoury. 2009. "Unbundling the Institution-Based View of International Business Strategy." In *Oxford Handbook of International Business*, edited by A. Rugman, and T. Brewer. Oxford: Oxford University.

Ping L., Plechero, M., and R. Basant. 2013. "International Human Resource Management Strategies of Chinese Multinationals Operating Abroad". *Asia Pacific Business Review* 19 (4): 526–556.

Porter, M. E., H. Takeuchi, and M. Sakakibara. 2000. *Can Japan Compete?*. Cambridge, MA: Perseus.

Posner, M. V. 1961. "International Trade and Technological Change." *Oxford Economic Papers* 13: 323–341.

Reuters. 2014. "Toyota to Miss China 2014 Sales Goal of over 1.1 Million Vehicles: Executives". Accessed May 2, 2015. http://www.reuters.com/article/2014/12/30/us-china-autos-toyota-idUSKBN0K806R20141230

Reuters. 2015a. "Toyota China Car Sales Weak in First Quarter". *Business News* April 1. Accessed June 14, 2015. http://uk.reuters.com/article/2015/04/01/uk-toyota-china-sales-idUKKBN0MS3HG20150401

Reuters. 2015b. "Exclusive: Toyota Ends Freeze on Expansion, Looks at Three New Plants". Accessed July 4, 2015. http://www.reuters.com/article/2015/01/12/us-autoshow-toyota-idUSKBN0KL2EU20150112

Robson, C. 2002. *Real World Research*. Oxford: Blackwell.

Rowley, C., and J. Bae. 1998. *Korean Business; Internal and External Industrialization and Management*. London: Cass.

Rowley, C., and J. Benson. 2002. "Convergence and Divergence in Asian Human Resource Management." *California Management Review* 44 (2): 90–109.

Rowley, C., and Y. Paik. 2009. *The Changing Face of Korean Management*. London: Routledge.

Rowley, C., and M. Warner, eds. 2015. *Management in South Korea Revisited*. Abingdon: Routledge.

Rugman, A. M. 1981. *Inside the Multinationals: The Economics of Internal Markets*. New York: Columbia University Press.

Rugman, A. M. 2010. "Reconciling Internalization Theory and the Eclectic Paradigm." *Multinational Business Review* 18 (2): 1–12.

Sako, M., and M. Kotosaka. 2012. "Institutional Change and Organizational Diversity in Japan." In *Capitalist Diversity and Diversity within Capitalism*, edited by Christel Lane and Geoffrey T. Wood, 132–156. Oxford: Oxford University Press.

Samsung Chairman Secretariat Office. 1998. *60-Year History of Samsung*. Seoul: Samsung Chairman Secretariat Office. (in Korean).

Samsung Electronics. 2014a. "Annual Report 2013." Accessed January 30, 2016. http://www.samsung.com/us/aboutsamsung/investor_relations/financial_information/downloads/2013/2013-samsung-electronic-report.pdf

Samsung Electronics. 2014b. "Samsung Electronics Sustainability Report 2013." Accessed January 18, 2016. http://www.samsung.com/common/aboutsamsung/download/companyreports/2013_Sustainability_Report.pdf

Saunders, M. N. K., Lewis, P., and A. Thornhill. 2012. *Research Methods for Business Students*. London: Financial Times / Prentice-Hall.

Sekiguchi, S. 1979. *Japan's Direct Foreign Investment*. NJ: Allanheld.

Song, H. 2013. *Supply Chain Perspectives and Issues in China: A Literature Review*. Hong Kong: Fung Business Intelligence Centre.

Statista. 2015. "Leading Automobile Manufacturers Worldwide in 2014, Based on Vehicle Sales (in million units)." Accessed January 18, 2016. http://www.statista.com/statistics/271608/

Statistics Bureau, MIAC (Ministry of Internal Affairs and Communications). 2015. Statistics Japan. Accessed January 18, 2016. http://www.stat.go.jp/data/nenkan/index1.htm

Technobuffalo. 2015. "Sony Considers Exit from Phone, TV Markets to Focus on Playstation." Accessed July 2, 2015. http://www.technobuffalo.com/2015/02/18/sony-considers-exit-from-phone-tv-markets-to-focus-on-playstation/

Tolentino, P. E. 2001. *Multinational Corporations: Emergence and Evolution*. London: Routledge.

Toyota. 2015. "Financial Results FY 2015". Accessed May 3, 2015. http://www.toyota-global.com/investors/financial_result

Trendforce. 2015. "Top Ten Smartphone Vendors Based on Market Share". Accessed June 12, 2015. http://it.sohu.com/20150121/n407947218.shtml

Trevor, M. 1983. "Quality - Japanese Re-Export." *Euro-Asia Business Review* 2.

UNCTAD (United Nations Conference on Trade and Development). 1996. *World Investment Report 1996: Investment, Trade and International Policy Arrangements*. Geneva: United Nations.

UNCTAD (United Nations Conference on Trade and Development). 2014. *World Investment Report 2014*. New York: United Nations.

UNCTAD (United Nations Conference on Trade and Development). 2015. "UNCTAD Statistics." Accessed January 18, 2016. http://unctad.org/en/Pages/Statistics.aspx

Vernon, R. 1966. "International Investment and International Trade in the Product Cycle." *The Quarterly Journal of Economics* 80 (2): 190–207.

Vernon, R. 1979. "The Product Cycle Hypothesis in a New International Environment." In *Oxford Bulletin of Economics and Statistics* 41 (4): 255–267.

Witt, M. 2014. "The Business System of Japan." In *Asian Business and Management: Theory, Practice and Perspectives*. 2nd Ed., 161–178, edited by H. Hasegawa, and C. Noronha, 61–78. Houndmills: Palgrave Macmillan.

World Bank. 2015. "World Bank Data. Exports of Goods and Services (% of GDP)." Accessed January 18, 2016. http://data.worldbank.org/indicator/NE.EXP.GNFS.ZS

WTO (World Trade Organization). 2015. "WTO Statistics Database." Accessed January 18, 2016. http://stat.wto.org/Home/WSDBHome.aspx?Language=E

Yamashita, N. 2010. *International Fragmentation of Production*. Cheltenham: Edward Elgar.

Yang, X., Y. Jiang, R. Kang, and Y. Ke. 2009a. "A Comparative Analysis of the Internationalization of Chinese and Japanese Firms." *Asia Pacific Journal of Management* 26 (1): 141–162.

Yang, X., Y. Lim, Y. Sakurai, and S. Seo. 2009b. "Internationalization of Chinese and Korean Firms." *Thunderbird International Business Review* 51 (1): 37–51.

Zeng, Y., O. Shenkar, S.-H. Lee, and S. Song. 2013. "Cultural Differences, MNE Learning Abilities, and the Effect of Experience on Subsidiary Mortality in a Dissimilar Culture: Evidence from Korean MNEs." *Journal of International Business Studies* 44 (1): 42–65.

Zhang, H., ed. 2013. *China's Outward Foreign Investment: Theories and Strategies*. Hong Kong: Enrich.

An empirical investigation into the internationalization patterns of Japanese firms

Pearlean Chadha and Jenny Berrill

School of Business, Trinity College, Dublin 2, Ireland

ABSTRACT
The existing theories of firm-level multinationality, together with the many patterns of internationalization traced by firms, suggest that there is no standard or optimal path of international expansion. Whether firms internationalize slowly or rapidly, the common dimension is time. We conduct a unique longitudinal analysis on the changing patterns of multinationality of Japanese firms listed on the Nikkei 225 over a 16-year time period from 1998 to 2013. We use the system developed by Aggarwal, Berrill, Hutson and Kearney (2011) to classify the degree of multinationality of each firm in each year using both accounting (sales) and non-accounting (subsidiary) data. We use three measures of multinationality–foreign sales per cent, location of sales and location of subsidiaries. Our results show that multinationality has increased over time and we find little evidence that firms are regional in their operations with a growing number of firms becoming trans-regional and global. Our industrial analysis shows Consumer Goods and Oil & Gas are the most multinational industries. While Consumer Services and Utilities are the least multinational.

Introduction

Internationalization is defined in existing literature as a process through which the level of international operations of a firm increases over a period of time (Aggarwal et al. 2011). The existing literature on firm-level multinationality and the process of internationalization followed by firms suggest that there is no one prescribed path followed by all (Buckley and Chapman 1997; Fillis 2001). Firms may internationalize slowly or rapidly according to different theories, such as a global strategy or the other a regional strategy (Chetty and Campbell-Hunt 2003). While many studies use cross-sectional data to study the multinationality of firms at one point in time (Rugman 2003; Rugman and Brain 2003; Rugman and Verbeke 2003, 2004; Rugman and Collinson 2005, 2008 and Rugman and Oh 2013), few studies provide a longitudinal analysis. The dearth of longitudinal studies of firm-level multinationality in the existing literature requires attention by International Business scholars and the merits of these studies have been highlighted by various authors (Contractor 2007; Hennart 2007; Glaum and Oesterle 2007; Asmussen, Benito, and Petersen 2009; Casillas and Acedo 2013).

We take up this challenge and conduct a unique longitudinal analysis on the changing patterns of multinationality of Japanese firms listed on the Nikkei 225 over a 16-year time period from 1998 to 2013. We use the classification system introduced by Aggarwal et al. (2011). We classify the degree of multinationality of each firm in each year using both accounting (sales) and non-accounting (subsidiary) data. We test the robustness of our findings using an additional measure of multinationality that is the foreign sales percentage, as this is the measure most commonly used in the literature. We further categorize our sample of 225 firms into 10 industries using the Industrial Classification Benchmark (ICB) categorization and compare changing patterns of multinationality across industries over time. Kundu and Merchant (2008) note that the multinationality of services is under-researched and find that studies on the service sector multinational firms are sparse. UNCTAD's World Investment Report (2012) notes the importance of this sector in today's global business environment given its high levels of foreign direct investment. The lack of academic research in this area calls for a comparative longitudinal analysis of service and non-service sector firms, which we undertake as part of our analysis.

We therefore provide an original and robust longitudinal analysis of Japanese firm-level multinationality. Our results contribute significantly to the regionalization/globalization debate in International Business, which, until recently, has been dominated by the use of cross-sectional and accounting data. We include hand-collected data on the geographical location of each firm's subsidiaries in each year. Previous studies investigating the multinationality of firms typically focus on US firms and are conducted at one point in time (Rugman 2003). They focus on only one measure of multinationality to classify firms. These methods range from foreign sales to number of foreign subsidiaries or simply choosing firms from lists compiled by FTSE (Antoniou, Olusi, and Paudyal 2010) and the Fortune 500 (Errunza, Hogan, and Hung 1999; Rugman and Verbeke 2004). We attempt to provide clarity on the issue of firm-level regionalization versus globalization, which is a source of much debate in the existing literature. We do this with what we believe is a more robust multinationality classification system and by adding a longitudinal dimension to the debate. This will add to the regionalization and globalization debate in International Business by investigating if firms internationalize to geographically close regions or further afield.

Our results, using all three measures (location of sales, location of subsidiaries and foreign sales percent), show that firm-level multinationality has increased over time. We find little evidence that firms are regional in their sales and subsidiaries operations with a growing number of firms becoming global. The industrial analysis shows that consumer goods, oil and gas and technology sectors are the most international, while consumer services and utilities are the least multinational using our measures of location of sales and location of subsidiaries. We also find that non-service firms are more multinational than service firms in each year. Our results for Japanese firms are in line with similar research for US firms (O'Hagan-Luff and Berrill 2016) and UK firms (Berrill and Hovey 2013).

The remainder of this paper is structured as follows. The next section provides a detailed review of existing literature on the classification of MNCs and the regionalization/globalization debate. We then outline the data and methodology used in our analysis. The subsequent section provides the results of our analysis. We then outline implications of our findings. Finally, we present our conclusion.

Literature review

There is no one classification system for the degree of firm-level multinationality that is accepted and used by all International Business researchers. Studies create samples of MNCs using various criteria and variables, often without theoretical basis or justification, leading to inconsistencies within the literature. Some studies have developed typologies. These include Perlmutter's (1969) threefold typology based on home country-oriented, host country-oriented and world-oriented firms. Bartlett and Ghoshal's (1989) fourfold typology categorizes firms based on organizational structure as multinational, international, transnational and global. Rugman's (2003) and Rugman and Verbeke's (2004) fourfold typology classifies firms sales as home-region oriented, host-region oriented, bi-regional and global. Sullivan (1994) uses the degree of internationalization (DOI) and transnationality index (calculated by United Nations Conference on Trade and Development) to rank 74 US manufacturing MNCs based on different measures. The DOI measure includes foreign sales percent, R&D intensity, assets, percentage foreign subsidiaries and managers' international experience, while the transnationality index is calculated using an average of three ratios; foreign sales to total sales, foreign assets to total assets and foreign employment to total employment. Aggarwal et al. (2011) measure international involvement of firms based on the breadth and depth of their operations across six geographic regions where breadth measures geographical spread and depth measures market penetration.

Many authors have noted the dearth of longitudinal studies of internationalization patterns of firms. Glaum and Oesterle (2007) note a longitudinal approach is more suited to study the complex process of internationalization but that most studies on firm internationalization use cross-sectional data. We believe a single measure is not able to capture the dynamic nature of multinationality. However, most studies focus on only one measure, which makes the classification one dimensional (Contractor 2007). Hennart (2007) suggests that the relationship between firm internationalization and performance should be analysed longitudinally. Asmussen, Benito, and Petersen (2009), Kuivalainen, Saarenketo, and Puumalainen (2012) and Casillas and Acedo (2013) suggest that the speed at which firms internationalize has often been ignored in the existing literature. The time dimension is essential to capture the firm-level internationalization patterns.

Much of the literature focuses on whether firms are regional or global in their operations. The regionalization/globalization debate has garnered the attention of International Business scholars in recent years. Doremus et al. (1998) argue that the concept of globalization is exaggerated and MNCs mostly have a regional focus. The literature is dominated by Rugman and his coauthors, who argue that most large MNCs are regional rather than global and term globalization as a myth (Rugman 2003; Rugman and Brain 2003; Rugman and Verbeke 2003, 2004; Rugman and Collinson 2005, 2008; Collinson and Rugman, 2007; Rugman and Oh 2013). Rugman and Verbeke (2004) classify firms with at least 50% of their sales in their home region as 'home region oriented'; firms with at least 20% of their sales in at least two regions, but less than 20% in any one region as 'bi-regional'; firms with more than 50% of their sales in a triad market other than their home region as 'host region oriented' and firms with sales of 20% or more in each of the three parts of the triad, but less than 50% in any one region as 'global'. Based on constituent firms in the 2001 Fortune 500 list complied using sales data, Rugman and Verbeke's (2004) findings conclude that these firms are regional in their operations and are moving towards adopting a regional business strategy rather than a global one. Rugman and Oh (2013) gather geographic sales, assets and subsidiaries data for 655 firms listed on the Fortune Global 500 between 2000 and 2007. They use variance component analysis and demonstrate that the world's largest MNCs are home region based in their operations. Dunning, Fujita, and Yakova (2007) find that MNCs have regional operations but this is influenced by macro-economic factors such as gross domestic product and trade of the countries, not the strategic focus of the firms.

Stevens and Bird (2004) point to shortcomings in Rugman's research. These include lack of a robust definition of globalization, ill-defined regions, using arbitrary thresholds for percentage foreign sales and the shortcomings arising from using only sales data. Aharoni (2006) argues that Rugman and his coauthors do not capture the dynamics of a firm's internationalization by focusing almost exclusively on cross-sectional data. Osegowitsch and Sammartino (2008) criticize the rationale behind Rugman's classification system. They find that large firms are becoming increasingly global by expanding sales outside their home region. Similar results are shown by Berrill (2015) for 1289 firms from G7 countries using the classification system developed by Aggarwal et al. (2011). The critiques of Rugman question the claim that globalization is not a myth and show that firms are moving towards a more transregional and global strategy.

Methodology

Our sample contains the 225 constituents of the Nikkei 225 index from 2013. The Nikkei 225 is a price-weighted market index for the Tokyo Stock Exchange and has been calculated since 1950. We classify each firm in each year from 1998 to 2013 based on the degree of multinationality using the ABHK model developed by Aggarwal et al. (2011). The following measurements of multinationality are used in our analysis:

(1) Location of sales.
(2) Location of subsidiaries.
(3) Percentage of foreign sales to total sales.

We collect our accounting data, that is, foreign sales and its geographic breakdown, from Datastream and Worldscope. Our non-accounting data (subsidiary data) are hand-collected each year from *Who Owns Whom* by Dun and Bradstreet (1998/1999 to 2012/2014). The Aggarwal et al. (2011) system divides the world into six geographic regions, namely Africa, Asia, Europe, North America, Oceania and South America. These six regions cover 193 countries and are based on geographical rather than economic or political borders that may change over time. We classify each firm into the following four categories, domestic (D), regional (R), transregional (T) and global (G). Domestic (D) firms have operations only in their home country; regional (R) firms have operations in their home region; transregional (T) firms have operations outside their home region and Global (G) firms have operations in all six geographical regions. The transregional category is further decomposed into T2 representing operations in two regions, T3 representing operations in three regions, T4 is operations in four regions and T5 equals to operations in five regions. Each category is given a score such that domestic firms score 0, regional firms score 1, T2 firms score 2, T3 firms score 3, T4 firms score 4, T5 firms score 5 and global firms score 6.

Our measures of multinationality help provide a more robust analysis of a firm's international operations. The ABHK model categorizes based on the existence of operations and does not take into account the percentage foreign sales in each region. For example, a firm with sales in all six regions is global according to the ABHK model, but the percentage of sales in each region may vary for different firms. On the other hand, the percentage of sales used on its own takes no account of geographical spread. Therefore, we use foreign sales percentage as an additional measure of multinationality in conjunction with the location of sales. For example, in 2013, Yahama Corporation has 54.82% foreign sales spread across all six geographic regions. Nissan Motors has 80.23% foreign sales that is higher than Yahama Corporation. But their sales are only in Asia, North America and Europe.

All firms are categorized into 10 industries using the Industrial Classification Benchmark (ICB)[1] as follows: Basic Materials, Oil and Gas, Telecommunications, Consumer Goods, Consumer Services, Industrials, Health Care, Financials, Technology and Utilities. We further classify firms as service and non-service firms.

Data analysis

We study changing pattern of multinationality for our 16-year time period (1998–2013) using the ABHK model. We determine the number of geographic regions each firm has operations in for each year. Results for sales and subsidiaries are shown in Tables 1 and 2 respectively.

Location of sales

Our findings show that the number of domestic firms in Japan (listed on the Nikkei 225) is 34 (21.21%) in 1998, fall to 16 (9.58%) in 2007 but rise to 40 (20.51%) in 2013. On average, 13.82% of firms are classified as domestic and is highest in 1999 (21.3%). The percentage of domestic firms remains above 10% in all years with the exception of 2007, when it is 9.50%. The number of regional firms is very low. There are no regional firms from 1998 to 2000. Toray industries is the only firm with regional sales in 2001 and Pacific Metals is the only firm with regional sales from 2002 to 2006. The number of firms with regional sales is highest in 2013 with seven firms (3.59%). The average percentage of regional firms in our sample period is as low as 0.75 percent suggesting that very few Japanese firms have sales operations solely in Asia.

The majority of firms have sales in two or more regions in all 16 years. Therefore, firms classified as transregional form the majority of the sample. The number of firms with sales in two regions (T2) ranges from 34 (21.12%) in 1998 to 39 (22%) in 2012. The overall trend is increasing from 27 (16.9%) in 1999 to 29 (17.79%) in 2006 and the peak at 39 (22.03%) in 2012 with a drop to 34 (17.44%) in 2013. The average percentage of T2 firms is 18.36% over the full sample period with the lowest at 15.5% in 2004 and highest at 22.03% in 2012. The number of T3 firms is 42 (26.09%) in 1998 and decreases to 38 (24.52%) in 2004. In 2007, the number of T3 firms increases to 48 (28.74%), the highest in our sample period but falls to 33 (16.92%) in 2013. The average percentage of T3 firms over the entire time period is 23.54% making this the second largest sales category. The percentage of T3 firms is the lowest at 14.77% in 2011, which is a sharp decline from 23.56% in 2010. In our sample, firms with sales in four regions (T4) form the majority with an average percentage of 29.78% over the 16-year time period. The number of T4 firms in 1998 is the lowest in the sample period at 35 (21.74%) and peak at 63 (38.80%) in 2011. The number of firms fell to 54 (27.69%) in 2013. The percentage of T4 firms in each year has been consistently above 21%. The percentage increases

Table 1. Number of firms in Japan based on measure of location of sales and foreign sales percentage.

Number of Firms	1998	1999	2000	2001	2002	2003	2004	2005	2006	2007	2008	2009	2010	2011	2012	2013
Panel A: Number of firms																
Domestic Japan Only (0)	34 (21.12)	34 (21.3)	31 (19.3)	25 (16.1)	21 (13.55)	19 (12.26)	17 (10.97)	17 (10.63)	18 (11.04)	16 (9.58)	18 (10.65)	17 (10.06)	18 (10.34)	22 (12.50)	20 (11.30)	40 (20.51)
Asia (1)	0 (0.00)	0 (0.00)	0 (0.00)	1 (0.6)	1 (0.65)	1 (0.65)	1 (0.65)	1 (0.63)	1 (0.61)	2 (1.20)	1 (0.59)	1 (0.59)	1 (0.57)	2 (1.14)	1 (0.56)	7 (3.59)
Two regions (2)	34 (21.12)	27 (16.9)	27 (16.8)	24 (15.5)	26 (16.77)	27 17.42)	29 (18.71)	28 (17.50)	29 (17.79)	30 (17.96)	31 (18.34)	32 (18.93)	34 (19.54)	37 (21.02)	39 (22.03)	34 (17.44)
Three regions (3)	42 (26.09)	40 (25.0)	43 (26.7)	35 (22.6)	36 (23.23)	37 (23.87)	38 (24.52)	44 (27.5)	44 (26.99)	48 (28.74)	44 (26.04)	41 (24.26)	41 (23.56)	26 (14.77)	28 (15.82)	33 (16.92)
Four regions (4)	35 (21.74)	41 (25.6)	42 (26.1)	50 (32.26)	52 (35.55)	51 (32.90)	48 (30.97)	45 (28.13)	46 (28.22)	47 (28.14)	48 (28.40)	54 (31.95)	55 (31.61)	63 (38.80)	59 (33.33)	54 (27.69)
Five regions (5)	14 (8.70)	16 (10.0)	17 (10.6)	19 (12.26)	18 (11.16)	20 (12.90)	21 (13.55)	24 (15.00)	23 (14.11)	23 (13.77)	25 (14.79)	22 (13.02)	23 (13.22)	24 (13.64)	25 (14.12)	25 (12.82)
Global	2 (1.24)	2 (1.3)	1 (0.6)	1 (0.65)	1 (0.65)	0 (0.00)	1 (0.65)	1 (0.63)	2 (1.23)	1 (0.60)	2 (1.18)	2 (1.18)	2 (1.15)	2 (1.14)	5 (2.82)	2 (1.03)
Average	2.58	2.69	2.75	2.94	3	3.03	3.07	3.09	3.08	3.08	3.1	3.11	3.1	3.06	3.13	2.7
Total number of firms	161	160	161	155	155	155	155	160	163	167	169	169	174	176	177	195
Panel B: % Foreign sales																
No foreign sales	35	36	30	29	26	23	22	16	13	9	9	9	8	11	12	41
Total	163	163	163	163	163	163	163	163	163	163	163	163	163	163	163	163
Average % Foreign Sales	45	34.63	35.4	32.67	31.19	31.39	27.04	28.34	29.78	32.82	33.91	33.29	33.11	38.67	38.5	33.86
Panel C: Regional analysis																
Domestic	34	34	31	25	21	19	17	17	18	16	18	17	18	22	20	40
Asia	69	73	78	75	77	82	93	96	105	115	115	117	121	126	127	129
Europe	71	74	78	76	78	81	83	87	86	92	95	93	95	91	91	92
South America	14	16	18	23	25	29	31	33	34	35	37	37	37	33	34	34
North America	84	95	96	101	102	105	105	107	109	111	112	112	115	103	107	108
Africa	2	2	1	1	1	1	1	1	1	1	2	3	3	5	6	5
Oceania	15	17	15	16	16	12	14	16	16	18	19	19	22	23	24	23
Other	96	99	103	105	106	103	101	105	108	104	105	107	108	126	132	107
Total observations	161	160	161	155	155	155	155	160	163	167	169	169	174	176	177	195

Note: This table shows the number of Japanese firms in each year based on data on foreign sales. Panel A shows number of firms that are domestic, regional, transregional and global. Transregional firms are broken down into firms with sales in two, three, four or five regions. For example, number of purely domestic firms in 2013 is 40 (20.51%) and in 1998 are 34 (21.12%). The percentage of firms that are domestic, regional, transregional and global in each year from 1998–2013 are shown in brackets in Panel A. For example, percentage of global firms in 2012 was 2.8% of the 177 firms for which full data was available in that year. Panel B shows the number of firms with no foreign sales, followed by the average foreign sales of all firms in each year. Panel C shows the number of firms that report sales in each of the six regions. For example, in 2008, 109 Japanese firms reported sales in North America and only one firm reported sales in Africa.

Table 2. Number of firms in Japan based on measure of location of subsidiaries.

Number of Firms	1998	1999	2000	2001	2002	2003	2004	2005	2006	2007	2008	2009	2010	2011	2012	2013
Panel A: Number of firms																
Domestic Japan Only (0)	5 (2.82)	5 (2.82)	12 (6.81)	13 (7.38)	0 (0)	18 (10.1)	19 (9.54)	18 (9.09)	18 (8.69)	19 (9.17)	20 (9.43)	23 (11.11)	–	15 (7.01)	–	14 (6.48)
Asia (1)	9 (5.08)	9 (5.08)	5 (2.84)	4 (2.27)	8 (4.49)	4 (2.24)	6 (3.01)	9 (4.54)	6 (2.89)	5 (2.41)	5 (2.36)	7 (3.38)	–	10 (4.65)	–	5 (2.31)
Two regions (2)	28 (15.8)	28 (15.8)	25 (14.2)	26 (14.7)	28 (15.7)	27 (15.1)	28 (14.0)	22 (11.1)	24 (11.5)	26 (12.5)	25 (11.79)	17 (8.21)	–	27 (12.62)	–	31 (14.35)
Three regions (3)	64 (36.1)	64 (36.1)	72 (40.9)	57 (32.3)	57 (32.0)	59 (33.1)	61 (30.6)	65 (32.8)	65 (31.4)	54 (26.0)	54 (25.47)	54 (26.09)	–	70 (32.71)	–	55 (25.46)
Four regions (4)	46 (25.9)	46 (25.9)	49 (27.8)	55 (31.2)	46 (25.8)	51 (28.6)	46 (23.1)	46 (23.2)	45 (21.7)	51 (24.6)	56 (26.42)	49 (23.67)	–	41 (19.16)	–	51 (23.61)
Five regions (5)	23 (12.9)	23 (12.9)	23 (13.0)	29 (16.4)	32 (17.9)	30 (16.8)	26 (13.0)	23 (11.6)	29 (14.0)	30 (14.4)	31 (14.62)	36 (17.39)	–	27 (12.62)	–	42 (19.44)
Global	2 (1.12)	2 (1.12)	2 (1.13)	5 (2.84)	7 (3.93)	7 (3.93)	13 (6.53)	15 (7.57)	20 (9.66)	22 (10.6)	21 (9.91)	21 (10.14)	–	24 (11.21)	–	18 (8.33)
Average	3.2	3.2	3.15	3.29	3.49	3.22	3.19	3.22	3.34	3.4	3.4	3.41	–	3.36	–	3.48
Total number of firms	177	177	176	176	178	178	199	198	207	207	212	207	–	215	–	216
Panel B: Regional analysis																
Domestic	5	5	13	19	17	18	19	18	18	19	20	23	–	21	–	18
Asia	170	170	175	176	179	179	180	181	189	189	192	186	–	198	–	197
Europe	145	145	154	157	157	154	156	154	163	159	165	161	–	166	–	170
South America	40	40	32	47	48	53	50	61	67	70	173	170	–	183	–	182
North America	150	150	155	155	155	160	160	162	167	167	73	72	–	79	–	80
Africa	2	2	4	8	12	11	22	23	24	25	24	28	–	33	–	32
Oceania	57	57	71	79	73	77	66	59	81	98	93	95	–	66	–	83
Total observations	177	177	176	176	178	178	199	198	207	207	212	207	–	215	–	216

Note: This table shows how many Japanese firms have subsidiaries in each year based on data on foreign subsidiaries. From 1998–2013, Panel A shows number of firms that are domestic, regional, transregional and global. Transregional firms are broken down into firms with subsidiaries in two, three, four or five regions. For example, number of purely domestic firms in 1998 is five and in 2013 are 19. The percentage of firms that are domestic, regional, transregional and global in each year from 1998–2007 are shown in brackets in Panel A. For example, percentage of global firms (in terms of foreign subsidiaries) in 1998 is 1.12% and in 2007 global firms constitute 10.6% of the total firm for which full data was available in that year. Panel B shows the number of firms that report subsidiaries in each of the six regions. For example, in 2011, 198 Japanese firms reported subsidiaries in Asia and 331 firms reported sales in Africa.

to 35% in 2002 then falls to 28.40% in 2008 and increasing thereafter. T5 firms with sales in five regions forms the smallest proportion of transregional firms in the sample. The number of T5 firms increase steadily through the sample period from 14 (8.70%) in 1998 to the highest in 2008 and 2013 at 25 (14%). The average percentage of T5 firms is 12.75%. The number of firms classified as global is 2 (1.24%) in 1998 and falls to 1 (0.56%) in the following years till 2005 with no firm reporting global sales in 2003. This number sharply increases to 5 (2.82%) in 2012 but fell to 2 (1.03%) in 2013. These findings show that very few firms have global sales spread across all six regions of the world. The overall pattern in our findings, based on location of sales indicates that although very few firms have sales in all six regions, globalization is increasing with firms moving away from a domestic focus and expanding sales across regions outside their home region.

We also calculate the percentage foreign to total sales for each firm and are presented in Panel B of Table 1. The average percentage foreign sales over the 16-year period is 34% ranging from 45% in 1998 to 27.04% in 2004 and increasing to 38.50% in 2012. We next analyse the location of sales data. Results detailing the regional spread of sales are presented in Panel C of Table 1. The number of firms with sales in Asia increased from 69 in 1998 to 129 in 2013. There was a similar increase in the number of firms with sales in Europe from 71 in 1998 to 92 in 2013. Although the number of firms with sales in Africa is very few, they have increased from two in 1998 to five in 2013. Similar increasing trends exist for North America, South America and the Oceania regions.

Location of subsidiaries of Japanese firms

We next analyse our subsidiary data and present results in Table 2.[2] There is a steady increase in the number of purely domestic firms from 5 (2.82%) in 1998 to 23 (11.11%) in 2009. This figure then falls to 14 (6.48%) in 2013. The number of regional firms with subsidiaries only in Asia is 9 (5.08%) in 1998 and falls to 4 (2.24%) in 2003. The number increases to 10 (4.65%) in 2011 but falls to five (2.31%) in 2013.

The majority of the firms have subsidiaries in two or more regions in our sample period (1998–2013). Therefore, firms classified as transregional form the majority of the sample. The number of T2 firms with subsidiaries in two regions outside Asia steadily fall from 28 (15.8%) in 1998 to 17 (8.21%) in 2009 and increases to 31 (14.35%) in 2013. The number of T3 firms with subsidiaries in three regions also decreases over our sample period from 64 (36.1%) in 1998 to 55 (25.46%) in 2013. The highest number of T3 firms is in 2000 (40.9%). The number of T4 firms is 46 (25.9%) in 1998 and 51 (23.61%) in 2013. The number of T5 firms increases from 23 (12.9%) in 1998 to 42 (19.44%) in 2013. A significant feature of our findings is the increase in the number of global firms with subsidiaries in all six regions from only 2 (1.12%) in 1998 to 24 (11.21%) in 2011. The number of global firms in 2013 is 18 (8.33). The average percentage of firms with regional and global subsidiaries is the smallest with 3.5% and 4.85%, respectively. The average number of regions Japanese firms have subsidiaries in is steady at three regions with an overall increase from 3.20 regions in 1998 to 3.44 in 2009. The number of firms with subsidiaries in Asia is the highest with an average of 182 firms followed by Europe and North America with an average number of 158 and 135 respectively. The most striking increase in firms with foreign subsidiaries is in Africa (from 2 in 1998 to 32 in 2013). The number of firms in South America and Oceania also increase over the time period. The majority of firms have transregional subsidiaries in each year. This internationalization pattern suggests that Japanese firms have expanded their operations beyond their home region and are moving towards a global strategy rather than a regional one.

Taxonomic classification of Japanese firms

Next, we combine the two measures of location of sales and subsidiaries and classify firms into 16 categories using a matrix of the two dimensions (breadth and depth). In Table 3, we show the ABHK matrix using the two measures of multinationality and classify the constituents of the NIKKEI 225 in to 16 types of MNCs. These categories range from purely domestic firms with sales and subsidiaries in Japan to global firms with sales and subsidiaries in all six regions. The number of purely domestic firms falls from 33 (15.71%) in 1998 to 8 (3.81%) in 2013. The majority of firms are classified in the transregional sales and subsidiaries category. The number of T2, T3, T4 and T5 firms with sales and subsidiaries in more than two regions (outside Asia) are 105 (50%) in 1998. These firms rise to 121 (57.67%) in 2009 and slightly fall to 118 (56.19%) in 2013. The number of trans-regional sales and global subsidiaries that is T2, T3, T4 and T5 firms using measure of sales and Global firms using measure of subsidiaries rises from 2 (0.95%) in 1998 to 22 (10.43%) in 2011 but falls to 10 (4.76%) in 2013. Our data set shows that Japanese firms are more multinational in terms of investments (subsidiaries) than trade (sales).

Industrial analysis

We use the Industrial Classification Benchmark (ICB) system to categorize our sample of 225 firms into 10 industries as follows: Oil and Gas (3 firms), Basic Materials (31 firms), Industrials (66 firms), Consumer Goods (43 firms), Health Care (10 firms), Consumer Services (22 firms), Telecommunications (4 firms), Utilities (5 firms), Financials (27 firms) and Technology (14 firms). We compare the multinationality levels across each industry level.[3]

Based on our sales figures, consumer goods is the most multinational with an average score of 3.54. The score implies that firms in the consumer goods industry had sales in an average of 3.54 regions in our 16-year sample period. The consumer goods industry is followed by technology and industrials with an average number of regions score of 3.48 and 3.45, respectively. The least multinational industries based on location of sales are consumer services and oil and gas with an average score of 0.66 and 1.38. The measure of location of sales is increasing on average for all industries in the ICB system with the exception of financials and oil and gas, where the average number of regions with sales in decreasing. The location of sales measure of multinationality shows that the greatest increase in multinationality is in the health care sector with an average of three regions in 1998 rising to the highest average of 4.10 regions in 2013.

According to our subsidiary data, the most multinational industry is oil and gas with an average score of 4.33. This score implies that on average, across our sample of three oil and gas firms in Japan have subsidiaries in 4.33 regions. The number of firms in the industry is small and since Japan does not hold oil and gas resources, these firms have a wide spread of subsidiaries across the world. Oil and gas is outward FDI intensive as Japan and all firms in the sector have transregional and global subsidiaries in all years. The second most multinational industry is the technology sector followed by the consumer goods sector with average scores of 3.71 and 3.63, respectively. The least multinational industry based on the

Table 3. Taxonomic classification of Japanese firms.

	Symbol	MNC type	1998	1999	2000	2001	2002	2003	2004	2005	2006	2007	2008	2009	2010	2011	2012	2013
		Purely domestic firm																
1	DT-DI	Domestic trading, domestic investments Regional and transregional firms	33(15.7)	34(16.1)	37(17.5)	39(18.4)	34(16.1)	35(16.5)	33(15.5)	32(15.0)	28(13.2)	27(12.7)	24(11.3)	28(13.2)	–0	17(8.05)	–0	8(3.80)
2	RT-DI	Regional trading, domestic investments	0(0)	0(0)	0(0)	0(0)	1(0.47)	1(0.47)	1(0.47)	1(0.47)	1(0.41)	0(0)	1(0.47)	1(0.47)	–0	1(0.47)	–0	0(0)
3	TT-DI	Transregional trading, domestic investments	15(7.14)	14(6.66)	7(3.31)	7(3.31)	7(3.31)	6(2.83)	7(3.30)	7(3.30)	3(1.41)	5(2.36)	5(2.36)	7(3.31)	–0	3(1.42)	–0	14(6.66)
4	DT-RI	Domestic trading, regional investments	7(3.33)	7(3.33)	2(0.94)	0(0)	7(3.31)	3(1.41)	4(1.88)	8(3.77)	5(2.35)	4(1.89)	4(1.89)	6(2.84)	–0	8(3.79)	–0	1(0.47)
5	RT-RI	Regional trading, regional investments	0(0)	0(0)	0(0)	0(0)	0(0)	0(0)	0(0)	0(0)	0(0)	1(0.47)	0(0)	0(0)	–0	0(0)	–0	0(0)
6	TT-RI	Transregional trading, regional investments	1(0.47)	1(0.47)	2(0.94)	0(0)	1(0.47)	1(0.47)	2(0.94)	1(0.47)	1(0.47)	0(0)	1(0.47)	1(0.47)	–0	2(0.94)	–0	3(1.42)
7	DT-TI	Domestic trading, transregional investments	47(22.3)	47(22.3)	45(21.3)	42(19.9)	39(18.4)	40(18.8)	39(18.3)	31(14.6)	36(16.9)	32(15.1)	34(16.1)	27(12.7)	–0	35(16.5)	–0	44(20.9)
8	RT-TI	Regional trading, transregional investments	0(0)	0(0)	0(0)	1(0.47)	0(0)	0(0)	0(0)	0(0)	0(0)	1(0.47)	0(0)	0(0)	–0	1(0.47)	–0	5(2.38)
9	TT-TI	Transregional trading, transregional investments	105(50)	105(50)	116(54.9)	115(54.5)	115(54.5)	119(56.1)	114(53.7)	117(55.1)	119(56.1)	119(56.3)	121(57.3)	121(57.3)	–0	121(57.3)	–0	118(56.1)

(Continued)

Table 3. (Continued).

	Symbol	MNC type	1998	1999	2000	2001	2002	2003	2004	2005	2006	2007	2008	2009	2010	2011	2012	2013
		Global firms																
10	GT-DI	Global trading, domestic investments	0(0)	0(0)	0(0)	0(0)	0(0)	0(0)	0(0)	0(0)	0(0)	0(0)	0(0)	0(0)	–0	0(0)	–0	0(0)
11	GT-RI	Global trading, regional investments	0(0)	0(0)	0(0)	0(0)	0(0)	0(0)	0(0)	0(0)	0(0)	0(0)	0(0)	0(0)	–0	0(0)	–0	0(0)
12	GT-TI	Global trading, transregional investments	0(0)	0(0)	0(0)	0(0)	0(0)	0(0)	0(0)	0(0)	0(0)	0(0)	0(0)	0(0)	–0	0(0)	–0	0(0)
13	DT-GI	Domestic trading, global investments	0(0)	0(0)	0(0)	0(0)	0(0)	0(0)	0(0)	0(0)	0(0)	0(0)	1(0.47)	0(0)	–0	0(0)	–0	6(2.85)
14	RT-GI	Regional trading, global investments	0(0)	0(0)	0(0)	0(0)	0(0)	0(0)	0(0)	0(0)	0(0)	0(0)	0(0)	0(0)	–0	0(0)	–0	1(0.47)
15	TT-GI	Transregional trading, global investments	2(0.95)	2(0.95)	2(0.94)	5(2.36)	7(3.31)	7(3.30)	11(5.18)	14(6.60)	17(8.01)	22(10.4)	19(9.00)	19(9.00)	–0	22(10.4)	–0	10(4.76)
16	GT-GI	Global trading, global investments	0(0)	0(0)	0(0)	0(0)	0(0)	0(0)	1(0.47)	1(0.47)	2(0.94)	0(0)	1(0.47)	1(0.47)	0	1(0.47)	0	0(0)
		Total	210	210	211	211	211	212	212	212	212	211	211	211	–	211	–	210

Note: This Table uses a simplified matrix of my two-dimensional measure of multinationality to describe 16 types of MNC, ranging from a purely domestic firm to a fully global corporation. For example, there are 33 firms with purely domestic operations in 1998 and they fall to eight firms in 2013. The number of transregional trading and investments firms are 105 (50%) in 1998 and 118 (56%) in 2013.

Table 4. Industrial analysis.

Year	1998	1999	2000	2001	2002	2003	2004	2005	2006	2007	2008	2009	2010	2011	2012	2013
Panel A: Industrial Analysis for Sales																
Basic materials	2.42	2.67	2.58	2.39	2.35	2.35	2.35	2.39	2.32	2.27	2.27	2.29	2.1	2.18	1.95	1.95
Consumer goods	3.29	3.67	3.63	3.65	3.82	3.69	3.63	3.63	3.68	3.64	3.61	3.61	3.55	3.26	3.18	3.15
Consumer services	0.6	1	0.92	0.86	0.86	0.8	0.86	0.71	0.58	0.58	0.42	0.58	0.54	0.5	0.38	0.38
Financials	2.14	2.07	2.58	2.92	2.83	3	3.56	3.11	3.33	3.33	3.33	2.86	2.6	3.25	3	3
Health care	4.1	3.9	3.7	3.22	3.22	3	3	3	3	2.86	2.86	2.88	3.13	2.5	3	3
Industrials	3.16	3.52	3.38	3.51	3.54	3.53	3.48	3.57	3.58	3.63	3.55	3.55	3.57	3.33	3.31	3.05
Oil and gas	1.67	2.33	3.5	2	2	3	1.5	0	0	0	0	0	0	3	0	3
Technology	3.93	3.71	3.5	3.46	3.38	3.67	3.38	3.67	3.31	3.38	3.31	3.46	3.75	3.31	3.23	3.15
Telecommunications	–	–	–	–	–	–	–	–	–	–	–	–	–	–	–	–
Utilities	–	–	–	–	–	–	–	–	–	–	–	–	–	–	–	–
Services	2.28	2.32	2.40	2.33	2.30	2.27	2.47	2.27	2.30	2.26	2.20	2.11	2.09	2.08	2.13	2.13
Non-services	2.89	3.18	3.32	3.00	3.02	3.25	2.87	2.65	2.58	2.58	2.55	2.58	2.59	3.02	2.33	2.86
Panel B: Industrial analysis for subsidiaries																
Basic materials	2.76	2.76	2.83	3.13	3.52	3.19	3.19	3.04	3.25	3.29	3.04	3.19	–	2.97	–	3.65
Consumer goods	3.5	3.5	3.66	3.74	3.69	3.67	3.47	3.43	3.66	3.79	3.7	3.87	–	3.57	–	3.56
Consumer services	2.75	2.75	2.7	2.76	2.85	2.73	2.68	2.9	2.95	2.95	3.14	3.33	–	3.19	–	2.9
Financials	3	3	3	3.25	3.36	3.04	3.21	3.38	3.24	3.46	3.6	3.12	–	3.12	–	3.15
Health care	3.38	3.38	3	2.86	3.5	3	2.78	3	2.78	2.78	2.89	3	–	2.7	–	3.78
Industrials	3.27	3.27	3.15	3.31	3.56	3.19	3.2	3.16	3.33	3.26	3.31	3.31	–	3.5	–	3.62
Oil and gas	4.5	4.5	4	4.5	4.5	4	3.67	4	3.67	4.67	4.33	5	–	5	–	4.33
Technology	3.5	3.5	3.42	3.45	4.11	3.73	3.67	3.83	3.92	4.08	3.83	3.67	–	3.77	–	3.43
Telecommunications	3.25	3.25	3.25	3.25	3	3	3.5	3.5	3.5	3.75	4	3.75	–	3.75	–	3
Utilities	2.5	2.5	2.5	2.75	2.75	2.25	1.75	1.5	2.8	2.8	2.8	3	–	3	–	3.6
Services	3.04	3.04	2.90	2.96	3.24	2.92	2.89	3.09	2.99	3.06	3.21	3.15	–	3.00	–	3.28
Non-services	3.51	3.51	3.41	3.63	3.88	3.56	3.44	3.49	3.57	3.82	3.64	3.81	–	3.76	–	3.72

Note: This Table shows the average level of multinationality for each industry in each year using our measures of internationalization. Panel A shows results using the location of sales measure, Panel B using the location of subsidiaries measure. Firms are categorized into ten ICB industries. For example, in 1998, firms in the oil and gas industry had an average score of 1.67 using the location of sales measure and an average score of 4.50 using the location of subsidiaries measure.

location of subsidiaries data is utilities with an average number of subsidiaries in 2.61 regions. Our measure of location of subsidiaries is increasing for all industries with an exception of the health care sector where the average number of foreign subsidiaries is decreasing. In the case of industrials and technology sector the trend is steady over the time period. Firms in the utilities sector have an increasing number of foreign subsidiaries. The number fell to 1.50 in 2005 from 2.50 in 1998 but increases to 3.60 in 2013. Inpex in the oil and gas sector shows a large global presence with subsidiaries in all six regions 2005 onwards. Trend micro in the technology sector is also a global firm with subsidiaries in all six regions in more than 11 years of our sample period. Our findings using both measures for the location of sales and subsidiaries show that most industries exhibit an increasing trend in multinationality over the time period. Using these two measures together we can see that industries with a high degree of foreign sales may not have a high level of foreign subsidiary holdings. A particular case of the Oil & Gas sector in Japan shows us a low average score of 1.68 in the location of sales measure while it emerges the most multinational sector based on our location of subsidiaries measure.

We further categorize firms into Service (63 firms) and non-service firms (162 firms). Results are presented in Table 4. In every year, the non-service firms are more multinational than service firms. Using our measure of location of sales measure, service sector firms have sales in 2.28 geographic regions in 1998, whereas non-service sector firms have sales in 2.89 regions in 1998. In 2011, the service sector has sales in 2.08 regions and the non-service sector has sales in 3.02 regions. Next, we use our measure of location of subsidiaries. We find that in 1998 the service sector has subsidiaries in 3.04 regions, while the non-service sector has subsidiaries in 3.51 regions. In 2013, the service sector firms have subsidiaries in 3.28 regions and the non-service sector firms have subsidiaries in 3.72 regions. We conclude that the non-service sector is consistently more multinational than the service sector in each year of our sample.

Implications

Our results expand on previous studies and provide evidence of increasing multinationality of Japanese firms using both dimensions of multinationality – sales and subsidiaries. The ABHK matrix shows the number of firms that are domestic in terms of both their sales and subsidiaries has decreased dramatically over the time period. Few firms are classified as purely domestic in sales (13.82%) and subsidiaries (7.05%) suggesting that most Japanese stocks provide international exposure to investors. About 84.42% of the firms in our sample have transregional sales and 83.59% of the firms have trans-regional subsidiaries. About 55% of firms have transregional sales and subsidiaries based on the ABHK matrix. This highlights the necessity for firms to expand beyond their home market and emphasizes the globalization of firms. The Nikkei index, which is used to measure the performance of the Japanese domestic market, actually contains many MNCs with foreign exposures (transregional firms). This may not give an accurate measure of the domestic Japanese market and investors in Japanese stocks are getting high degree of international exposure.

The pattern of internationalization of Japanese firms is in line with those of the US and UK firms. The number of Japanese firms with regional and global operations forms a small proportion of the sample, while there is an increase in the number of firms with trans-regional operations. O'Hagan-Luff and Berrill (2016) categorize 396 US firms using the ABHK system and find that the number of firms with sales in 4, 5 and 6 regions outside North America has increases between 1996 and 2010. They also note that firms with sales in all six regions, that is global firms are only a maximum of eight out of 396 firms over the time period. Berrill and Hovey (2013) study the internationalization pattern for 600 UK firms and find little evidence that firms are regional in their sales and an equally small number of firms are global. Delios and Beamish (2005) analyse 1229 Japanese firms and find that firms with home-region-based strategy have lower performance than firms with host oriented, bi-regional or global strategy. Berrill (2015) show a decrease in the number of Japanese firms with purely domestic sales and increase in number of firms with regional sales. These can be compared to our sales data that also shows a decrease in domestic firms up until 2012. While in our dataset the increase in the number of regional firms is only seen in 2013.

Our findings update and extend the studies by Rugman and his coauthors on the myth of globalization. Rugman and Verbeke (2004) demonstrates that only nine out of the Fortune 500 firms were truly global with sales of 20% or more in each of the three parts of the triad (North America, Europe and Asia), but less than 50% in any one region of the triad. Their study is based predominantly on sales data from 2001 and they classify the majority of their sample as home region oriented while only 30.9% of the firms are classified as host region oriented. This cross-sectional analysis shows a limited view and contrasts with our findings spanning over 16 years of sales and subsidiary data. We refute the claim made by Rugman and Oh (2010, 2013) that globalization is a myth because firms concentrate on a regional strategy. Firms with trans-regional sales and subsidiaries dominate our sample of 225 firms listed on the Nikkei index. We find some evidence that firms focus on the triad regions as highlighted by Rugman and his coauthors. In our analysis, the majority of firms have exposure to North America, Europe and Asia throughout the time period. However, the number of firms with operations in Africa, South America and Oceania are increasing over the 16 years. These findings suggest that investing in Japanese stocks provides investors with exposure to more geographic regions over time. This is crucial for investor awareness and may impact investment decisions of domestic investors.

Our findings are a significant expansion to previous studies as we include subsidiary data on Japanese firms. We find a similar pattern for Japanese firms' subsidiaries to that of sales but firms tend to be more multinational in their investments than trade. This suggests a strong commitment by Japanese firms to international markets. The number of firms categorized as regional and global for their location of subsidiaries are small and the majority of firms are trans-regional. Foreign direct investment (FDI) outflows from Japan have increased overall from $31 billion in 2004 to $138 billion in 2013 making Japan the second largest investing country in the world after the United States (OECD FDI Report, 2013). FDI figures from the UNCTAD World Investment Report (2015) tie in with our findings as they suggest a decline in FDI outflows from Japan to other Asian countries but an increase in FDI to Africa reaching a record high of $4.5 billion. Our subsidiary data shows a dramatic increase in number of firms with subsidiaries in Africa from two in 1998 to 32 in 2013 and the number of Japanese firms with subsidiaries only in Asia has fallen from nine in 1998 to five in 2013. An increase in FDI figures from Japan over time supports the internationalization pattern of increasing foreign engagement found in our firm-level analysis of foreign subsidiaries.

Conclusion

Our paper conducts a longitudinal analysis on the pattern of multinationality of firms listed on the Japanese stock index Nikkei 225 constituting 225 firms over a 16-year sample period from 1998 to 2013. The analysis is based on the ABHK model developed by Aggarwal et al. (2011). We use three measures of multinationality – percentage of foreign sales, location of sales and location of subsidiaries. We conduct a unique firm-level and industry-level analysis of Japanese firms using robust longitudinal data. The use of accounting data and non-accounting data captures different aspects of multinationality. Our study provides meaningful direction to the conflicting results present in existing literature that leave the internationalization patterns of firms ambiguous. We can conclude that multinationality has increased over time and only the degree of increase varies in the measures we use. Our first measure of foreign sales percent shows an overall increase in multinationality with an average foreign sales percentage of 34% over the 16-year time period. The number of T4 firms forms the majority of our sample and there is an increasing trend for all firms using the sales measure. Japanese firms have sales in an average of 3 regions in our sample. The average number of regions using the subsidiaries measure is also three regions. Our industrial analysis also shows an overall increasing trend in internationalization. In terms of sales financials and oil and gas have decreased in multinational-ity while in terms of subsidiaries the health care sector shows a decreasing trend. This internationalization pattern suggests that Japanese firms have expanded their operations beyond their home region and are moving towards a more global strategy rather than a regional one. Our analysis adds a new dimension to the contentious regionalization/globalization debate in International Business.

Notes

1. The Industrial Classification Benchmark (ICB) is a categorization system maintained by FSTE International Limited. It categorizes over 70,000 companies and 75,000 securities worldwide, enabling a comparison of companies across four levels of classification. It uses a system of 10 industries, partitioned into 19 supersectors, that are further divided into 41 sectors, that then contain 114 subsectors.
2. Subsidiary data for the years 2010 and 2012 is unavailable.
3. Firms classified as Telecommunications and Utilities do not have data available for location of sales.

Disclosure statement

No potential conflict of interest was reported by the authors.

References

Aggarwal, R., J. Berrill, E. Hutson, and C. Kearney. 2011. "What is a Multinational Corporation? Classifying the Degree of Firm-level Multinationality." *International Business Review* 20 (5): 557–577.

Aharoni, Y. 2006. "Book Review: Alan M Rugman, The Regional Multinationals. MNEs and Global Strategic Management." *International Business Review* 15 (4): 439–446.

Antoniou, A., O. Olusi, and K. Paudyal. 2010. "Equity Home-Bias: A Suboptimal Choice for UK Investors?" *European Financial Management* 16 (3): 449–479.

Asmussen, C. G., G. R. Benito, and B. Petersen. 2009. "Organizing Foreign Market Activities: From Entry Mode Choice to Configuration Decisions." *International Business Review* 18 (2): 145–155.

Bartlett, C., and S. Ghoshal. 1989. *Managing Across Borders: The Transnational Solution*. Boston, MA: Harvard Business School Press.

Berrill, J. 2015. "Are the World's Largest Firms Regional or Global?" *Thunderbird International Business Review* 57 (2): 87–101.

Berrill, J., and Hovey, M. (2013). An Empirical Investigation into the Internationalisation Patterns of UK Firms. Available at SSRN 2358727.

Buckley, P. J., and M. Chapman. 1997. "The Perception and Measurement of Transaction Costs." *Cambridge Journal of Economics* 21 (2): 127–145.

Casillas, J., and F. J. Acedo. 2013. "Speed in the Internationalization Process of the Firm." *International Journal of Management Reviews* 15 (1): 15–29.

Chetty, S., and C. Campbell-Hunt. 2003. "Paths to Internationalisation Among Small-to Medium-sized Firms: A Global Versus Regional Approach." *European Journal of Marketing* 37 (5/6): 796–820.

Collinson, Simon, and Alan M. Rugman. 2007. "The Regional Character of Asian Multinational Enterprises." *Asia Pacific Journal of Management* 24 (4): 429–446.

Contractor, F. J. 2007. "Is International Business Good for Companies? The Evolutionary or Multi-stage Theory of Internationalization vs. the Transaction Cost Perspective." *Management International Review* 47 (3): 453–475.

Delios, A., and P. W. Beamish. 2005. Regional and Global Strategies of Japanese Firms. *MIR: Management International Review* 45 (1): 19–36.

Doremus, P., W. Keller, L. Pauly, and S. Reich. 1998. *The Myth of the Global Corporation*. Princeton, NJ: Princeton University Press.

Dun and Bradstreet. [1998/1999] 2012/14, Who Owns Whom? London: Dun & Bradstreet International.

Dunning, J., M. Fujita, and N. Yakova. 2007. "Some Macro-data on the Regionalisation/Globalisation Debate: A Comment on the Rugman/Verbeke Analysis." *Journal of International Business Studies* 38 (1): 177–199.

Errunza, V., K. Hogan, and M. W. Hung. 1999. "Can the Gains From International Diversification Be Achieved without Trading Abroad?" *The Journal of Finance* 54 (6): 2075–2107.

Fillis, I. 2001. "Small Firm Internationalisation: An Investigative Survey and Future Research Directions." *Management Decision* 39 (9): 767–783.

Glaum, M., and M.-J. Oesterle. 2007. "40 years of Research on Internationalization and Firm Performance: More Questions Than Answers?" *Management International Review* 47 (3): 307–317.

Hennart, J.-F. 2007. "The Theoretical Rationale for a Multinationality-performance Relationship." *Management International Review* 47 (3): 423–452.

Kuivalainen, O., S. Saarenketo, and K. Puumalainen. 2012. "Start-up Patterns of Internationalization: A Framework and its Application in the Context of Knowledge-intensive SMEs." *European Management Journal* 30 (4): 372–385.

Kundu, S., and H. Merchant. 2008. "Service Multinationals: Their Past, Present, and Future." *Management International Review* 48 (4): 371–377.

OECD. 2013. FDI figures report. The Organisation for Economic Co-operation and Development (OECD).

O'Hagan-Luff, M., and J. Berrill. 2016. "US Firms–How Global are they? A Longitudinal Study." *International Review of Financial Analysis* 44: 205–216.

Osegowitsch, T., and A. Sammartino. 2008. "Reassessing (home-)Regionalisation." *Journal of International Business Studies* 39 (2): 184–196.

Perlmutter, H. 1969. "The Tortouous Evolution of the Multinational Corporation." *Colombia Journal of World Business* 4 (1): 9–18.

Rugman, A., and C. Brain. 2003. "Multinational Enterprises Are Regional, Not Global." *Multinational Business Review* 11 (1): 3–12.

Rugman, A., and S. Collinson. 2005. "Multinational Enterprises in the New Europe: Are They Really Global?" *Organizational Dynamics* 34 (3): 258–272.

Rugman, A., and S. Collinson. 2008. "The Regional Nature of Japanese Multinational Business." *Journal of International Business Studies* 39 (2): 215–231.

Rugman, A., and R. Hodgetts. 2001. "The End of Global Strategy." *European Management Journal* 19 (4): 333–343.

Rugman, A. M., and C. H. Oh. 2010. "Does the Regional Nature of Multinationals Affect the Multinationality and Performance Relationship?" *International Business Review* 19 (5): 479–488. doi:http://dx.doi.org/10.1016/j.ibusrev.2009.02.012

Rugman, A. M., and C. H. Oh. 2013. "Why the Home Region Matters: Location and Regional Multinationals." *British Journal of Management* 24 (4): 463–479. doi:http://dx.doi.org/10.1111/j.1467-8551.2012.00817.x

Rugman, A., and A. Verbeke. 2003. "Regional Transnationals and Triad Strategy." *Transnational Corporation* 13 (3): 1–20.

Rugman, A. 2003. "Regional Strategy and the Demise of Globalization." *Journal of International Management* 9 (4): 409–417.

Rugman, A. M., and A. Verbeke. 2004. "A Perspective on Regional and Global Strategies of Multinational Enterprises." *Journal of International Business Studies* 35 (1): 3–18.

Stevens, M. J., and A. Bird. 2004. "On the Myth of Believing that Globalization is a Myth: Or the Effects of Misdirected Responses on Obsolescing an Emergent Substantive Discourse." *Journal of International Management* 10 (4): 501–551.

Sullivan, D. 1994. "Measuring the Degree of Internationalization of a Firm." *Journal of International Business Studies* 25 (2): 325–342.

UNCTAD. 2012. "*World Investment Report 2012: Towards a New Generation of Investment Policies.*" United Nations Conference on Trade and Development: New York and Geneva.

UNCTAD. 2015. "World Investment Report 2012: Towards a New Generation of Investment Policies." United Nations Conference on Trade and Development, New York and Geneva.

Japanese production networks in India: spatial distribution, agglomeration and industry effects

Sierk A. Horn[a] and Adam R. Cross[b]

[a]Japan Centre, Ludwig-Maximilians-University Munich, München, Germany; [b]International Business School Suzhou (IBSS), Xi'an Jiaotong-Liverpool University (XJTLU), Suzhou, P.R. China

ABSTRACT
This paper examines the determinants of subnational location choice of Japanese multinational enterprises (JMNEs) in India to investigate whether or not conventional investment behaviour as 'foot-loose' and one-off investments has given way to an agglomeration logic as Japanese foreign direct investment has intensified. Using geographic information system analysis of investment project numbers, we find that Japanese MNE behaviour in India is evolving, with complementing but complex subnational interactions of economic, institutional and infrastructure factors serving as strong determinants of location choice consistently across key phases of India's liberalization. We argue that Japanese investment decisions in India have followed a self-reinforcing dynamic whereby prior investments indeed attract further investment.

Introduction

Research on the internationalization motives and behaviour of Japanese multinational enterprises (JMNEs) is now substantial (e.g. Delios and Beamish 2005; Delios and Henisz 2003; Farrell 2008; Farrell, Gaston, and Sturm 2004; Kiyota and Urata 2007; Siddharthan and Lakhera 2005; Tomiura 2005; Yoshida and Ito 2006). Within this literature, various key characteristics of Japanese firm internationalization have been investigated, most notably inherent network effects and, in particular, the role of *keiretsu*-type organizational forms (e.g. Abo 2008; Ernst 1994; Guiheux and Lecler 2000; Mody, Dasgupta, and Sinha 1998; Mody and Srinivasan 1998; Sakakibara and Serwin 2000), cluster formation and agglomeration effects (e.g. Chung and Song 2004; Doner 1991; Mayer and Mucchielli 1998; Nopprach 2006), the relocation and configuration of Japanese production networks across the Asia Pacific region (e.g. Ernst 2006; Itagaki 1997; Yusuf 2004), and the determinants of location choice at the national level (e.g. Cassidy and Andreosso-O'Callaghan 2006; Somlev and Hoshino 2005). One commonality associated with most of these studies is that they predominantly examine Japanese corporate behaviour in developed country contexts. To date, little attention has been given to contemporary developments concerning location choice at a subnational level, nor to the activities of Japanese MNEs in emerging economies, especially in contexts outside of China and Thailand (on which, see Beamish and Jiang 2002; Belderbos and Carree 2002; Buckley and Horn 2009; Cheng 2007; Marukawa 2004; Ma and Delios 2007; Wakasugi 2004). Moreover, industry effects are usually excluded from extant research. Crucially, this may oversimplify our understanding of agglomerative behaviour amongst Japanese firms. The present study addresses each of these lacunae. Our focus on India can be justified on the basis that it is fast becoming an important destination for foreign direct investment (FDI) by JMNEs (Horn, Forsans, and Cross 2010; JETRO 2013; Horn 2016), not least because of the size and potential of the markets it offers, its 'embryonic' state as an investment hub, and its greater openness to foreign business. At the same time, the regions of India offer highly divergent opportunities as FDI destinations because of profound yet evolving differences in economic, institutional and infrastructure-related factors. This means that India represents a timely context in which to examine the localization behaviour of Japanese companies in emerging markets at a subnational level, and whether or not this behaviour has changed in recent times.

With these considerations in mind, our study evaluates Indo–Japanese relations at the corporate level with the specific objective of identifying the determinants of subnational location choice and whether or not geographic concentration and agglomeration effects – a prevalent characteristic of Japanese corporate behaviour that is well documented in both industrialized and developing countries – are observable in the distribution of Japanese-owned operations across India. *A priori*, two divergent scenarios can be envisaged. On the one hand, a tendency may be observed for Japanese firms to increasingly colocate in geographic clusters over time as 'footloose' and 'one-off' pioneer investments give way to a greater engagement with the local business community – including the development of localized production networks – as India becomes increasingly established as an important middle- to long-term production base for JMNEs. On the other, a tendency away from geographic clustering at a subnational level may be observed as JMNEs reveal a growing trend to replace established business relationships that coalesce around traditional *keiretsu*-type organizational structures with more flexible and streamlined inter-firm linkages (Abegglen 2006; Economist 2009; Horn and Cross 2009; McGuire and Dow 2009) and distributed offshore production networks. Expressed another way, a growing propensity for JMNEs to adjust their international supply networks and to 'fine-slice' their operations on an ever more precise calculus, whereby optimal locations and ownership strategies are chosen in order to minimize total costs and to reach markets (Buckley 2009), may now engender new forms of localization behaviour among Japanese firms in developing economies such as India, especially among those with little to no prior investments in the country. For this reason, our country analysis is conducted in the context of ongoing reform of the Japanese production system worldwide, and, in particular, the changing nature of inter- and intracorporate Japanese business networks (Horn and Cross 2009). Four key research questions are examined in this study:

(1) How do subnational location characteristics influence the geographic dispersion of Japanese operations in India (as measured by investment project numbers)?;
(2) can firm-level and industry-level variations in dispersion be detected?;
(3) to what extent is agglomerative behaviour – one of the key facets of Japanese corporate behaviour – observed?; and
(4) can trends in the subnational distribution of investment project numbers be detected over time?

The remainder of the paper is organized as follows. First, the background to location choice in general and the determinants of Japanese investment location decisions in particular is charted. This synthesis of current knowledge on the determinants of the geographic distribution of JMNEs (in emerging economies) and their strategic orientation is used to inform our spatial analysis of Japanese operations in India. We go on to develop nine research propositions that we derive from an evaluation of extant literature. We then provide a brief account of the methodological approach used, especially concerning data collection and the analysis of spatial information, to test these propositions in the case of India. We explain how the application of geographic information system (GIS) analysis techniques in this study expands upon conventional measures of firm agglomeration. We go on to employ firm- and state-level data to investigate the evolution of the subnational investment behaviour of Japanese firms in India, from which we draw inferences about their strategic intent and localization behaviour. To discern nuances over time, our data are examined across two peak periods of Japanese investment in India (1995–1998 and 2004–2008). We conclude with a discussion of key findings and suggestions for further research.

Literature review

In recent times, considerable scholarly attention has been given to understanding the determinants of the spatial distribution of FDI by foreign firms in emerging economies. Location choice has been established as a central component of the theory of corporate internationalization (Dunning and Lundan 2008; Hymer 1976; Vernon 1974). This theory has established the notion that location per se contributes to the global competitiveness of MNCs and moderates their existing ownership-specific advantages (Collinson and Rugman 2008; Dicken 2003; Dunning 1998; Porter 2000). Country-specific location factors are also relevant to the formulation of national economic policies (Balasubramanyam and Greenaway 1992; Dicken 2003; Kimura and Ando 2004; Urata and Kawai 2000). The institutional framework *and* non-policy incentives have been identified as key enablers of FDI (Nicholas, Purcell, and Gray 2001). Even though a consensus on the relative importance and impact of discrete FDI determinants has yet to form (Chakrabarti 2001), the positive effects of FDI on economic development is widely acknowledged (e.g. Blomstrom and Kokko 1998; Borensztein, De Gregorio, and Lee 1998; Markusen and Venables 1998). Given that trade and investment barriers around the world are falling, renewed interest in those forces which determine FDI – especially FDI directed towards emerging economies – is not surprising (e.g. Altomonte and Guagliano 2003; Bevan and Estrin 2004; Chakraborty and Nunnenkamp 2008; Coughlin and Segev 2000; Meyer 2004; Nunnenkamp 2002; Wei et al. 1999). Because of the longstanding history of Japan as a major source of FDI, as well as the prominence of Japanese firms in international production networks and their success in the global market place, the location behaviour of Japanese MNEs has attracted much scholarly attention, and knowledge is comparatively advanced. A large empirical literature has now accumulated on the determinants of Japanese investment in both the industrialized and developing economies. In addition to country effects (such as incentives and factor endowments), studies have detected variant behaviour at the firm-level and industry-level according to a number of determinant factors. These include firm experience (e.g. Delios and Beamish 2005), size and orientation (e.g. Belderbos and Carree 2002; Mody, Dasgupta, and Sinha 1998), industry (that is, manufacturing vs. services) (e.g. Cieślik and Ryan 2002; Yamawaki 2006), vertical versus horizontal

FDI (e.g. Fukao and Wei 2008), home-country market share and R&D expenditures (e.g. Head, Ries, and Swenson 1995).

Theoretical framework and hypothesis development

Most prior studies on the determinants of Japanese FDI are positioned at the cross-country level. Few make direct reference to factors which influence subnational location decisions, despite the fact that *ex post* effects at the subnational level are likely, especially in large, heterogeneous markets such as India (e.g. Belderbos and Carree 2002; Thiran and Yamawaki 1995). At the same time, when viewed collectively, the findings of studies on those host economy-specific antecedents that are likely to attract Japanese investments are inconclusive. This can be attributed to (i) differences in data availability, sample selection and region of assessment, (ii) the application of different conceptual frameworks and statistical models that incorporate location-based determinants, and (iii) different levels of abstraction and time frames. All this resonates with the observations of Chakrabarti (2001), who concludes that most studies of FDI location determinants are driven less by theory and more by *ex post* explanations based on the selection of particular variables for modelling. Despite these conceptual weaknesses, certain commonalities amongst the explanatory variables employed in these studies can be identified: namely, market size and growth, human capital, infrastructure, agglomeration, and manufacturing density. We therefore use these six components to derive nine propositions concerning the likely spatial determinants of subnational location choice by JMNEs in India.

Market size and market growth

Despite their diverse scope, most prior studies identify market size and market potential as common and significant predictors of Japanese location decisions. Japanese firms have been shown to be attracted by market size due to the prospect of income generation, with positive effects demonstrated both at the national and subnational levels (e.g. Chen 1997; Fung, Iizaka, and Parker 2002). Following the assumption that the economic size of a market determines the likelihood of attracting Japanese FDI (Zhou, Delios, and Yang 2002), data on Gross Domestic Product (GDP) and GDP per capita (as a measure for consumer income and purchasing power) have been widely used as independent variables. Economic development across India varies greatly (MOSPI 2009), and in part, this has given rise to highly segmented subnational markets. This suggests the following:

Proposition 1: Japanese firms preferentially establish larger numbers of operations in more economically advanced regions of India.

A salient feature of emerging markets is that the tapping of market potential is often more important to prospective firms than is current absolute market size (Enderwick 2007). Projections of future market size and rising income thresholds, based on the extrapolation of growth rates and population size (with local liberalization policy as a constant), illustrate that access to markets is not only a matter of current demand but also one of securing future anticipated income streams. The long-term orientation of JMNEs is well documented (e.g. Delios and Keeley 2000; Maskin 1995), and market growth is therefore commonly hypothesized as a prime location determinant under the assumption that investments are, at least in part, market seeking (e.g. Cieślik and Ryan 2004; Somlev and Hoshino 2005). The regions of India not only vary significantly in terms of population size but also in economic growth (MOSPI 2009). According to a contemporary JBIC report (2009) market potential is the predominant reason why India is considered to be a promising destination amongst the Japanese business community. Therefore:

Proposition 2:   Japanese firms preferentially establish larger numbers of operations in regions of India with higher economic growth rates.

Human capital

One of the most important – but at the same time most controversial and fragile – variables found to influence the inward investment behaviour of Japanese firms is that of labour cost. While most studies report a significant correlation between FDI levels and labour costs, some find the relationship to be negative (e.g. Belderbos and Carree 2002; Tokunaga and Ishii 1995) and others positive (e.g. Chen 1997; Somlev and Hoshino 2005). Explanations for the former finding include the prevalence of efficiency-seeking investment motives among firms while for the latter the need to access a stable and skilled labour pool has been advanced. Other studies report ambivalent evidence of this relationship (e.g. Fukao and Wei 2008). While industry, regional and trade-related production effects may help to explain these mixed results (at least in part), the majority of studies set in emerging or transitional economy contexts show that high wages in general deter Japanese investment (e.g. Urata and Kawai 2000). However, in light of inherent characteristics of human resource management (HRM) systems among JMNEs (such as multiskilling and stable employment) other studies (e.g. Mody, Dasgupta, and Sinha 1998; Wakasugi 2004) report that Japanese firms generally rely on developing skilled human resource capabilities (expressed in higher wages paid than competitors) and that low wages are equated to poor productivity. Given the disparity of economic development across India, it is not surprising that wage levels also vary appreciably.[1] We therefore posit that:

Proposition 3:   Japanese firms establish larger numbers of operations in regions of India with higher labour costs.

It is well known that labour quality (i.e. human capital) is a key concern for Japanese firms (Abegglen and Stalk 1985). It is therefore reasonable to argue that the subnational location decisions of Japanese firms (once the decision to enter the country has been made) should also be guided by considerations of workforce educational attainment levels. Many studies of subnational location choice have captured this determinant using literacy rates and (varying) levels of education as proxies (e.g. Cassidy and Andreosso-O'Callaghan 2006; Cheng 2006; Cheng and Stough 2006; Fukao and Wei 2008). Negative correlations between Japanese FDI levels and regional unemployment rates have been interpreted in the context of low labour quality in the respective location (e.g. Thiran and Yamawaki 1995). However, in contrast to US or European firms, which in general place emphasis on 'deep' knowledge and instant applicability of staff (i.e. the use of explicit job descriptions and few generalists among employees) (Carr and Pudelko 2006; Itô 2006; Pudelko 2006a, 2006b), the Japanese HRM system is largely geared towards generalist know-how, flexibility and continuous learning of its labour force (Aoki 1994; Keizer 2005; Woodward 1992). While Japanese firms might be attracted to the availability of educated personnel (and low cost may be desirable), we assume that the qualification of the workforce in terms of industrial experience is at least equally as important (Chen 1997; Mody, Dasgupta, and Sinha 1998; Nicholas, Purcell, and Gray 2001). Assessment of labour quality beyond educational indicators is difficult to capture, however. According to several JBIC surveys (2007, 2008, 2009), the availability of qualified human labour is a key reason why Japanese firms perceive India to be an attractive investment destination. These arguments give rise to the following:

Proposition 4: Japanese firms preferentially establish larger numbers of operations in regions of India with higher education attainment levels.

Infrastructure

The level and quality of infrastructure have largely been found to have positive effects on Japanese investment decisions (e.g. Belderbos, Capannelli, and Fukao 2001; Brimble and Urata 2006; Guiheux and Lecler 2000; Zhou, Delios, and Yang 2002). Superior infrastructure facilities generally act as pull factors for foreign firms, as they signal the status of economic development (Belderbos and Carree 2002) and serve as a significant determinant of operational efficiency and costs (Yamawaki 2006). Depending on the investment motivation, the inherent features of the Japanese production system, such as Just-in-Time (JIT) production methods (Smith and Florida 1994) and proximity to customers (Head and Mayer 2004), also highlight the requirement by JMNEs for a well-developed infrastructure. In prior literature, attention has focused on a variety of infrastructure-related factors, including the density of transport links (e.g. railways, surfaced roads), availability of services (e.g. electricity, telephone lines) and levels of regional development (e.g. GDP per capita) as influencing location choice (Belderbos and Carree 2002; Cassidy and Andreosso-O'Callaghan 2006; Nicholas, Purcell, and Gray 2001; Smith and Florida 1994; Thiran and Yamawaki 1995; Urata and Kawai 2000). Meanwhile, recent JBIC surveys (2006, 2007, 2008) consistently highlight physical infrastructure deficiencies, especially transport-related deficiencies (NKS 2007), as reducing the overall attractiveness of India as an investment destination for JMNEs. Thus:

Proposition 5: Japanese firms preferentially establish larger numbers of operations in regions of India with superior infrastructure.

Since access to transport hubs are of particular importance when investing in large emerging economies (Lall, Shalizi, and Deichmann 2004), we employ data on road and railway-related variables (adjusted for the geographical size of the state) and seaport availability (freight per annum) to explore the role of infrastructure as a location determinant for JMNEs in India.

As physical infrastructure quality can only be roughly estimated (Ford and Strange 1999), particularly in developing economies with geographically extensive subnational regions such as India, we also account for the regional importance of Special Economic Zones (SEZs) to capture positive infrastructure effects on location choice. As part of government policies to attract inward FDI to India (Nayak 2008), SEZs are not only important in terms of their effect on production costs (e.g. reduced tariffs, bureaucratic regime and so forth), but they also provide superior infrastructure and proximity to transportation hubs (e.g. seaports and airports). As a consequence of potential positive backward linkage effects (Panagariya 2009), SEZs also serve as an indicator of the level of regional economic development and therefore reflect infrastructure quality (Belderbos and Carree 2002). Finally, the presence of SEZs also signals a favourable policy regime towards foreign and domestic business. Given divergent attitudes towards business – and especially foreign business – among the governments of Indian states (Sinha 2005; Wells 1998), it is necessary to capture this important institution-related dimension (Meyer and Nguyen 2005). Since SEZs numbers are likely to be associated with certain types of investment-friendly policy-induced incentives and infrastructure-related determinants, we expect that:

Proposition 6: Japanese firms preferentially establish larger numbers of operations in regions of India with greater numbers of SEZs.

Agglomeration and manufacturing density

A key commonality among studies on the strategic location behaviour of Japanese firms is that of agglomeration effects. At the most abstract level, the geographical clustering of economic activity is an outcome of the pooled procurement of human resources and intermediate products (Marshall 1920) and is demonstrated by the centripetal forces of heavy manufacturing activities (e.g. Braunerhjelm and Svensson 1996; Wheeler and Mody 1992). Agglomeration also induces spill-over effects facilitated by information sharing and (local) experience accumulation (Fujita and Thisse 1996). Japanese firms have been shown to be especially responsive to geographical concentration effects (e.g. Belderbos, Capannelli, and Fukao 2001; Head, Ries, and Swenson 1995; Smith and Florida 1994; Woodward 1992). Studies by Head, Ries, and Swenson (1999) and Belderbos and Carree (2002) demonstrate an agglomeration sensitivity of Japanese firms at three levels: (a) the industry (density) level, (b) the national level (with Japan as the country of origin), and (c) the *keiretsu* (or business group affiliation) level. The underlying rationale for this self-perpetuating tendency has been linked to a number of factors, including: (i) the vertical fragmentation of Japanese manufacturing processes (Belderbos, Capannelli, and Fukao 2001; Hatani 2009); (ii) customer orientation and industry bandwagon effects (Hennart and Park 1994; Smith and Florida 1994; Zhou, Delios, and Yang 2002); (iii) risk reduction due to information and experience sharing (Ford and Strange 1999; Wakasugi 2005); (iv) the replication of home-market subcontracting relationships (Head, Ries, and Swenson 1995) and (v) efficiency considerations arising from the pooling of resources within horizontally organized business groups (Fukao and Wei 2008). Because of the early developmental state of Japanese investment in India (and, therefore, the reduced likelihood of *keiretsu*-specific accumulations of Japanese firms), we focus in this study on two potential agglomeration effects. The first is a consequence of home country origin. The ease of communication and local social infrastructure sharing of operational or managerial features (e.g. JIT production) across and between Japanese firms have been shown to have a positive co-location effect on Japanese FDI (Belderbos and Carree 2002). Initiatives, such as local JETRO representation and the establishment of 'national' SEZs (with General Trading Houses, or Sôgô Shôsha serving as *agent provocateurs*), may also positively encourage the agglomeration of Japanese-owned activities. These 'country of origin' effects give rise to the following:

Proposition 7: Japanese firms preferentially establish larger numbers of operations in regions of India with higher numbers of prior Japanese-owned investment cases.

Following the approach of Zhou, Delios, and Yang (2002), we capture national agglomerative forces in terms of the number of Japanese enterprises present prior to the investment of a JMNE in a particular region of India.

The second agglomeration effect that we examine relates to manufacturing density. It has been found that agglomeration is highly correlated with nationality-independent externalities, including proximate location of (related) manufacturing activities (Belderbos and Carree 2002; Woodward 1992) and labour market conditions (Mayer and Mucchielli 1998; Yamawaki 2006). Because of both divergent economic development levels across India and Japan's manufacturing heritage, we expect geographical clusters of Japanese firms to emerge in regions of India in the following way:

Proposition 8: Japanese firms preferentially establish larger numbers of operations in regions of India with higher levels of manufacturing activity.

Since new investments by Japanese firms are likely to gravitate towards indigenous manufacturing activities (Woodward 1992), we capture manufacturing density in this study in terms of a region's labour force employed in the secondary sector (following Smith and Florida 1994). However, we recognize that counts of firms by region or density measurements must be considered only as rough proxies for the realities of clustering effects. Important factors, such as subregional characteristics, geographic size of region, cross-border linkages, subnational discrepancies in investment cost and longitudinal developments, are usually lost when analysing agglomerative firm behaviour. In this study, we address such issues through the application of GIS-based analysis techniques. This approach offers the potential of calibrating the evaluation of location choice in terms of 'buffering prior investment' cases (i.e. spherical computation of firms within a certain radius at a particular point in time; in this case, the geographical location of new investment projects) – solely based on latitude and longitude coordinates. Arguably, the location decisions of some firms may be driven by cost minimization motives (as a consequence of regional cost incentives, tax exemptions and so forth) that at the same time may allow for a proximity to other firms located in a neighbouring region or state. Our analysis of location by specific state is therefore here fine-tuned by including measures of geographic proximity that disregard state boundaries. This, we believe, will generate a more accurate picture of agglomeration effects than has hitherto been achieved in studies of Japanese firms in emerging markets. At the same time, by expanding on conventional measurements of corporate concentration (Porter 1998), GIS analysis techniques enable us to control for longitudinal effects using a stepwise, year by year, analysis of agglomeration. Instead of a cross-sectional analysis, we use proximity counts based upon year of entry information. Following the above discussion of the propensity for JMNEs to build clusters in new environments, we assume that this should be reflected in greater concentrations of other Japanese firms in their vicinity than is evident among other nationality firms. In other words:

Proposition 9: Japanese firms are more likely to preferentially establish larger numbers of operations in regions of India with higher levels of manufacturing density than are other foreign firms.

For Japanese production networks distance matters (Dyer 1994). In this study, we capture geographic proximity as the count of firms within a radius of 35 and 75 km respectively of the focal case location of a JMNE.

Methodology

In order to test our propositions, we populated a list of Japanese-owned operations in India using a variety of sources, including the electronic version of the Japanese Overseas Investment Database 2008 (Kaigai Shinshutsu Kigyô Sôran), published by Tôyô Keizai, the 2009 printed version of the same database, and the Crown Group's 'Japanese companies in India handbook' (Indo Nikkei Kigyô Nenkan 2008). For triangulation purposes and to explore the possibility of missing cases, our data set was complemented with project-level data from the annual editions of the Japanese Overseas Investment Directory, or Kaigai Shinshutsu Kigyô Sôran (Tôyô Keizai 1999, 2007). Our final data set comprises information on location, year of entry, industry category and authorized capital for a total of 518 affiliates in which Japanese firms hold at least 5% equity. As the authorized capital variable showed a high degree of inconsistency across our data sources (for reasons, *inter alia*, of missing data as well as currency fluctuations and conversion irregularities) and in line with similar prior studies (e.g. Delios and Beamish 2005; Smith and Florida 1994; Zhou, Delios, and Yang 2002) we use investment project numbers as the dependent variable. This enables us to classify each investment in terms of its location by Indian state, year of establishment and industry affiliation. Our premise is that states containing larger numbers of investment project numbers exhibit superior location-specific advantages for JMNEs than do those where smaller numbers are found (Delios and Beamish 2005). Data specific to the operations of non-Japanese firms in India were collected using the Prowess database provided by the Centre for Monitoring the Indian Economy (CMIE 2008). To our knowledge, this is the most comprehensive and accurate database of firm-level financial information available for India. Using information on ownership we identified 848 foreign firms in India that are non-Japanese. For the spatial analysis, location information (i.e. address and postcode) on 474 Japanese firms and 806 foreign firms of other nationalities (after data cleaning) was converted into longitude and latitude coordinates. Using the GIS software Mapinfo Professional we generated measures of interfirm proximity. We first created 'buffers' around each investment case (defined by latitude, longitude and year of investment) using 35 and 75 km radii. We then identified the number of investment cases based on whether or not these fall inside or outside the boundary of this buffer at a specific point in time. Next, we transferred the resultant firm counts to the statistical package SPSS for further analysis, including measures of correlation and regression.

To assess the strategic intent and localization behaviour of Japanese firms in India two categories of independent variable need to be considered at the subnational level: location endowments (including SEZ numbers) and firm-level factors (to capture agglomeration effects). For reasons of data availability, the chosen unit of analysis is the subnational administrative region of India. India is composed of 28 states and seven union territories (including the national capital). The distinction is that each state has its own elected government, while a union territory is ruled directly by the federal government. For purposes of exposition, we refer to both as 'states'. Measures on each of the 35 administrative regions (i.e. 'states') were obtained from various official Indian databases, including the Ministry of Statistics and Program Implementation (MOSPI), the Labour Bureau Government of India (LBGI), the Ministry of Human Resource Development (MHRD), the Ministry of Road Transport and Highways, and the Bank of India. Socio-demographic information was gathered from the

Ministry of Home Affairs (MHA, Census 2001) and Bose, Singh, and Adhikary 1991 (Census 1991).

To test each of our propositions, data were collected on regional GDP, GDP per capita and market growth (percentage change in GDP per capita), wages (labour cost and ability), literacy rates and education levels (education attainment) as well as length of roads and railways and number of SEZs per region. Measures of infrastructure are complemented by GIS-generated proximity measures (the distance of firm location to nearest seaport and airport). Finally, in order to explore Japanese corporate behaviour in terms of agglomeration effects, we use counts of already existing operations in a specific region to capture established 'nationality' and 'industry' relationships in investment behaviour. In addition to both these measures, and following Yamawaki (2006), we also use manufacturing density (measured first as labour force employed in the secondary sector, and second as the ratio of state population to total employment in the secondary sector) as a further indicator of industry agglomeration. Because agglomeration effects involve complex relationships of investment behaviour (e.g. new investors may cause wage levels to change), it is likely that the influence of the eventual covariates will be moderated by other economic indicators (such as regional GDP, GDP per capita and wage levels) which have been shown to be crucial covariate location determinants of agglomerative behaviour (Chakrabarti 2001). This is reflected in our analysis.

Historical analysis of key trends in Japanese investment in India has documented the responsiveness of Japanese firms to institutional change (Nayak 2008). Following significant economic reform in the 1990s, and India's gradual opening towards foreign capital, two distinct peaks of Japanese investment can be discerned between the years of 1995–1998 and 2004–2008 (Buckley, Cross, and Horn 2012). These two periods are aligned closely to the characterization by Buckley, Cross, and Horn (2012) of the evolution of India's FDI policy and concomitant effects on Indo-Japanese corporate relations that the authors label as 'Phase 4: liberalization phase' and 'Phase 6: new experimental phase', respectively. The former period captures a time when India abandoned planned economy thinking and introduced stronger market mechanisms and reforms. This saw Japanese investment inflows increase, especially in 'beachhead' production facilities mainly in transport machinery, electronics and machinery, with a distinct peak in 1997. The latter period captures a time when Japanese FDI increased sharply in response to continued investment and trade liberalization efforts, including the opening of additional sectors to FDI, raising of equity caps, 'automatic' investment approvals, currency convertibility, tariff cuts and various incentives and benefits offered to foreign firms operating in SEZs (for more detail, see Table 4 in Buckley, Cross, and Horn 2012). Hence, these two periods (1995–1998 and 2004–2008) are used to undertake a comparative analysis of variation and evolution of Japanese investment behaviour in India over time.

Data analysis

The limited number of administrative regions in India necessitates a conservative empirical analysis of subnational location choice. Table 1 reports the overall findings of correlation analysis (Pearson's *r*) for each of the two time periods in question, and Table 2 provides a breakdown by major industry. A positive coefficient indicates a positive relationship between

Table 1. Correlation matrix of subnational location determinants and Japanese investment numbers in India.

Subnational determinant	1995/1998 Cor.	1995/1998 Sig.	2004/2008 Cor.	2004/2008 Sig.	Diff-Sig
Market size and growth variables					
GDP	0.520**	0.001	0.452**	0.005	0.739
GDP per capita	0.21	0.128	0.314*	0.007	0.676
Market growth (% change in GDP per capita)	−0.005	0.49	−0.052	0.391	0.86
Labour cost variable					
Wages	0.453**	0.008	0.440**	0.418	0.952
Human capital variables					
Literacy rate	−0.031	0.433	0.141	0.209	0.504
Enrolment in secondary education	0.502**	0.002	0.358*	0.022	0.503
Enrolment in higher education	0.502**	0.003	0.304*	0.045	0.369
Infrastructure variables					
Road network (length in km)	0.244	0.78	−0.005	0.488	0.31
Railway network (length in km)	0.442**	0.004	0.491**	0.001	0.802
Seaport (tonnage per annum)	0.069	0.346	−0.054	0.38	0.622
SEZ number	0.297*	0.8	0.464**	0.003	0.433
Agglomeration effect variables					
Number of prior Japanese firms	0.826**	0	0.910**	0	0.159
Manufacturing density (absolute numbers of employees in the Indian manufacturing sector)	0.507**	0.002	0.463**	0.004	0.848
Manufacturing density (labour force employed in the secondary sector)	0.197	0.144	−0.151	0.217	
Manufacturing density (ratio of state population to total employment in the secondary sector)	−0.008	0.484	0.116	0.278	

*<0.05,
**<0.01.

Table 2. Correlation matrix of subnational location determinants and Japanese investment numbers in India by industry.

Subnational determinant (by state)	Transport 1995/1998	Transport 2004/2008	Electronics 1995/1998	Electronics 2004/2008	Machinery 1995/1998	Machinery 2004/2008	Chemicals 1995/1998	Chemicals 2004/2008	IT 1995/1998	IT 2004/2008
Market size variables										
GDP	0.336*	0.256	0.318*	482**	0.530**	0.339*	0.481**	0.445**	0.546**	0.288
	−0.032	−0.082	−0.041	−0.003	−0.001	−0.031	−0.003	−0.006	−0.001	−0.058
GDP per capita	−0.006	0.031	0.271	0.281	0.16	0.284	0.195	0.308*	0.112	0.279
	−0.488	−0.435	−0.07	−0.063	−0.196	−0.063	−0.147	−0.046	−0.274	−0.065
Labour cost variable										
Wages	0.272	0.248	0.177	0.547**	0.471**	0.314*	0.475**	0.407*	0.494**	0.199
	−0.081	−0.089	−0.184	0	−0.006	−0.043	−0.005	−0.012	−0.004	−0.142
Human capital variables										
Literacy rate	−0.179	−0.091	0.034	0.158	−0.047	0.117	0.138	0.154	−0.017	0.159
	−0.168	−0.302	−0.428	−0.182	−0.401	−252	−0.229	−0.188	−0.464	−0.18
Enrolment in secondary education	0.403*	0.285	0.338*	0.363*	0.474**	0.328*	0.366*	0.353*	0.547**	0.238
	−0.011	−0.057	−0.029	−0.021	−0.003	−0.033	−0.02	−0.024	−0.001	−0.095
Enrolment in higher education	0.368*	0.193	0.326*	0.229	0.523**	0.119	0.341*	0.398*	0.552**	0.226
	−0.019	−0.145	−0.034	−0.103	−0.001	−0.258	−0.028	−0.012	−0.001	−0.106
Infrastructure variables										
Road network (length in km)	−0.124	−0.04	0.517**	−0.012	0.138	0.037	0.222	−0.007	0.166	0.015
	−0.239	−0.409	−0.001	−0.473	−0.215	−0.416	−0.1	−0.485	−0.177	−0.467
Railway network (length in km)	0.115	0.097	0.624**	0.411**	0.283*	0.561**	0.421**	0.448**	0.298*	0.510**
	−0.256	−0.29	0	−0.007	−0.05	0	−0.006	−0.003	−0.041	−0.001
Seaport (tonnage per annum)	−0.055	−0.051	−0.066	−0.03	−0.063	−0.038	−0.026	−0.054	−0.042	−0.049
	−0.377	−0.385	−0.353	−0.433	−0.359	−0.415	−0.441	−0.379	−0.406	−0.39
SEZ number	−0.03	0.365*	0.254	.524**	0.179	0.291*	0.643**	0.409**	0.288*	0.244
	−0.432	−0.016	−0.07	−0.001	−0.152	−0.045	0	−0.007	−0.047	−0.079
Agglomeration effect variables										
Number of prior Japanese firms	0.626**	0.829.**	0.148	0.905**	0.804**	0.281	0.527**	0.644**	0.625**	0.666**
	0	0	−0.199	0	0	−0.051	−0.001	0	0	0
Manufacturing density (absolute numbers of employees in the Indian manufacturing sector)	0.315*	0.289	0.259	0.515**	0.523**	0.329*	0.479**	0.442**	0.538**	0.264
	−0.042	−0.057	−0.08	−0.002	−0.001	−0.035	−0.003	−0.006	−0.001	−0.076
Manufacturing density (labour force employed in the secondary sector)	0.197	−0.161	0.01	−0.169	0.164	−0.123	0.169	−0.087	0.168	−0.12
	−0.144	−0.202	−0.48	−0.191	−0.189	−0.262	−0.182	−0.327	−0.184	−0.268

*<0.05,
**<0.01.

the location determinant and the number of investing firms or, in other words, an increase in the probability of Japanese investment cases.

Much of JMNE competitiveness is built on HRM and, in the case of operations abroad, on the international transfer of these practises. Labour productivity, labour quality and their interplay therefore deserve particular attention: When we control for subnational labour productivity in India (partial correlation of Wages × GDP: 1998: $r = 0.957$, $p = 0.000$; 2004: $r = 0.929$, $p = 0.000$) the effects of wages on Japanese investment numbers diminishes. This correlation can also be demonstrated at the industry level.[2] It is important to note that the medium to strong positive effects of wage structure on Japanese investment is not only relativized controlling for GDP at a subnational level. In the cases of the transport and electronic industry, the algebraic sign changes towards a negative relationship in the 1995/1998 period. Subsequent multiple regression analysis reveals that in both our time periods Japanese corporate behaviour in India is driven more by labour productivity than wage considerations (1995/1998: Adjusted $R^2 = 0.208$, $p = 0.011$; 2004/2008: Adjusted $R^2 = 0.198$, $p = 0.015$).

Education enrolment figures are also an indicator of the quality of local labour. Like productivity, this dimension has explanatory power as a proxy for the propensity for JMNEs to search for and recruit higher quality labour in India. Subsequent analysis reveals that wage levels and educational enrolment variables are highly correlated ($r = 0.859$, $p < 0.001$ in the case of secondary education enrolment and $r = 0.911$, $p < 0.001$ in the case of higher education enrolment). When controlling for education effects on Japanese investment (irrespective of industry affiliation), partial correlations show that the relationship between wage levels and investment cases diminishes. This decrease in significance can also be demonstrated at the industry level, with the notable exception of the chemicals industry. It seems that in this industry wage structure and educational enrolment are perceived not as exclusive but complementary location determinants within India.

GIS-generated data help to further refine our understanding of the propensity for Japanese firms to colocate in India. A comparison of the count of firms present in a state prior to investment reveals significant variation across Japanese and other nationality firms, as Table 3 shows.

The dominance of country of origin effects on location choice is substantiated by the subsequent analysis of covariates. Controlling for market size, labour, education, infrastructure and manufacturing density, partial correlations show that the relationship between subnational agglomeration effects and investment cases in India remains very strong and significant (see Table 4). This can be demonstrated for both time periods and all industries. This finding points towards a consistent location determinant for Japanese firms at the subnational level. Table 5 reports that our GIS data analysis confirms an intensification of agglomerative tendency among JMNEs in India over the two periods under investigation.

In order to further explore the spatial spread and quality of Japanese investment at the subnational level, we categorize Indian states in terms of their location characteristics. Hierarchical cluster analysis (using Euclidian distance) of the location determinants in respect to market size, labour, educational attainment and infrastructure provides evidence of three distinct profiles for Indian states. Subsequent variable analysis indicates that state groupings can be established based upon distinctiveness across all parameters, with Indian states exhibiting homogeneously 'low', 'medium' and 'high' levels of development in their respective group. Confirmatory cluster analysis shows that our categorization is stable for both periods

Table 3. Agglomeration effects by country of origin.

	Japanese firms	Other foreign firms	t-test (2-tailed)
Number of firms within 35 km radius (prior to investment)	84	65	0.000***
Number of firms within 75 km radius (prior to investment)	122	78	0.000***
Number of Japanese firms within 75 km radius (prior to investment)	41	11	0.000***
By industry (within 75 km radius)			
Automobiles	97	30	0.002**
Electronic	68	43	0.000***
Machinery	9	5	0.000***
Chemicals	19	21	0.71

**<0.01,
***<0.001.

Table 4. Dominance of country of origin effect (partial correlation).

	Period of assessment	
Control variables	1995/1998	2004/2008
SEZ number	0.770 (0.000)***	0.904 (0.000)***
Educational attainment	0.757 (0.000)***	0.917 (0.000)***
Wages	0.787 (0.000)***	0.908 (0.000)***
Manufacturing density	0.766 (0.000)***	0.902 (0.000)***
GDP	0.744 (0.000)***	0.902 (0.000)***
Infrastructure	0.796 (0.000)***	0.922 (0.000)***

***<0.001.

Table 5. Agglomerative effects of Japanese investment (number of firms with low, medium or high count of firms in their vicinity).

	35 km radius			75 km radius		
Agglomeration (firm count)	1995/1998	2004/2008		1995/1998	2004/2008	
Low	31	25	χ^2 26.427	34	27	χ^2 58.036
Medium	39	53	df 2	45	38	df 2
High	19	88	$p=0.000$	10	101	$p=0.000$

1995/1998 and 2004/2008. Examination of the geographic spread of Japanese investment cases (Table 6) reveals that the majority of Japanese firms are located in states with low to medium levels of development. Only 20% of Japanese firms are located in a group of states characterized by comparatively high levels of education, infrastructure, wages and so forth. This distribution indicates that, collectively, Japanese firms seem to be insensitive to levels of social, economic or infrastructure development in India.

Discussion

Location factors drive FDI and the question that we want to answer here is: What determinants best explain the subnational investment patterns of JMNEs operating in India? We first discuss our findings in terms of the key investment determinants identified in our theoretical

Table 6. State profile effects on JMNE location by industry (investment numbers).

Industry	State development level				In 1995/1998				In 2004/2008			
	Low	Med	High	Sig.	Low	Med	High	Sig.	Low	Med	High	Sig.
Transport	51	38	11	0.438 (0.377)	10	13	1	0.656 (0.356)	15	7	2	0.889 (0.972)
Electronics	27	45	11	0.041 (0.002)	6	5	1	0.074 (0.052)	7	8	4	0.055 (0.004)
Machinery	24	30	18	0.106 (0.001)	4	6	3	0.006 (0.009)	12	10	2	0.612 (0.107)
Chemicals	16	9	11	0.000 (0.000)	4	2	1	0.148 (0.171)	7	1	4	0.007 (0.000)
Synthetic Resin	1	3	3		0	0	0		1	2	1	
Rubber, Rubber goods	7	1	0		3	1	0		2	0	0	
Ceramics, Glass	5	4	0		0	0	0		2	1	0	
Steel, Metal products	12	7	2		1	1	0		6	3	0	
Optical, Medical Instruments, Watches	5	12	7		1	3	2		1	4	2	
Finance	3	2	8		0	0	1		2	0	5	
Transport, Warehouse	10	8	7		0	1	1		6	1	3	
Mass Media, Publishing, Advertising	7	1	4		0	0	1		2	0	0	
IT	9	28	4	0.051 (0.028)	1	4	1	0.002 (0.002)	7	6	1	0.573 (0.075)
Trade	9	5	9		3	1	0		4	0	5	
Real Estate, Construction, Engineering	11	4	3		2	2	0		5	0	2	
Foodstuffs, Agriculture, Fishery	5	4	2		0	0	0		2	0	0	
Petroleum, Mining	1	3	0		0	0	0		1	1	0	
Textiles, Textile Products	4	3	0		2	0	0		1	2	0	

framework. Adopting an overview – a spatial analysis approach – then allows us to explore the potential alignment of individual location factors that operate at state level.

Investment determinants

Market size and growth

In both our time periods (1995/1998 and 2004/2008), the effects of subnational market size is large and positive. Consistent with earlier studies (e.g. Belderbos and Carree 2002; Cieślik and Ryan 2004; Delios and Keeley 2000; Ford and Strange 1999; Friedman, Gerlowski, and Silberman 1992; Fung, Iizaka, and Parker 2002; Head and Mayer 2004; Kumar 2001; Somlev and Hoshino 2005; Urata and Kawai 2000; Woodward 1992; Zhou, Delios, and Yang 2002), we find JMNEs to exhibit a tendency to preferentially locate in regions of India characterized by high GDP levels. This finding holds irrespective of industry affiliation. Thus, we find strong support for Proposition 1. The relationship between market size and investment numbers is particularly strong in the machinery, chemicals and information technology (IT) industries. Moreover, the finding is stable across both periods of assessment (especially in electronics, machinery and chemicals).

In contrast, GDP per capita has only a small effect on investment numbers (being moderately significant for the more recent investment period only). Consequently, Proposition 2 is not fully supported. With regards to industry, only the correlation results for investments in the chemicals industry in the 2004/2008 period are significant at the 5% level. This proxy indicates that for both periods Japanese firms appear less concerned with the overall level of economic development of Indian states. Interestingly, a comparison of results for our two time periods indicates that these considerations are gathering momentum. In general, across all industries the strength of relationship between GDP per capita and investment project numbers increases, suggesting greater sensitivity to demand conditions over time. Investments between 2004 and 2008 are found to be influenced significantly by diverging regional economic externalities. We observe JMNEs to increasingly invest in states with high GDP per capita figures, potentially indicating a formation period of emerging epicentres, whereby economic development attracts further investment. At the same time, regions that are not participating fully in the growth of the Indian economy are falling further behind in terms of FDI by JMNEs.

In contrast to earlier research, a pronounced long-term orientation of Japanese investment in foreign markets has not been confirmed in the case of India. Subnational economic growth has been shown to be insignificant (and even slightly negatively correlated) to Japanese investment numbers during both time periods. For an emerging economy such as India, this orientation towards the present is somewhat surprising. While JBIC surveys (2006–2009) of Japanese firms consistently rate the future market potential of India as a main criterion of investment attractiveness, this appears not to be translated into positive investment decisions at the subnational level. We infer from this that once the decision to invest in India and participate in (future) economic growth has been reached, Japanese firms give more prominence to pragmatic location determinants and focus on the pursuit of present rather than long-term strategic objectives at a subnational level.

Labour costs

Empirical findings indicate moderate effects between the wage structure of a state and investment project numbers. We therefore find some support for Proposition 3. Labour costs are positively and significantly correlated with Japanese FDI project numbers at the subnational level in both our time periods. However, the range of correlation coefficients suggests divergent relationships at the industry level, with medium to strong effects confined to the electronics, machinery, chemical and IT sectors. Even though subsequent analysis does not reveal significant differences across our two time periods, the distinct increase in effect in the electronics industry and the distinct decrease in effect in the IT industry are noted and require further scrutiny in future research.

Following the argumentation of Chen (1997) and Wei et al. (1999), it is important that labour cost is contextualized by taking efficiency levels into account. Our findings suggest that Japanese investment numbers across Indian states are associated with higher wages if higher productivity levels can be achieved. Contrary to the common and well-documented assumption that Japanese FDI in emerging economies is driven by efficiency-seeking motives (e.g. Belderbos and Carree 2002; Cheng 2007), our findings indicate that the picture in India is more complex. While early investments in some industries seems to have been driven, at least in part, by efficiency-related motives (with potential indirect effects on subsequent wage structures), the overall thrust of our findings is that Japanese investors seem to accept higher wages if and when these are offset by higher productivity levels. Despite industry variations and changes of investment behaviour over time, our study finds that most JMNEs preferentially locate in Indian regions with high wage levels and tend to avoid regions with low wage levels. Only in the most recent period are industry effects negligible, and this suggests that higher labour costs are not necessarily detrimental to Japanese investment because JMNEs take into account regional variation in productivity levels.

Human capital

Indicators for quality of human capital at the state-level (namely enrolment in secondary and higher education) are found to have a positive relationship with investment numbers. We therefore find strong support for Proposition 4. In other words, the higher the availability of educated personnel within a state the more likely that instances of Japanese FDI will be observed. Literacy rates at the state level are not significant and have very weak effects as a subnational location determinant. Differences across the two time periods are not detected, so the relationship between investment cases and secondary and higher education enrolment can be assumed to be stable over time. While this finding is reconfirmed at the industry level, the overall decrease in the strength of relationship over time across all major industries (from medium to strong to small effects) points towards 'lead' Japanese investors placing greater emphasis on educational attainment levels as a location determinant compared to subsequent investing firms.

Contrary to the common assumption that industrialized country FDI in emerging economies is primarily driven by cost-reducing motives, our empirical analysis and the subsequent post hoc exploration reveals a much more nuanced and complex picture of Japanese investment behaviour at a subnational level in the case of India. Generally, JMNEs are found to prefer locations characterized by a productive, educated and skilled workforce. The relationships between these location determinants and Japanese investor behaviour are positive and strong. Arguably, this reflects the idiosyncrasies of Japanese HRM systems, which are generally built around flexibility, group cohesion and multiskilling, all of which require a certain level of educational attainment among the workforce. For this, JMNEs seem prepared to accept higher wage structures in Indian states.

Infrastructure

The empirical analysis of the effect of Indian infrastructure on Japanese location decisions shows mixed results. For reasons of data availability (roads and rail networks measured in kilometres per state, and ports measured in freight tonnage per annum) and stark differences in the geographical size of individual states, all infrastructure variables have been relativized according to geographic size of the host state. While during the period 1995/1998, all correlation coefficients indicate a positive relationship with investment cases (with small effects for road infrastructure and medium effects for railway networks), the latter period (2004/2008) only shows a positive effect for railways. Consequently, of the two infrastructure variables that capture domestic transportation potential only rail network extent is found to have a significant effect on location choice at the subnational level. Subsequent analysis shows no significant differences between the two periods of assessment, suggesting insensitivity to transport infrastructure-related variables among the Japanese business community over time. These empirical findings are reconfirmed at the industry level, even though noteworthy variations have been detected. Neither the extent of road nor rail infrastructure appears to be relevant location determinants for the transport industry. Conversely, investments by electronics industry firms are related to the extent of road networks in states in the first period of assessment, but this relationship significantly decreases in the second.

In short, our analysis reveals only partial support for Proposition 5. The limited effects of infrastructure development on Japanese FDI location decisions contrast to the findings of various JBIC surveys that regularly report infrastructure deficiencies as a barrier to Japanese investment. Despite the positive effects of rail infrastructure development, the extent of road networks and seaport facilities are found to be largely irrelevant to the location decision process. Our findings for the seaport variable (irrespective and respective of industry effects) are interesting in that they indicate that import and export considerations seem unimportant to the location decision process at the subnational level. Arguably, the non-existent relationship between seaport facilities and investment cases may indicate that Japanese firms have perceived India primarily as a target market rather than an export platform. For example, it may be that goods are manufactured primarily for, and are transported to, the domestic market, with the extent of railway infrastructure a significant factor as a means of distributing finished and intermediate products. Confirming the findings of Anand and Delios (1996), this result may also reflect the institutional heritage of the Indian government's import substitution policy: many JMNEs have expanded into a market that traditionally was protected from imports by high tariff and non-tariff barriers.

Special export zones

The Indian government announced in 2000 a plan to proactively support the establishment of SEZs as engines for regional economic growth (mirroring similar policies in China and other emerging countries). Under this initiative, Indian states have the right to individually formulate and enact a legal framework towards SEZs at the subnational level. In this way, SEZs – and their associated (regional) tax incentives, advanced infrastructure and simplified investment procedures – have become a powerful investment incentive for foreign companies. The number of SEZs in a state also reflects how 'friendly' state governments are towards foreign (and domestic) business. In addition to the conversion of eight existing export processing zones (EPZs), more than 500 zones have been formally approved in India since the ratification of the SEZ Act in 2005. While questions remain about the efficacy of the dramatic growth of SEZs across India, with regional competition a particular concern (Panagariya 2009), we find a positive effect for this policy initiative, at least with respect to Japanese FDI. In both our periods of assessment, the existence of EPZs (1995/1998) and SEZ numbers (2004/2008) are positively correlated to Japanese investment numbers. Strong support is therefore found for Proposition 6. While insignificant, direct comparison of the correlation coefficients shows a closer relationship since the introduction of SEZs in 2005. This finding can be interpreted in two ways. On the one hand, JMNEs may be responding positively to the extent of state-level openness to foreign and domestic business, and a commitment to attract FDI (i.e. a policy incentive). On the other, JMNEs may be directly locating in SEZs or close to other companies that have already done so. In either case, the policy of the Indian government to promote SEZs (accompanied by regionally targeted tax concessions and improved infrastructure) appears to have enhanced location attractiveness for Japanese companies. Indeed, our results lend some support to the view that the Indian government has successfully transplanted the positive and consistent effects of SEZs demonstrated previously by the case of China (Chen 1997).

Subsequent analysis at the industry level shows that investments by Japanese electronics and chemicals companies are particularly associated with SEZs (with medium to strong effects), perhaps indicating an export-orientation amongst these firms. Except for the chemicals industry the strength of relationship with SEZ numbers (in the case of the transport industry, $p<0.1$) has increased over the two periods of assessment. This finding points towards a strategic shift in investment motivations across our focal industries and reconfirms the positive effects of the introduction of SEZs and the associated improvements in investment conditions as a consequence of fiscal advantages, infrastructure quality and a 'pro-business' stance of local government.

Agglomeration effects

Our findings indicate that Japanese firms are highly responsive to agglomeration effects in India. For both time periods, the correlation coefficients are significant and their size indicates the strong effect of prior Japanese investment projects as a location determinant. Thus, strong support is found for Proposition 7. In comparison to other independent variables this particular country of origin effect is by far the strongest. It is especially strong in the transport, electronics, chemicals and IT industries. Moreover, statistical comparison shows a significant increase in relationship strength for the transport and electronics industries over the two periods of assessment. Rather than confirming the assumption that agglomeration effects would diminish over time due to regional expansion of Japanese business networks (Delios, Beamish, and Zhao 2009) or a weakening of network cohesion in the home market (Cross and Horn 2009; Lincoln and Shimotani 2009; McGuire and Dow 2009), our findings indicate that JMNE investments in India seem to be largely unrelated to developments in other emerging economies or in Japan itself in terms of the propensity to cluster geographically. The diminishing strength of relationship in the case of the machinery industry is, however, counter-intuitive to this argument and needs to be investigated in future research. In addition, our findings are confirmed by subsequent analysis of GIS-generated data. For both distance measures employed, JMNEs are more likely to locate in areas with higher firm concentrations than are other nationalities of foreign firms, verifying our a priori assumption of a more pronounced colocation strategy among JMNEs. Thus, Proposition 9 is supported. Furthermore, analysis of 'national' agglomeration supports this finding. The effect of the number of prior Japanese-owned operations as an investment determinant is considerably more strongly pronounced than it is for other foreign firms. These findings are state-independent and are therefore arguably a more robust reflection of investment drivers. A strong tendency towards agglomerative behaviour and geographic concentration among Japanese firms in India must therefore be concluded. This effect can be demonstrated for the main industry sectors, namely the automobile, electronics and machinery industries, in which JMNEs exhibit stronger agglomerative behaviour than do other nationality firms (albeit less so in the case of the chemicals industry). This sectoral variation points towards concentration effects at the industry level.

The fact that we reveal agglomeration externalities beyond nationality effects highlights an interesting disparity in terms of absolute numbers and ratio. Manufacturing density (measured by absolute numbers of employees in the Indian manufacturing sector) is strongly and positively correlated to Japanese investment numbers at the subnational level, a finding that is consistent across both periods of assessment. Consequently, we find strong support for Proposition 8: Japanese firms preferentially locate in Indian states with a nominally large manufacturing base. However, when measured against the overall population and working population of the state, this positive relationship diminishes. Hence, the comparisons of manufacturing density measurements indicate that Japanese firms seem to be primarily concerned with the availability of adequate personnel, but that agglomeration effects are relatively weak in this respect. Noteworthy industry-level effects have not been found.

When Indian states are divided into those evidencing low, medium and high agglomerative effects, a notable shift towards higher geographical concentrations of firms is apparent. For both our measures of geographical concentration, empirical exploration highlights substantial agglomerative variance, clearly indicating a self-perpetuating and reinforcing trajectory of Japanese investment. This agglomeration towards prior Japanese subsidiaries may be explained by spill-over effects arising from factors such as interfirm linkages, information sharing and common location requirements. Arguably, imponderables of the Indian market environment may lead to nuanced corporate compatriot effects. Our findings mirror evidence of Japanese corporate behaviour in China between 1997 and 2003 (Chen 1997), but whereas in China agglomerative behaviour has been less in evidence in more recent years (Delios, Beamish, and Zhao 2009), it has been much more sustained in the case of India. It is possible to speculate that these strong national agglomeration effects in the case of India are largely due to an uncertain market environment fuelled by a government experimenting with deregulation. In such an environment, risk reduction can be achieved by tapping into the experience of other nearby firms that share the same country of origin and, therefore, cultural heritage. If the Japanese experience in India is to follow the same trajectory as for China, agglomeration effects may alleviate over time.

Spatial analysis

While the effect of subnational development levels varies across both periods of assessment, the location parameters (irrespective of industry affiliation) are at first sight indiscriminate to investment behaviour by JMNEs. However, with respect to industry effects, significant differences in investment strategies can be observed for firms from the electronics, chemical and IT sectors. Following the argumentation of Dostal (2008), it is feasible that investments in New Delhi[3] have been motivated by its capital city status, a trend that has been observed in the transitional economies of Eastern Europe and China (Ma and Delios 2007). While the position of New Delhi is arguably less monocentric than the dominant capital cities of the post-communist countries, it nevertheless is a gateway to India in terms of innovation, accelerated institutional interaction and as an epicentre of transformational change. This may explain why New Delhi receives the majority of FDI to India (next to Maharashtra) (MCI 2009), despite weak location-specific advantages arising from its relatively low GDP and manufacturing intensity (which, of course, are also related to population size). Firms from all industries, except transport, show a high degree of tailoring investments to levels of subnational development. Accordingly, our findings underscore the fallacy of assuming homogeneous investment patterns among Japanese firms. We observe in both time periods a pragmatic process of location selection, whereby a distinct set of location determinants have driven firm-level strategies. A comparison of Japanese FDI by state groupings shows that in the mid-1990s investments by Japanese firms were primarily directed towards those states with low to medium levels of development, while in the 2004/2008 period, a rise in investment numbers in states with comparatively high levels of development can be observed. As the importance of investments in less developed states also increases, dual investment strategies seem to be emerging whereby efficiency seeking considerations are paired with motivations directed towards tapping the potential of a more developed workforce.

Subsequent analysis at the industry-level reconfirms these location choice variations. In the 1995/1998 period, firms from the electronics and machinery industries located particularly in states with low levels of development, while IT-related firms tended to opt for medium levels of development. Most recent investments in the electronics, machinery and IT industries follow earlier patterns of efficiency-seeking investments, while an increasing number of firms in the chemical industries have shifted their focus towards more advanced areas. For transport-related firms, no diverging investment patterns across the groupings have been found, indicating strategies of best corporate fit. In sum, our analysis of investment cases vis-à-vis homogeneous groups of states has highlighted distinct industry responses to subnational location determinants, but that further investigation is required in order to explain why this has occurred.

Implications

While much has been written about the investment behaviour of JMNEs in the industrialized world, less is known about their activities in developing countries. In this paper, we have sought to shed light on one important question concerning the activities of Japanese companies in developing countries, namely how subnational location characteristics influence the numbers and geographic dispersion of Japanese operations, and whether firm-level and industry-level variation are detectable. India represents a useful context in which to investigate this issue, not only because Indo–Japanese economic relations are rapidly evolving, but because the market size, growth and deregulation trajectory of India suggests that the already strong presence of Japanese companies is likely to intensify in future years, despite significant geographical and psychological distances between the two countries. Indeed, what we observe in this study may be a consequence of the comparatively nascent state of JMNE engagement with the Indian market, and our findings should serve as a useful benchmark against which to compare the investment behaviour of JMNEs should they, as in the case of China, distribute their activities more widely across the country.

Several location specific factors have been found to affect positively the numbers of Japanese investment projects in Indian states. At the subnational level, overall market size, wage levels, educational attainment and institutional framework (captured by SEZ numbers) are found to be significant catalysts for investment project numbers, irrespective of industry. These effects are found to be strong and to some extent deepen across our two periods of assessment, confirming findings reported in previous studies. However, contrary to expectation, our findings in respect to income levels (measured as GDP per capita), the long-term orientation of Japanese firms (captured by market growth), human capital (measured as literacy and education rates) and infrastructure quality (extent of roads and proximity to seaports in particular) are inconclusive. It would seem that, in the case of India, Japanese firms are insensitive to these types of spatial determinants compared to other country destinations. This may be attributed to the traditional manufacturing orientation of JMNEs that sits in contrast to the rapid expansion of the services sector in India as the prime driver of national economic growth.

Using GIS data to conduct a more fine-grained analysis of infrastructure-related factors in particular, we find that although infrastructure quality is less relevant at the aggregate national level, proximity to transportation hubs is indeed an important location determinant for Japanese FDI. Arguably, this finding may point towards nuanced strategies among Japanese investors that combine both international network integration imperatives (e.g. in relation to supply chain management, access to resources or efficiency gains) with market-seeking motives. Overall, our empirical analysis draws attention to a complementary and iterative interaction of economic (market access, labour quality), institutional (regional openness) and infrastructure (or accessibility)-related factors that underpin the bulk of Japanese FDI in India. Moreover, when these factors are investigated longitudinally they are found to be stable across key phases of India's post-1991 liberalization process.

Among the location determinants we investigate, agglomeration effects are by far the most prominent. In line with earlier research in both the developed and developing economies (e.g. Belderbos and Carree 2002; Cheng 2007; Chung and Song 2004; Fukao and Wei 2008; Head, Ries, and Swenson 1999; Mayer and Mucchielli 1998; Wakasugi 2004; Zhou, Delios, and Yang 2002), our study has confirmed that the presence of foreign-owned (both Japanese and non-Japanese) operations at the subnational level enhances the probability of further investment projects by JMNEs in geographic concentrations. This agglomerative tendency of JMNEs has been captured via a variety of measures, including number of firms by state, industry density, as well as GIS-generated proximity counts.

While our analysis of the spatial determinants of Japanese investment in India may help to guide inward investment-related policy formulation, it is worth noting that persistence in the disparity of regional development levels across India may give rise to an investment decision process among JMNEs that has its own, self-reinforcing dynamic. In other words, the coevolution of corporate behaviour and investment location quality may follow (and give rise to) an agglomeration logic, with more frequent and larger clusters of Japanese companies becoming evident. If the probability of investment is triggered by a certain set of location determinants (that discriminate both in terms of the corporate decision process and enduring regional disparities, which are likely in transitional economies such as India), then from a local policy perspective those initiatives that reflect and nurture nascent or emergent Japanese investment clusters become paramount to economic development. Our findings suggest that it will be difficult for individual Indian states to close the gap on lead investment destinations. Even wage-level rises, a likely effect of agglomeration as ever more firms compete for labour, seem not to deter or redirect Japanese investors to laggard regions. The same is found for infrastructure quality, which suggests that recent efforts by the Indian government to improve this feature of the country's investment climate may not bear fruit in terms of proactively encouraging JMNEs to invest in locations in which they are currently relatively inactive. In short, we see little evidence that JMNEs will relocate to the more remote and less-developed regions of India, despite policy initiatives in this direction.

Conclusion

India's position within Japanese global production networks is unusual. Highly demanding in terms of operation modes, India is neither culturally nor geographically close to Japan. Perhaps not surprisingly, therefore, India is regularly ranked as a high-risk investment destination among JMNEs. Yet, Japanese operations in India are substantial and growing. It would be a mistake, however, to assert that because India is a comparatively poor nation that Japanese FDI is motivated by low-labour cost-related factors: productivity levels appear also to be an important subfacet of investment considerations. In the case of JMNEs, development-related advances (e.g. educational attainment, infrastructure and so forth) do not necessarily translate into improved location attractiveness. Indeed, our findings suggest that it is difficult to identify a coherent 'Japanese' investment strategy in India, as no single location-specific approach dominates besides geographic concentrations of activity. This is in line with earlier studies that so far have produced largely inconclusive results. Accordingly, our findings offer further contextualization, by looking in more detail into to date under-documented industry-specific requirements and considerations. Those industries that account for the bulk of Japanese FDI in India (transport, electronics, machinery, chemicals and IT) exhibited varying sensitivity towards the location-specific factors that determine the presence of JMNEs. While market-related considerations and educational attainment levels are shown to be high and stable predictors, the role of institutional incentives, labour costs and infrastructure as location determinants varies significantly across these key sectors. This finding may be explained by fluctuating industry-specific antecedents that dictate FDI motives (e.g. labour intensity, need for educated labour, infrastructure and so forth). Interestingly, we also find that the investment profile (by industry) is evolving over time, and factors that contribute to a firm's subnational location choice are changing. Most notably, for all key sectors, the relevance of educational attainment as an investment trigger was more pronounced during the early phases of investment than in more recent times. Industry-specific investment incentives as regards wages, infrastructure and institutional framework have also been observed.

This, however, does not mean that Japanese firms are departing from the overall agglomerative trajectory (unlike the current shift in location strategy currently under way in China). Rather, it seems to point towards a change in risk perceptions among later investors, corporate learning effects, evolving investment motives and the availability of trained personnel. Changes at the interface between corporate behaviour and location determinants continue to be confined to the subnational level and do not necessarily mean that JMNEs are seeking to diversify their location portfolio in India. The accelerating engagement of Japanese firms in India presents numerous scholarly challenges. Japan's substantial role as FDI source country, the global competitiveness and lead role of Japanese MNEs, and their performance as change catalyst of key Indian industries necessitate a deeper, firm-level understanding. Research opportunities emerge from two particular areas.

First, while our analysis has been able to make transparent overall FDI trends and Japanese reaction to institutional change vis-à-vis other source countries, one thing it cannot account for is that investment decisions are always part of an individual firm's specific competitive situation and that this may be determined, at least in part, by industry effects. Our findings should therefore be enriched by firm-level investigations into Indian market entry motivations. In this way, the interaction between subsidiary strategy, MNC strategy and the influence of the institutional environment and industry effects can be elucidated. Moreover, data quality in emerging economies such as India is notoriously difficult to ascertain. A detailed, case-by-case investigation into the triggers of investment by Japanese MNEs may yield important information about how institutional change resonates with the decision profiles of multinational firms.

Second, emerging markets feature strongly in the strategic planning of Japanese MNEs, not least because of perceptions of vast and untapped customer bases. However, despite the evidently growing market potential, many firms may fail to notice the gap between a marketing portfolio geared towards industrialized markets and needs and wants of emerging market customers. India is a case in point, particularly for Japanese firms. Combinations of high purchasing power and big population do not necessarily equate to a large customer base, and nor do they capture the de facto stark contrasts of subnationally divergent economic realities. Indian customers are not only geographically and socioculturally dispersed; incongruent income distribution has also led to immense variations in disposable income levels. In short, for many Japanese companies (and the products and services they provide), the Indian market potential is latent and not (yet) fully realized. As a consequence research on customized marketing approaches towards emerging markets that are likely to be counter-intuitive to the predominant global marketing logic should be deepened.

Notes

1. The reliability and stability of labour relations have been shown to be important factors in Japanese investment decisions (Taylor 1993), with unionization levels commonly portrayed as a (country) risk factor. In addition to potential increases in labour cost, problems transferring home country practice of non-confrontational enterprise unions (Ford and Strange 1999) may discourage investment (Shimada 2005). With its distinct political heritage of state control, Indian labour unions continue to be considered as influential entities, and strikes as a legitimate tool of industrial relations. Contemporary surveys of Japanese firms rank labour relations as an important dimension of the local business environment (JBIC 2008; JETRO 2007a, 2007b). Unfortunately, an analysis of the effects of the unionization rate in the present study was not possible here due to incomplete data on all Indian states.
2. These results are not reported here but are available from the authors on request.
3. It is worth noting that if New Delhi is removed from the group allocation, significant effects of subnational development level on Japanese investment numbers become apparent.

References

Abegglen, J. C. 2006. *21st-Century Japanese Management*. New York: Palgrave Macmillan.
Abegglen, J. C., and G. Stalk. 1985. *Kaisha, the Japanese Corporation*. New York: Basic Books.
Abo, T. 2008. *Japanese Hybrid Factories: A Comparison of Global Production Strategies*. Houndmills: Palgrave MacMillan.
Altomonte, C., and C. Guagliano. 2003. "Comparative Study of FDI in Central and Eastern Europe and the Mediterranean." *Economic Systems* 27 (2): 223–246.
Anand, J., and A. Delios. 1996. "Competing Globally: How Japanese MNCs Have Matched Goals and Strategies in India and China." *The Columbia Journal of World Business* 31 (3): 50–62.
Aoki, M. 1994. "The Japanese Firm as a System of Attributes: A Survey and Research Agenda." In *The Japanese Firm*, edited by M. Aoki and R. Dore, 11–40. Oxford: Oxford University Press.
Balasubramanyam, V. N., and D. Greenaway. 1992. "Economic Integration and Foreign Direct Investment: Japanese Investment in the EC." *JCMS: Journal of Common Market Studies* 30 (2): 175–194.
Beamish, P. W., and R. Jiang. 2002. "Investing Profitably in China: Is It Getting Harder?" *Long Range Planning* 35: 135–151.
Belderbos, R., G. Capannelli, and K. Fukao. 2001. "Backward Vertical Linkages of Foreign Manufacturing Affiliates: Evidence from Japanese Multinationals." *World Development* 29 (1): 189–208.
Belderbos, R., and M. Carree. 2002. "The Location of Japanese Investments in China: Agglomeration Effects, Keiretsu, and Firm Heterogeneity." *Journal of the Japanese and International Economies* 16: 194–211.
Bevan, A. A., and S. Estrin. 2004. "The Determinants of Foreign Direct Investment into European Transition Economies." *Journal of Comparative Economics* 32 (4): 775–787.
Blomstrom, M., and A. Kokko. 1998. "Multinational Corporations and Spillovers." *Journal of Economic Surveys* 12 (3): 247–277.
Borensztein, E., J. De Gregorio, and J.-W. Lee. 1998. "How Does Foreign Direct Investment Affect Economic Growth?" *Journal of International Economics* 45 (1): 115–135.
Bose, A., V. K. Singh, and M. Adhikary. 1991. *Demographic Diversity in India, 1991 Census: State and District Level Data*. Delhi: B.R. Publishing.
Braunerhjelm, P., and R. Svensson. 1996. "Host Country Characteristics and Agglomeration in Foreign Direct Investment." *Applied Economics* 28 (7): 833–840.
Brimble, P., and S. Urata. 2006. "Behaviour of Japanese, Western and Asian MNCs in Thailand." *Japan Centre for Economic Research* 105: 1–32.
Buckley, P. J. 2009. "The Impact of the Global Factory on Economic Development." *Journal of World Business* 44 (2): 131–143.
Buckley, P. J., A. Cross, and S. A. Horn. 2012. "Japanese Foreign Direct Investment in India: An Institutional Theory Approach." *Business History* 54 (5): 657–688.
Buckley, P. J., and S. A. Horn. 2009. "Japanese Multinational Enterprises in China: Successful Adaptation of Marketing Strategies." *Long Range Planning* 42 (4): 495–517.
Carr, C., and M. Pudelko. 2006. "Convergence of Management Practices in Strategy, Finance and HRM between the USA, Japan and Germany." *International Journal of Cross Cultural Management* 6 (1): 75–100.
Cassidy, J. F., and B. Andreosso-O'Callaghan. 2006. "Spatial Determinants of Japanese FDI in China." *Japan and the World Economy* 18: 512–527.
Chakrabarti, A. 2001. "The Determinants of Foreign Direct Investments: Sensitivity Analyses of Cross-Country Regressions." *Kyklos* 54: 89–114.

Chakraborty, C., and P. Nunnenkamp. 2008. "Economic Reforms, FDI, and Economic Growth in India: A Sector Level Analysis." *World Development* 36 (7): 1192–1212.

Chen, C. 1997. "Provincial Characteristics and Foreign Direct Investment Location Decision within China." Chinese Economies Research Centre Working Paper 97_16. Adelaide: University of Adelaide.

Cheng, S. 2006. "The Role of Labour Cost in the Location Choices of Japanese Investors in China." *Papers in Regional Science* 85 (1): 121–138.

Cheng, S. 2007. "Structure of Firm Location Choices: An Examination of Japanese Greenfield Investment in China." *Asian Economic Journal* 21 (1): 47–73.

Cheng, S., and R. Stough. 2006. "Location Decisions of Japanese New Manufacturing Plants in China: A Discrete Choice Analysis." *The Annals of Regional Science* 40 (2): 368–387.

Chung, W., and J. Song. 2004. "Sequential Investment, Firm Motives, and Agglomeration of Japanese Electronics Firms in the United States." *Journal of Economics and Management Strategy* 13 (3): 539–560.

Cieślik, A., and M. Ryan. 2002. "Characterising Japanese Direct Investment in Central and Eastern Europe: A Firm Level Investigation of Stylised Facts and Investment Characteristics." *Post-Communist Economies* 14 (4): 509–527.

Cieślik, A., and M. Ryan. 2004. "Explaining Japanese Direct Investment Flows into an Enlarged Europe: A Comparison of Gravity and Economic Potential Approaches." *Journal of the Japanese and International Economies* 18: 12–37.

CMIE (Centre for Monitoring the Indian Economy) 2008. *Prowess Database*. Mumbai: CD-Rom.

Collinson, S., and A. M. Rugman. 2008. "The Regional Nature of Japanese Multinational Business." *Journal of International Business Studies* 39: 215–230.

Coughlin, C. C., and E. Segev. 2000. "Foreign Direct Investment in China: A Spatial Econometric Study." *The World Economy* 23 (1): 1–23.

Cross, A. R., and S. A. Horn. 2009. "The Changing Role of China in the Transformation of Corporate Japan." *Asia Pacific Business Review* 15 (3): 463–476.

Crown Group. 2008. *Indo Nikkei Kigyô Nenkan 2008–2009* [Japanese Companies in India Handbook]. Bangkok: Comm Bangkok.

Delios, A., and P. W. Beamish. 2005. "Regional and Global Strategies of Japanese Firms." *Management International Review* 45: 19–36.

Delios, A., P. W. Beamish, and X. Zhao. 2009. "The Evolution of Japanese Investment in China: From Toys to Textiles to Business Process Outsourcing." *Asia Pacific Business Review* 15 (3): 323–345.

Delios, A., and W. J. Henisz. 2003. "Policy Uncertainty and the Sequence of Entry by Japanese Firms, 1980–1998." *Journal of International Business Studies* 34: 227–241.

Delios, A., and T. D. Keeley. 2000. "Japanese Foreign Direct Investment in Thailand: An Empirical Analysis and Qualitative Post-crisis Analysis." *Journal of International Business and Economy* 1 (1): 91–118.

Dicken, P. 2003. *Global Shift*. London: Sage.

Doner, R. F. 1991. *Driving a Bargain: Automobile Industrialisation and Japanese Firms in Southeast Asia*. Berkley: University of California Press.

Dostal, P. 2008. "The Post-communist Capital City Effect, Transnational Activities and Regional Development in the Czech Republic in the 1990s." In *City and Region: Papers in Honour of Jiri Musil*, edited by W. Strubelt and G. Gorzelak, 15–42. Opladen: Budrich University Press.

Dunning, J. H. 1998. "Location and the Multinational Enterprise: A Neglected Factor?" *Journal of International Business Studies* 29 (1): 45–66.

Dunning, J. H., and S. M. Lundan. 2008. *Multinational Enterprises and the Global Economy*. Cheltenham: Edward Elgar.

Dyer, J. H. 1994. "Dedicated Assets: Japan's Manufacturing Edge." *Harvard Business Review* 72 (6): 174–178.

Economist. 2009. "Corporate Restructuring in Japan: Breaking Free." *Economist Magazine*, June 18. Accessed June 21, 2009. http://www.economist.com/businessfinance/displaystory.cfm?story_id=13871842

Enderwick, P. 2007. *Understanding Emerging Markets*. Abingdon: Routledge.

Ernst, D. 1994. "Carriers of Regionalisation: The East Asian Production Networks of Japanese Electronics Firms." Working Paper Series 32007. Berkeley, CA: UCAIS Berkeley Roundtable on the International Economy, UC Berkeley.

Ernst, D. 2006. "Searching for a New Role in East Asian Regionalisation – Japanese Production Networks in the Electronics Industry." In *Beyond Japan*, edited by P. Katzenstein and T. Shiraishi, 161–187. Ithaca, NY: Cornell University Press.

Farrell, R. 2008. *Japanese Investment in the World Economy*. Cheltenham: Edward Elgar.

Farrell, R., N. Gaston, and J.-E. Sturm. 2004. "Determinants of Japan's Foreign Direct Investment: An Industry and Country Panel Study, 1984–1998." *Journal of the Japanese and International Economies* 18 (2): 161–182.

Ford, S., and R. Strange. 1999. "Where Do Japanese Manufacturing Firms Invest in Europe and Why?" *Transnational Corporations* 8 (1): 117–139.

Friedman, J., D. A. Gerlowski, and J. Silberman. 1992. "What Attracts Foreign Multinational Corporations? Evidence from Branch Plant Location in the United States." *Journal of Regional Science* 32 (4): 403–418.

Fujita, M., and J.-F. Thisse. 1996. "Economics of Agglomeration." *Journal of the Japanese and International Economies* 10: 339–378.

Fukao, K., and Y. Wei. 2008. "How Do the Location Determinants of Vertical FDI and Horizontal FDI Differ?" Hi-Stat Discussion Paper Series d07-233. Tokyo: Hitotsubashi University, Institute of Economic Research.

Fung, K. C., H. Iizaka, and S. Parker. 2002. "Determinants of U.S. and Japanese Direct Investment in China." *Journal of Comparative Economics* 30 (3): 567–578.

Guiheux, G., and Y. Lecler. 2000. "Japanese Car Manufacturers and Component Makers in the ASEAN Region." In *Global Strategies and Local Realities: The Auto Industry in Emerging Markets*, edited by J. Humphrey, Y. Lecler, and M. S. Salerno, 207–233. Houndmills: Palgrave Macmillan.

Hatani, F. 2009. "Pre-clusterization in Emerging Markets: The Toyota Group's Entry Process in China." *Asia Pacific Business Review* 15 (3): 369–387.

Head, C. K., and T. Mayer. 2004. "Market Potential and the Location of Japanese Investment in the European Union." *Review of Economics and Statistics* 86: 959–972.

Head, C. K., J. C. Ries, and D. L. Swenson. 1995. "Agglomeration Benefits and Location Choice: Evidence from Japanese Manufacturing Investments in the United States." *Journal of International Economics* 38 (3–4): 223–247.

Head, C. K., J. C. Ries, and D. L. Swenson. 1999. "Attracting Foreign Manufacturing: Investment Promotion and Agglomeration." *Regional Science and Urban Economics* 29: 197–218.

Hennart, J.-L., and Y.-R. Park. 1994. "Location, Governance, and Strategic Determinants of Japanese Manufacturing Investment in the United States." *Strategic Management Journal* 15 (6): 419–436.

Horn, S. A. 2016. "Subsidiary Capacity Building in Emerging Markets." *Thunderbird International Business Review* 58 (1): 55–74.

Horn, S. A., and A. R. Cross. 2009. "Japanese Management at a Crossroads? The Changing Role of China in the Transformation of Corporate Japan" *Asia Pacific Business Review* 15 (3): 285–308.

Horn, S. A., N. Forsans, and A. R. Cross. 2010. "The Strategies of Japanese Firms in Emerging Markets: The Case of the Automobile Industry in India." *Asian Business & Management* 9: 341–378.

Hymer, S. H. 1976. *The International Operations of Firms: A Study on Foreign Direct Investment*. Cambridge: MIT Press.

Itagaki, H. 1997. *The Japanese Production System: Hybrid Factories in East Asia*. Houndmills: Palgrave MacMillan.

Itô, K. 2006. *Gendai No Rômu Kanri* [Contemporary Labour Management]. Tokyo: Minerva Shobô.

JBIC (Japan Bank for International Cooperation). Various years. *Survey Report on Overseas Business Operations by Japanese Manufacturing Companies*. Tokyo: JBIC.

JETRO (Japan External Trade Organization) 2007a. *White Paper on International Trade and Foreign Direct Investment: Increasing Utilization of Asian FTAs and Growth Strategies for Japanese Companies*. Tokyo: JETRO.

JETRO (Japan External Trade Organization) 2007b. "Kyûshin Indo no Bijinesu Risuku [Business Risk of Fast Developing India]." *JETRO Sensâ*, August, 6–31.

JETRO (Japan External Trade Organization) 2013. *Japanese Trade and Investment Statistics*. http://www.jetro.go.jp/en/stats/statistics/.

Keizer, A. B. 2005. "The Changing Logic of Japanese Employment Practises: A Firm-level Analysis of Four Industries." PhD thesis published at the Erasmus Research Institute of Management. Erasmus University, Rotterdam.

Kimura, F., and M. Ando. 2004. "Two-dimensional Fragmentation in East Asia: Conceptual Framework and Empirics." *International Review of Economics and Finance* 14: 317–348.

Kiyota, K., and S. Urata. 2007. "The Role of Multinational Firms in International Trade: The Case of Japan." Working Papers 560. Research Seminar in International Economics, Ann Arbor, MI: University of Michigan.

Kumar, N. 2001. "Determinants of Location of Overseas R&D Activity of Multinational Enterprises: The Case of US and Japanese Corporations." *Research Policy* 30: 159–174.

Lall, S., Z. Shalizi, and U. Deichmann. 2004. "Agglomeration Economies and Productivity in Indian Industry." *Journal of Development Economics* 73 (2): 643–673.

Lincoln, J. R., and M. Shimotani. 2009. "Whither the Keiretsu, Japan's Business Networks? How Were They Structured? What Did They Do? Why Are They Gone?" Working Paper Series. Institute for Research on Labor and Employment, Institute of Industrial Relations, Berkeley, CA: UC Berkeley.

Ma, X., and A. Delios. 2007. "A New Tale of Two Cities: Japanese FDIs in Shanghai and Beijing, 1979–2003." *International Business Review* 16: 207–228.

Markusen, J. R., and A. J. Venables. 1998. "Foreign Direct Investment as a Catalyst for Industrial Development." *European Economic Review* 43 (2): 335–356.

Marshall, A. 1920. *Principles of Economics*. London: Macmillan.

Marukawa, T. 2004. "Towards a Strategic Realignment of Production Networks: Japanese Electronics Companies in China." In *Regional Strategies in a Global Economy: Multinational Corporations in East Asia*, edited by R. Haak, and D. S. Tachiki, 99–117. Tokyo: Deutsches Institut für Japanstudien (DIJ).

Maskin, E. S. 1995. "Long-term Investment by Japanese and American Firms." *Japan and the World Economy* 7 (2): 249–254.

Mayer, T., and J.-L. Mucchielli. 1998. "Strategic Location Behaviour: The Case of Japanese Investments in Europe." *Journal of Transnational Management Development* 3 (3): 131–167.

McGuire, J., and S. Dow. 2009. "Japanese Keiretsu: Past, Present, Future." *Asia Pacific Journal of Management* 26: 333–351.

MCI (Ministry of Commerce and Industry) 2009. *India: Share of Top Investing Countries FDI Inflows*. Accessed June 19, 2009. http://www.dipp.nic.in/fdi_statistics/India_top_countries.pdf

Meyer, K. E. 2004. "Perspectives on Multinational Enterprises in Emerging Economies." *Journal of International Business Studies* 35: 259–276.

Meyer, K. E., and H. V. Nguyen. 2005. "Foreign Investment Strategies and Sub-national Institutions in Emerging Markets: Evidence from Vietnam." *Journal of Management Studies* 42 (1): 63–93.

MHA (Ministry of Home Affairs) Census 2001. Accessed May 20, 2009. http://www.censusindia.gov.in/

Mody, A., S. Dasgupta, and S. Sinha. 1998. "Japanese Multinationals in Asia." *Oxford Developmental Studies* 27: 149–164.

Mody, A., and K. Srinivasan. 1998. "Japanese and U.S. Firms as Foreign Investors: Do They March to the Same Tune?" *The Canadian Journal of Economics/Revue Canadienne D'Economique* 31 (4): 778–799.

MOSPI (Ministry of Statistics and Program Implementation). 2009. Various Reports. Accessed July 3, 2009. http://www.mospi.gov.in/mospi_cso_rept_pubn.htm

Nayak, A. K. J. R. 2008. *Multinationals in India*. Houndmills: Palgrave Macmillan.

Nicholas, S., W. Purcell, S. Gray. 2001. "Regional Clusters, Location Tournaments and Incentives: An Empirical Analysis of Factors Attracting Japanese Investment to Singapore." *Asia Pacific Journal of Management* 18 (3): 395–405.

NKS (Nihon Keizai Shinbunsha) 2007. *Indo* [India]. Tokyo: Toppan Insatsu.

Nopprach, S. 2006. "Supplier Selection in the Thai Automotive Industry." Hi-Stat Discussion Paper Series D06-186. Tokyo: Institute of Economic Research, Hitotsubashi University.

Nunnenkamp, P. 2002. "Determinants of FDI in Developing Countries: Has Globalization Changed the Rules of the Game?" Kiel Working Papers 1122. Kiel: Kiel Institute for the World Economy.

Panagariya, A. 2009. *India: The Emerging Giant*. Oxford: Oxford University Press.

Porter, M. E. 1998. "Clusters and the New Economics of Competition." *Harvard Business Review* 76 (6): 77–90.

Porter, M. E. 2000. "Locations, Clusters and Company Strategy." In *The Oxford Handbook of Economic Geography*, edited by G. L. Clark, M. P. Feldman, and M. S. Gertler, 253–274. Oxford: Oxford University Press.

Pudelko, M. 2006a. "A Comparison of HRM Systems in the USA, Japan and Germany in Their Socio-economic Context." *Human Resource Management Journal* 16: 123–153.

Pudelko, M. 2006b. "German Human Resource Management: A Source of Inspiration." *European Management Journal* 24 (6): 430–438.

Sakakibara, M., and K. Serwin. 2000. "U.S. Distribution Entry Strategy of Japanese Manufacturing Firms: The Role of Keiretsu." *Journal of the Japanese and International Economies* 14: 43–72.

Shimada, T. 2005. *Indo No Subete* [All about India]. Tokyo: Diayamondo.

Siddharthan, N. S., and M. L. Lakhera. 2005. "Foreign Direct Investment and Location Advantages: Japanese Perceptions of India Compared to China and ASEAN." *Journal of International and Area Studies* 12 (1): 99–110.

Sinha, A. 2005. *The Regional Roots of Developmental Politics in India: A Divided Leviathan*. Bloomington: Indiana University Press.

Smith, D. F., Jr., and R. Florida. 1994. "Agglomeration and Industrial Location: An Econometric Analysis of Japanese-Affiliated Manufacturing Establishments in Automotive-Related Industries." *Journal of Urban Economics* 36: 23–41.

Somlev, I. P., and Y. Hoshino. 2005. "Influence of Location Factors on Establishment and Ownership of Foreign Investments: The Case of the Japanese Manufacturing Firms in Europe." *International Business Review* 14: 577–598.

Taylor, J. 1993. "An Analysis of the Factors Determining the Geographical Distribution of Japanese Manufacturing Investment in the UK, 1984–91." *Urban Studies* 30 (7): 1209–1224.

Thiran, J. M., and H. Yamawaki. 1995. "Regional and Country Determinants of Locational Decisions: Japanese Multinationals in European Manufacturing." Discussion Papers 1995017. Louvain-la-Neuve: Université catholique de Louvain, Institut de Recherches Economiques et Sociales (IRES).

Tokunaga, S., and R. Ishii. 1995. "Nihon Kigyô no Gurobâru Oyobi Higashi Ajia ni Okeru Chokusetsu Tôshi Kettei ni Kansuru Keiryô Bunseki." [Foreign direct investments in the world and Asia, a quantitative analysis.] In *EC, NAFTA Higashi Ajia to Gaikoku Chokusetsu Tôshi* [FDI in EC, NAFTA and East Asia], edited by K. Ohno and Y. Okamoto, 133–167. Tokyo: Ajia Keizai Kenkyûjo.

Tomiura, E. 2005. "Technological Capability and FDI in Asia: Firm-level Relationships among Japanese Manufacturers." *Asian Economic Journal* 19 (3): 273–289.

Tôyô Keizai. Various Reports. *Kaigai Shinshutsu Kigyô Sôran* [Japanese Overseas Investment Directory]. Tokyo: Tôyô Keizai.

Urata, S., and H. Kawai. 2000. "How Do the Location Determinants of Vertical FDI and Horizontal FDI Differ?" *Small Business Economics* 15: 79–103.

Vernon, R. 1974. "The Location of Economic Activity." In *Economic Analysis and the Multinational Enterprise*, edited by J. H. Dunning, 89–114. London: Allan & Unwin.

Wakasugi, R. 2005. "The Effects of Chinese Regional Conditions on the Location Choices of Japanese Affiliates." *The Japanese Economic Review* 56 (4): 390–407.

Wei, Y., X. Liu, D. Parker, and K. Vaidya. 1999. "The Regional Distribution of Foreign Direct Investment in China." *Regional Studies* 33: 857–867.

Wells, L. T., Jr. 1998. "Multinationals and the Developing Countries." *Journal of International Business Studies* 29 (1): 101–114.

Wheeler, D., and A. Mody. 1992. "International Investment Location Decisions: The Case of US Firms." *Journal of International Economics* 33: 57–76.

Woodward, D. P. 1992. "Locational Determinants of Japanese Manufacturing Start-ups in the United States." *Southern Economic Journal* 58 (3): 690–708.

Yamawaki, H. 2006. "The Location of American and Japanese Multinationals in Europe." *International Economics and Economic Policy* 3 (2): 157–173.

Yoshida, Y., and H. Ito. 2006. "How Do the Asian Economies Compete with Japan in the US Market? Is China Exceptional? A Triangular Trade Approach." *Asia Pacific Business Review* 12 (3): 285–307.

Yusuf, S. 2004. "Competitiveness through Technological Advances under Global Production Networking." In *Global Production Networking and Technological Change in East Asia*, edited by S. Yusuf, M. A. Altaf, and K. Nabeshima, 1–34. Oxford: Oxford University Press.

Zhou, C., A. Delios, and J. Y. Yang. 2002. "Location Determinants of Japanese Foreign Direct Investment in China." *Asia Pacific Journal of Management* 19 (1): 63–86.

MNCs from the Asia Pacific in the global economy: examples and lessons from Japan, Korea, China and India

Robert Fitzgerald[a] and Chris Rowley[b,c,d,e]

[a]Royal Holloway, University of London, UK; [b]Cass Business School, City University, London, UK; [c]IHCR, Korea University, Seoul, Korea; [d]Institute of Asia and Pacific Studies, Nottingham University, Nottingham, UK; [e]Griffith Business School, Griffith University, Nathan, Australia

ABSTRACT

The Japanese multinational company (JMNC), after rapid internationalization in the 1980s and 1990s, had to adjust its strategies, organization and capabilities in the response to subsequent changes in the global economy. While JMNCs had once been highly researched, we know too little about these businesses in recent decades. We call for more extensive in depth research of JMNCs, and then analyse issues around the adoption of new strategies or organizational forms; the application of influential international business theories in interpreting Asia Pacific MNCs; comparisons of JMNCs with MNCs from China and Korea; the lessons JMNCs hold for Asia Pacific and emerging economy MNCs; and the management and operations of JMNC subsidiaries in host economies.

Introduction: reviewing and comparing

The Japanese multinational company (JMNC), after its rapid internationalization from the 1980s, had to adjust its strategies, organization and capabilities in response to changes in the global economy that became evident from the late 1990s. 'Globalization' was hardly a new phenomenon historically speaking, but the term rapidly gained currency after 1992, even if it was overused to explain almost every trend in politics, economics and society (Fitzgerald 2015; Rowley and Oh 2016a, 2016b; Dicken 2003). In international business, the period was distinguished by shifts towards the lowering of government controls on trade and cross-border investment; the geographical extension of the international economy into the former Communist bloc; the rise in international mergers and acquisitions (M&A); increases in service industry foreign direct investment (FDI); the switch of inward FDI flows to developing nations; greater reliance on cross-border production networks, contracting-out, and off-shoring; and the ever more noticeable presence of the 'dragon multinational' and competition from emerging economies. JMNCs were no different to other MNCs in having to fashion strategic and organizational responses to transforming competitive realities.

For the period of the 1980s and 1990s, in which manufacturers from Japan led the world in FDI and management methods, the JMNC was arguably the most highly researched form of business organization. Since that period, interest for very justifiable reasons turned towards China and other emerging economies. We know, as a result, too little about the policies of JMNCs in more recent decades, despite the fact that Japan remains one of largest sources of FDI. This volume redresses this gap, offering insights into the continued evolution of the JMNC, while advocating the need for more extensive in-depth research. The contributors considered, in summary, a number of vital questions about the JMNC in comparison to the Korean MNC (KMNC) and the Chinese MNC (CMNC):

(1) To what extent have JMNCs attempted to adopt or develop new strategies and styles of organization, and how different are the outcomes from previous practice?
(2) How effectively do existing influential theories about international business offer insights into the JMNC and into rivals from the Asia Pacific more generally?
(3) How different was the experience of the JMNC to MNCs from the other two major Asia Pacific economies, China and Korea?
(4) To what extent can MNCs from the Asia Pacific and emerging economies learn lessons from the experience of JMNCs?
(5) In addition to matters of global strategy, how are JMNC subsidiaries adapting and operating at the level of host nations?

Long-term evolution of the JMNC

The fact of Japan's low growth and perceived decline in competitiveness affects our perception of JMNCs, but there has been a lack of contemporary in-depth research. Longitudinal analysis of JMNCs, during the period 1998–2003, shows a continued strategic commitment to higher levels of international engagement. We can see through data on foreign sales percentage, the location of sales and the location of subsidiaries that, overall, JMNCs have grown in their 'multinationality'. The results indicate that many of them have retained their pursuit of a global as opposed to an Asia Pacific regional strategy. In achieving their aims, during the twenty-first century, JMNCs have encountered technological change, the rise of new competitors, reform of the Japanese business system and the restructuring and relocation of global production and major industries such as electronics.

A comparison of JMNCs during the period of their rapid internationalization and competitive success in the 1980s and 1990s (see Rowley 1996) with later decades highlights a number of relevant factors, including strategic intent, the cross-border transfer of capabilities, and the costs and benefits of parental firm control versus subsidiary autonomy. Manufacturing JMNCs had undertaken their major phase of FDI by transferring domestically well-entrenched capabilities to developed economies in Europe and the United States. In doing so, they revealed what analysts conceived as strong 'strategic intent' and long-term strategic planning. Having established themselves as leading MNCs, Japanese companies appeared less clear in their strategic aims and long-term planning became identified with slow responses to competitive trends. The localization of decision-making or research and development (R&D), contracting-out, strategic alliances in product development or production, host market customization and responsiveness, the accessing of low-cost sites, and the deepening integration of global production chains required changes to traditions of strong parent company control and organizational centralization. Nonetheless, many JMNCs retained globally competitive capabilities in management, technology, production, products and brands.

FDI theory and Asia Pacific MNCs

We can see from the available case studies and analysis that, in the space of 30 years or so, the strategic aims and organizational structures of JMNCs have evolved significantly. Their example points to the need for theories that are dynamic in approach, and for explanations that incorporate both path dependency and critical breaks with the past. The 'Eclectic Paradigm' requiring evaluation of ownership, localization and internalization (OLI) factors and the Uppsala school (using a template of institutional and cultural characteristics) are fundamentally static in their approach. While the 'International Product Life Cycle' (IPLC) theory undoubtedly describes dynamics, it concentrates almost exclusively on product development within a firm to the exclusion of organizational, production, and marketing considerations and wider national and international contexts. Case studies of Asia Pacific MNCs highlight the need to evaluate factors of international political economy. Developmental states in the region, albeit applying differing institutional arrangements and policies, have played a central role in national economic development, technology acquisition and the fostering of enterprises with competitive capabilities. The raising of tariffs and the imposition of import quotas by governments in Western Europe and the United States explain the conversion of Japanese manufacturers from exporters into multinational investors, and they contributed to the internationalization decisions of KMNCs.

Government in Japan supported the FDI initiatives of JMNCs, and financing reflected the priorities of domestic and international policies, firstly facilitating the relocation of labour-intensive sectors and the accessing of raw materials or key components overseas, subsequently the founding of large-scale manufacturing subsidiaries in developed markets, and lastly, the establishment of operations in emerging economies and the international acquisition of technology and management knowledge. Both the Korean and Chinese governments encouraged firms to globalize. A large number of leading CMNCs are state-owned and supported by state-owned banks, and intergovernment agreement has determined the locational choices made by CMNCs, most obviously in Africa. Both the IPLC theory and the OLI model have been criticized for their firm-level perspectives. The Kojima–Ozawa approach emphasizes comparative levels of economic development and technology, the role of trade and trading relationships and the importance of government. In other words, it identifies business topics that are specifically international as opposed to those that are predominantly firm level.

The IPLC and OLI framework are predicated on firms with defined boundaries, while studies of Asia Pacific business have stressed the permeability of government–business relationships and interfirm networks. FDI theories in their origins emerged from research into Western or US MNCs, and they may, it is argued, be a more partial predictor of internationalization by Asia Pacific MNCs. The debate about how much we can refer to the Asia Pacific MNC, however, remains unresolved, and case-study evidence so far points to the danger of covering over substantive differences between nations, industries and firms.

Comparing Asia Pacific MNCs: implications for convergence and globalisation

Interesting parallels can be found in the internationalization of MNCs from Japan, China and Korea, but we can discover also important points of divergence. In terms of strategy, JMNCs and KMNCs have made an impact on the developed host markets of North America and Europe, while, with noted exceptions, CMNCs have achieved their most prominent breakthroughs in emerging economies. JMNCs and then KMNCs demonstrated strong strategic intent in their internationalization, whereas the approach of CMNCs appears more opportunistic. As seen from their operations in China, and despite perhaps too easy assumptions about cultural affinity, KMNCs have shown themselves to be more flexible, risk-taking and rapid in strategic decision-making and implementation than JMNCs. In this, they have been assisted by top-down, family-owned corporate structures, within the *chaebol*, but significant and costly mistakes can derive from the lack of strategic planning (Rowley and Bae 1998; Rowley, Sohn, and Bae 2002; Rowley and Paik 2009; and Jun and Rowley 2014).

Organizationally, MNCs from Japan, Korea and China have relied on strong parental firm control and centralization, which have complemented strategies of transferring of home-grown resources and competitive advantages to host economies. With regard to core capabilities, JMNCs have long been identified with leadership in management, technology, production methods and product quality. KMNCs have shown a capacity for mass production and low costs, but some, most prominently Samsung Electronics, have secured reputations for R&D, quality and brands. CMNCs, overall, have relative competitive capabilities in emerging economies, although, in manufacturing and services, Huawei stands as a model for CMNCs aspiring to own global ownership advantages. Centralized management enables JMNC and KMNC subsidiaries to call on the managerial or technological resources of the parent firm or global networks, and it allows CMNC subsidiaries to call on extensive human resources and a low-cost supply chain. Case-studies indicate the strategic advantages of centralized organization, as well as the drawbacks in the empowering of subsidiaries, the local customizing of products and marketing, or the building of global enterprises. Firms have attempted, with partial success, to balance the utility of centralized resources with the decentralization of decision making.

Lessons from MNCs

To what extent does the earlier internationalization of Japanese firms provide lessons for other Asia Pacific MNCs, and, in reverse, what lessons can JMNCs take through comparisons with their regional counterparts? As we have noted, Japanese manufacturers with unique management systems and technologies led the first phase of FDI to developed markets and gave precedence to parent firm control and capability transfer to subsidiaries. By the turn of the century, many JMNCs were conscious of the need to address declining competitiveness through a greater profit orientation, strategic alliances over R&D or production, the relocation of global production, contracting-out, increased host market product customization or enhanced subsidiary decision-making and capabilities. Questions remained, however, over the extent to which JMNCs adapted to the latter phase of their internationalization. KMNCs, too, ultimately confronted similar issues to JMNCs, and they had to improve investments in R&D and product quality, for which they received the support of their government. CMNC managers acknowledged their achievements as MNCs, but appeared less confident about a second phase of FDI based on distinctive products and management systems, perceiving government as failing to assist adequately with this strategic aim.

Case-study evidence from the JMNCs underlines the need to reconsider firm-level strategies after an initial stage of rapid internationalization and emphasizes how firms should do so in parallel with an assessment of changes in the structures of the global economy. Analysis suggests that long-term and short-term strategy must be balanced and mutually supportive. Without a long-term strategy, MNCs can neglect R&D or not sustain competitiveness; if failing on short-term targets, MNCs overlook customers in rapidly transforming markets and undermine the prospects of long-term planning. The history of JMNCs and CMNCs indicates important differences and effects from government policies in support of internationalization.

Localization and MNC subsidiaries

As well as re-evaluating their global strategy and organization, JMNCs had to consider policies in host markets and, particularly, in fast-growing emerging economies. The restructuring and relocation of electronics production to low-cost areas inevitably affected JMNCs that had internationalized as world leaders and as major investors in developed markets. Japanese automobile makers and other manufacturers did establish regional subsidiaries, invested in local R&D and sought to employ greater numbers of indigenous managers, but internal consideration of the extent to which parental firm control had been or should be released continued. Japanese trading companies, *sogososha*, continued to be major presences in developing nations heavily reliant on trade and commodities and needing advice on markets and international logistics. There were also Korean general trading companies applied similar strategies (Jun and Rowley 2014).

In China, Japanese manufacturers were among the earliest investors in the 1990s. There is evidence of cases in which JMNCs adapted to changes in China's institutional and economic policies, but also pointing to JMNCs that have been less successful in responding to broader trends and new competitors. While effecting a partial withdrawal from China, Suzuki demonstrated flexibility over matters of ownership and joint ventures in India and evolved into one of its most significant automobile producers. Research into the behaviour of JMNCs in India challenges the idea that investment behaviour is 'footloose'. It shows the importance of agglomeration patterns by firms at the national and subnational level, which complement and interact with economic, institutional and infrastructure factors. As well as revealing the importance of business networks in determining JMNC strategy, prior investment and location decisions assist corporate learning and the recruitment of trained personnel and obviate the levels of risk, as does the use of joint ventures. More research evaluating the influence of industry versus national effects in investment decisions is needed, and it is an open question about how effectively JMNCs can adapt and exploit their opportunities in fast expanding emerging markets. We know little, as yet, about the impact of Japanese FDI on India's economy and competitiveness, and about the role of JMNC subsidiaries in global production networks.

Conclusion

This volume makes a case for renewed interest in Asian MNCs, especially the JMNC during the era of low growth in Japan and rapid expansion and transformation in the global economy. It has presented data and a wide range of case evidence on the historical development of MNCs and noted contemporary challenges in strategy, management structures and organizational learning. To evaluate Asia Pacific MNCs more generally, the importance of comparative analysis is apparent, as is research that considers and contrasts global-, national-, subnational-, industry-, parent firm- and subsidiary-level factors.

Our work and evidence provides useful countervailing views to the overly dominant ethnocentric and a historical US perspectives implicit in too much business and management study (Rowley and Oh 2016a, 2016b). They are also a clarion call for others to continue along this route. Indigenous theory and research, rather than replication with the naïve and simplistic transplanting of 'Western' perspectives and theories to other contexts, is needed.

Acknowledgement

The support of the Korea Foundation is noted.

Disclosure statement

No potential conflict of interest was reported by the authors.

References

Dicken, P. 2003. *Global Shift*. London: Sage.
Fitzgerald, R. 2015. *The Rise of the Global Company: Multinationals and the Making of the Modern World*. Cambridge: Cambridge University Press.
Jun, I. W., and C. Rowley. 2014. "Changes & Continuity in Management Systems & Corporate Performance: HRM, Corporate Culture, Risk Management & Corporate Strategy in South Korea." *Business History* 56 (3): 485–508.
Rowley, C. 1996. "Are We Turning Japanese? Review Article." *Asia Pacific Business Review* 3 (1): 73–80.
Rowley, C., and J. Bae, eds. 1998. *Korean Businesses: Internal and External Industrialization*. London: Frank Cass.
Rowley, C., T.-W. Sohn, and J. Bae, eds. 2002. *Managing Korean Business: Organization, Culture Human Resources and Change*. London: Frank Cass.
Rowley, C., and Y. Paik, eds. 2009. *The Changing Face of Korean Management*. London: Routledge.
Rowley, C., and I. Oh. 2016a. "Business Ethics & the Role of Context: Instutionalism, History & Comparisons in the Asia Pacific Region." *Asia Pacific Business Review* 22 (3): 353–365.
Rowley, C., and I. Oh. 2016b. "Relinquishing Business Ethics from a Theoretical Deadlock: The Requirement for Local Grounding & Historical Comparisons in the Asia Pacific Region." *Asia Pacific Business Review* 22 (3): 516–521.

Index

Abegglen, J.C. 91, 94
Abo, T. 16, 90
Ackroyd, S.S. 16
Africa 31, 38, 67, 76, 80, 86, 121; see also individual countries
Aggarwal, R. 73, 74, 75, 76, 87
agglomerative behaviour of JMNEs in India 10, 90–113, 123
Aharoni, Y. 45, 50, 76
Alder, P.S. 16
Aliber, R.Z. 65
Allen, G.C. 14
Altomonte, C. 92
Anand, J. 107
Ando, K. 15
Ando, N. 65
Angola 39
Antoniou, A. 74
Aoki, M. 94
Apple 60, 62
Argentina 20
Asmussen, C.G. 74, 75
Australia 17
automobile industry: China 17, 18, 20; Beijing Auto 23, 58, 59; FAW Group Corporation 57; GAC Group 57; Hyundai 47, 55, 58–9, 61–2, 63, 64; Nanjing Automobile Corporate (NAC) 35, 36; SAIC 35, 36; Suzuki 20–1, 23–4, 25, 26, 123; Toyota 55–8, 61–2, 63, 64; Zhejiang Geely Holding Group 66
automobile MNCs, Japanese 13, 15, 19, 27, 48, 52, 55, 123; Suzuki (motorcycles and cars) 20–1, 23–4, 25, 26, 123; Toyota 4, 13, 14, 19–20, 22–3, 25, 36, 38, 47, 48, 55–8, 61–2, 63, 64
automobile MNCs, Korean 48, 55

Balasubramanyam, V.N. 92
banks: China 18, 36, 121; Japan 22, 27, 28
Bartlett, C.A. 69, 75
Beamish, P.W. 91
Beijing Auto 23, 58, 59
Belderbos, R. 16, 49, 91, 92, 93, 94, 95, 96, 97, 105, 106, 111

Berrill, J. 74, 76, 86
Bevan, A.A. 92
bias, challenging Western research see comparative analysis of expansion into Mainland China by JMNCs and KMNCs
Blomstrom, M. 92
Boisot, M. 19
Borensztein, E. 92
Bose, A. 99
'bottom of the pyramid' (BOP) lower income customers 31
Boyer, R. 65, 67
Bratton, J. 16
Braunerhjelm, P. 96
Brazil 20, 32, 38
Brimble, P. 95
Brunei 22
Buckley, P.J. 17, 45, 73, 91, 99

Cai, K.G. 17, 18
Campbell, N. 15
Canada 17, 20, 30, 58
capabilities 13–14, 16, 17, 18; CMNCs' internationalization 31–3; comparisons and contrasts: JMNCs and CMNCs 37–9; (implications and conclusions of survey) 40–1; JMNCs' internationalization 22–5
Carr, C. 94
Casillas, J. 74, 75
Cassidy, J.F. 90, 94, 95
chaebols 50, 122
Chakrabarti, A. 92, 93, 99
Chakraborty, C. 92
Chang, S.-J. 58, 59
Chang'an Motors 21, 23, 25
Changhe Motors 21, 23, 25
chemicals industry: JMNEs in India 105, 106, 108, 109, 110, 112
Chen, C. 93, 94, 95, 106, 108, 109
Cheng, S. 91, 94, 106, 111
Chetty, S. 73
Child, J. 17, 18

INDEX

China and CMNCs 1, 2, 109, 110, 112, 120, 121, 122–3, 123; comparative analysis of expansion into Mainland China by JMNCs and KMNCs *see separate entry*; comparison of JMNCs and CMNCs *see separate entry*; currency 65; literature review: rise of CMNCs 17–19
China Development Bank 18
China Export and Import Bank 18
China Hydro 32
China Wuyi 32
Chung Mong-koo 59
Chung, W. 90, 111
Cieślik, A. 92, 94
CNPC 29–30, 31, 34, 37, 39; production share agreement 30
Cold War 14
Collinson, S. 75, 92
Columbia Pictures 21
comparative analysis of expansion into Mainland China by JMNCs and KMNCs 8–9, 45–68; case studies 55; (Hyundai Motor) 47, 55, 58–9, 61–2, 63, 64; (Samsung Electronics) 47, 48, 55, 59–60, 61–3, 64; (Sony Corporation) 47, 48, 55, 60–2, 64, 65; (Toyota Motor) 47, 48, 55–8, 61–2, 63, 64; country-level overview analysis 52–5; discussion: (IPLC theory) 62–3, 65–6; (OLI paradigm) 63–4, 65–6; (similarities and differences between Japanese and Korean firms) 61–2; (Uppsala model) 64–5, 66, 67; implications 65–7; literature review 47–51; research methodology 51–2
comparison of JMNCs and CMNCs 5–7, 12–14, 122; CMNCs internationalization: (capabilities) 31–3; (corporate organization/structure) 33–4; (government support) 39–40; (motivation and strategy) 28–31; comparisons and contrasts: (capabilities) 37–9; (corporate organization/structure) 39; (government support) 39–40; (motivation and strategy) 36–7; implications and conclusion 40–1; JMNCs internationalization: (capabilities) 22–5; (corporate organization/structure) 25–7; (government support) 27–8; (motivation and strategy) 19–22; literature review: (rise of CMNCs) 17–19; (rise of JMNCs) 14–16; methodology 19
construction industry: China 19, 28–9, 31, 32, 33, 34, 37, 38, 39; CSCEC (China State Construction and Engineering Corporation) 28–9, 33, 37, 38
consumer goods: Japanese firms 74, 77, 81
consumer services: Japanese firms 74, 77, 81
Contractor, F.J. 74, 75
corporate organization/structure 13–14, 15–16, 18; CMNCs' internationalization 33–4; comparisons and contrasts: JMNCs and CMNCs 39; (implications and conclusions of survey) 40–1; JMNCs' internationalization 25–7, 62

Coughlin, C.C. 92
Cross, A.R. 16, 108
CSCEC (China State Construction and Engineering Corporation) 28–9, 33, 37, 38
Cusumano, M.A. 15
Czech Republic 21

Dai-ichi Kangyo Bank 22
Daiwa Securities 22
Das, D.K. 48
definition of MNC 47, 66
Delios, A. 16, 49, 50, 61, 86, 90, 92, 93, 98, 105, 108, 109
Deng, P. 17, 18
deregulation 22, 28, 109, 110
Dicken, P. 92, 119
Doner, R.F. 90
Doosan Corporation 55
Dore, R. 14
Doremus, P. 75
Dostal, P. 109
Dunning, J.H. 47, 62, 63, 64, 76, 92
Dyer, J.H. 97

East Asian model of MNC internationalization *see* comparative analysis of expansion into Mainland China by JMNCs and KMNCs
Eastern Europe 2, 20, 110
eclectic paradigm/ownership-location-internalization (OLI) model 47, 62, 63–4, 65–6, 121
Eisenhardt, K.M. 19
Electrolux 47
electronics industry: CMNCs 19, 20
electronics industry: JMNCs 19, 20, 21, 27, 37, 38, 48, 55, 123; Panasonic 4, 13, 21, 24, 48; Sanyo 21, 24, 26, 28, 36, 38; Sony 4, 13, 21, 24, 26, 38, 47, 48, 55, 60–2, 64, 65; subnational location choice of JMNEs in India 99, 102, 105, 106, 107, 108, 109, 110, 112
electronics industry: KMNCs 48, 52, 55; Samsung Electronics 47, 48, 55, 59–60, 61–3, 64, 122
Elger, T. 16
empirical study: internationalization patterns of Japanese firms 9–10, 73–87, 120; implications 85–6; industrial analysis 81–5; literature review 75–6; location of sales 77–80, 81, 85, 86, 87; location of subsidiaries 80–1, 85, 86, 87; methodology 76–85; non-service sector 74, 77, 85; regionalization/globalization 74, 75–6, 77, 80–1, 85–6, 87; service sector 74, 77, 85
Encarnation, D.J. 16
Enderwick, P. 93
Ericsson 60
Ernst, D. 90
Erramilli, M.K. 49
Errunza, V. 74
Ethiopia 31, 32
European Union/Community 2, 3–4, 20

INDEX

Farrell, R. 4, 5, 15, 27, 90
FAW Group Corporation 57
Fiat 35
Fillis, I. 73
Fitzgerald, R. 1, 2, 3, 4, 5, 14, 15, 21, 22, 36, 39, 46, 47, 62, 119
Florian, A. 16
Florida, R. 16
Ford 14, 23, 66
Ford, D. 48
Ford, S. 95, 96, 105
France 2, 21, 25
Fransman, M. 15
Friedman, J. 105
Fujita, M. 96
Fukao, K. 93, 94, 96, 111
Fung, K.C. 93, 105

GAC Group 57
Gamble, J. 59
gaming software 61
General Motors 4, 14, 20, 58
geographic information system (GIS) analysis 92, 97, 98, 102, 108, 111
Germany 2, 17, 21
Ghana 20
Glaum, M. 74, 75
globalization/regionalization debate 65, 74, 75–6, 77, 80–1, 85–6, 87
Goerzen, A. 50
government support 13–14, 17, 18–19, 59; CMNCs' internationalization 30, 34–6; comparisons and contrasts: JMNCs and CMNCs 39–40; (implications and conclusions of survey) 40–1; JMNCs' internationalization 14, 15, 27–8
Gree 30, 32, 37, 38
Griffiths, M.B. 62
Groot, L. 15
Guiheux, G. 90, 95
Guillén, M.F. 49

Haier 30, 37, 38, 39
Hamel, G. 13, 15
Harbin Power Equipment Corporation (HPEC) 34–5
Harzing, A.W. 15
Hasegawa, H. 16
Hatani, F. 96
Hatch, W. 15
Head, C.K. 93, 95, 96, 105, 111
Hemmert, M. 48, 49, 51, 61
Hennart, J.-F. 74, 75, 96
Hitachi 21–2
Hitt, M. 18
Hollensen, S. 47
Honda 13
Hong Kong 21, 30, 46, 64
Hood, N. 46

Horaguchi, H. 16
Horn, S.A. 91
Huawei 13, 29, 30–1, 32, 33, 34, 38, 39, 41, 62, 122
Hungary 20, 21, 24
Hymer, S.H. 45, 92
Hyundai 47, 55, 58–9, 61–2, 63, 64

IBM 15
import substitution policy 107
India 20, 21, 24, 29, 30, 38, 58, 123; Japanese production networks in 10, 90–113, 123
information technology (IT) industry: JMNEs in India 105, 106, 108, 109, 110, 112
INPEX Corporation 85
intellectual property 18, 19, 35; patents 62
international economy and MNC strategy 2–5
International Product Life Cycle Theory (IPLC Theory) 47, 62–3, 65–6, 121
Iraq 29, 30
isomorphic peer pressure 49, 50
Itagaki, H. 90
Italy 21
Itô, K. 94
Itochu 13
Iveco 35

Jackson, K. 51
Japan Bank for International Cooperation (JBIC) 28
Japan Export-Import Bank (JEXIM) 28
Japan External Trade Organization (JETRO) 27, 28, 96
Japanese MNCs 1–2, 3–4, 60, 119–20, 122–3, 124; comparative analysis of expansion into Mainland China by JMNCs and KMNCs *see separate entry*; comparison of JMNCs and CMNCs *see separate entry*; empirical investigation into internationalization patterns 9–10, 73–87, 120; FDI theory and Asia Pacific MNCs 121; literature review: (internationalization of Korean MNCs and JMNCs) 47–51; (internationalization patterns of Japanese firms) 75–6; (location behaviour of JMNEs) 92–3; (rise of JMNCs) 14–16; long-term evolution of 120–1; parent control 15–16, 26–7, 37, 38, 39, 50, 120–1, 122, 123; subnational location choice of JMNEs in India *see separate entry*
Johanson, J. 45, 47, 48, 50, 62, 64
joint ventures 3, 7, 47; CMNCs 17, 18, 29, 34, 35, 40; JMNCs 15–16, 20, 21, 23, 24, 37, 41, 50, 57, 61, 123; KMNCs 58, 59, 64; OLI paradigm 63
Jun, I.W. 1, 122, 123
Jung, J.C. 50
just-in-time (JIT): inventory management 48; production methods 95, 96

kaizen 48
Kawabe, N. 14

INDEX

Kazakhstan 29, 30, 39
Keizer, A.B. 94
Kenney, M. 16
Kenya 32
Kimura, F. 92
Kiyota, K. 90
Kojima, K. 15, 46, 51, 121
Korea and KMNCs 1, 13, 20, 121, 122, 123; comparative analysis of expansion into Mainland China by JMNCs and KMNCs see separate entry; literature review: internationalization of Japanese MNCs and KMNCs 47–51
Kuivalainen, O. 75
Kumar, N. 105
Kundu, S. 74
Kuwait 29

Lall, S. 95
lean production 16, 19
learning-by-doing 29, 36
Lechevalier, S. 65, 67
Lee, K. 59, 60
Lenovo 29, 39, 61, 62
Ietto-Gillies, G. 46, 47, 48, 62, 63, 64, 65
LG 32, 48, 60, 62
Liker, J.K. 48
Lincoln, J.R. 108
literature review: internationalization of Japanese MNCs and Korean MNCs 47–51; internationalization patterns of Japanese firms 75–6; location choice, subnational 92–3; rise of Chinese MNCs 16–19; rise of Japanese MNCs 14–16
location choice of JMNEs in India, subnational 10, 90–113, 123
longitudinal analysis: internationalization patterns of Japanese firms 9–10, 73–87, 120
low-income markets 31, 32
Lu, J. 16, 49
Luo, Y. 17, 18, 19

Ma, X. 91, 110
Macau 46
McGuire, J. 91, 108
machinery industry: JMNEs in India 99, 105, 106, 108, 109, 110, 112
Makino, S. 16, 50
Malaysia 30
Malhotra, N.K. 66
Markusen, J.R. 92
Marshall, A. 96
Marubeni 13, 66
Marukawa, T. 91
Maskin, E.S. 93
Mason, M. 14
Matsushita-Panasonic 21, 24
Mayer, T. 90, 97, 111
Meyer, K.E. 92, 96

MG Rover 17, 35, 36
Miles Fletcher, W., III 51
mimetic internationalization behaviour 49
Mitsubishi Bank 22
Mitsubishi Corporation 13, 14, 22, 25, 26–7, 28, 55
Mitsubishi UFJ Financial Group 22
Mitsui & Co 14, 22, 26, 28, 66
Mizuho Group 22
model of MNC internationalization, East Asian see comparative analysis of expansion into Mainland China by JMNCs and KMNCs
Mody, A. 90, 92, 94, 95
Morris, J. 16
motivation and strategy 13–14, 15, 16, 17, 18; CMNCs' internationalization 28–31; comparisons and contrasts: JMNCs and CMNCs 36–7; (implications and conclusions of survey) 40–1; JMNCs' internationalization 19–22

Nanjing Automobile Corporate (NAC) 35, 36
Nayak, A.K.J.R. 95, 99
Nguyen, K. 61
Nicholas, S. 92, 95
Nintendo 13
Nissan 13, 14, 20, 38, 77
Nolan, P. 18
Nopprach, S. 90
North America 76, 80, 86, 122; see also individual countries
Nunnenkamp, P. 92

Oceania 80, 86
OECD (Organisation for Economic Co-operation and Development) 47
Oh, S.-Y. 58, 59
O'Hagan-Luff, M. 74, 85–6
Ohmae, K. 48
oil industry/oil and gas 17, 19, 39; CNPC 29–30, 31, 34, 37, 39; empirical study: internationalization patterns of Japanese firms 74, 77, 81, 85, 87; production share agreement 30; Sakhalin oil pipeline 28
Oliver, N. 16
Omron 24, 26
organizational learning 14, 37, 38, 49, 124
Osegowitsch, T. 76
Ouchi, W.G. 48
ownership-location-internalization (OLI) model 47, 62, 63–4, 65–6, 121
Ozawa, T. 15, 51, 121

Pacific Metals 77
Pakistan 20, 21
Panagariya, A. 95, 108
Panasonic 4, 13, 21, 48; Matsushita- 21, 24
parent control 41, 122; CMNCs 16, 33–4, 39, 122; JMNCs 15–16, 26–7, 37, 38, 39, 50, 120–1, 122, 123

INDEX

Park, Y.R. 50
Peng, M.W. 46
Perlmutter, H. 75
Philippines 63
Pilling, D. 13
Porter, M.E. 48, 92, 97
Posner, M.V. 62
Prahalad, C.K. 13
price wars 19
privatization 2, 3
production networks, Japanese 4; in India 10, 90–113
Pudelko, M. 94

Quan, Y. 17
quotas and tariffs 3–4, 14, 15, 20, 121

regionalization/globalization debate 65, 74, 75–6, 77, 80–1, 85–6, 87
Ren, Z.F. 32
Renault 38
research bias, challenging Western *see* comparative analysis of expansion into Mainland China by JMNCs and KMNCs
research and development 4, 37, 38, 41, 49, 75, 120, 122, 123; Chinese firms 18–19, 29, 30, 31, 32–3, 34, 35, 37, 40; Huawei 30, 31; Nanjing Automobile Corporate (NAC) 35; Sanyo 24, 26; Sony 24; Toyota 23, 25
return on investment 58, 64
risk avoidance 49
Robson, C. 51
Rowley, C. 1, 4, 5, 48, 51, 119, 120, 122, 124
Rugman, A.M. 13, 17, 45–6, 66, 73, 74, 75–6, 86
Rui, H. 17, 18
Russia 29, 33

Sachwald, F. 15
SAIC 35, 36
Saka, A. 16
Sakakibara, M. 90
Sakhalin oil pipeline 28
Sako, M. 49
Samsung Electronics 47, 48, 55, 59–60, 61–3, 64, 122
Sanwa Bank 22
Sanyo 21, 24, 26, 28, 36, 38
Saunders, M.N.K. 51–2
Schaede, U. 28
Seki, M. 15
Sekiguchi, S. 15, 48
Shanghai Fuhua 29
Shanghai Oriental Pearl 61
Shell 30
short-termism 37
Siddharthan, N.S. 90
Singapore 38
Sinha, A. 96
small and medium-sized enterprises (SMEs) 28

Smith, D.F., Jr 95, 96, 97, 98
Solis, M. 27
Somlev, I.P. 90, 94, 105
Song, H. 66
Sony 4, 13, 21, 24, 26, 38, 47, 48, 55, 60–2, 64, 65
South Africa 20
South America 76, 80, 86
Spain 21
special economic zones (SEZs) in India 95–6, 98, 99, 107–8, 111
spill-over effects 96, 109
Stevens, M.J. 76
Stewart, P. 16
Strange, R. 15
strategic alliances 3, 14, 15, 34, 38, 41, 120, 122
strategy, international economy and MNC 2–5
strategy and motivation 13–14, 15, 16, 17, 18; CMNCs' internationalization 28–31; comparisons and contrasts: JMNCs and CMNCs 36–7; (implications and conclusions of survey) 40–1; JMNCs' internationalization 19–22
subnational location choice of JMNEs in India 10, 90–113, 123; agglomeration and manufacturing density 96–7, 108–9, 111–12; data analysis 99–103; discussion 103–10; geographic information system (GIS) analysis 92, 97, 98, 102, 108, 111; human capital 94–5, 105–6, 111, 112; implications 110–12; infrastructure 95–6, 107–8, 111, 112; labour costs 94, 105–6, 111, 112; literature review 92–3; market size and growth 93–4, 105, 111, 112; methodology 98–9; research questions 91; spatial analysis 109–10; special economic zones (SEZs) 95–6, 98, 99, 107–8, 111; theoretical framework and hypothesis development 93–7
Sudan 29–30, 34, 39
Sullivan, D. 75
Sumitomo Corporation 13, 22, 26
Suzuki 20–1, 23–4, 25, 26, 123

Taiwan 46, 60, 64
tariffs and quotas 3–4, 14, 15, 20, 121
Taylor, B. 16
technology cooperation 15
technology sector: Japanese firms 74, 77, 81, 85
telecommunications: CMNCs 19; Huawei 13, 29, 30–1, 32, 33, 34, 38, 39, 41, 62, 122
telecommunications: Japanese firms 77, 81
Thailand 20, 21, 91
Thiran, J.M. 93, 94, 95
Three Gorges Dam construction 34–5
Thurow, L.C. 15
Tokunaga, S. 94
Tolentino, P.E. 50
Tomiura, E. 90
Tong, X, G. 29

129

INDEX

Toray Industries 77
Toshiba 13, 14
Toyota 4, 13, 14, 19–20, 22–3, 25, 36, 38, 47, 48, 55–8, 61–2, 63, 64
transaction costs 49, 63
transport industry: JMNEs in India 99, 102, 107, 108, 110, 112
Trevor, M. 15, 16, 48
Turkey 58
Turnbull, P. 16

Udagawa, M. 14
United Arab Emirates (UAE) 38
United Kingdom 2, 17, 20; internationalization patterns of UK firms 85, 86; Sanyo 21; Sony 21
United States 2, 3–4, 14, 15, 17, 20, 22, 45, 46, 120, 121, 124; Haier 38; internationalization patterns of US firms 85–6; Japanese management methods 16; sanctions 29; Sanyo 21; Sony 21, 24, 26; Toyota 4, 56
Uppsala model 45, 47–8, 49, 62, 64–5, 66, 67, 121
Urata, S. 92, 94, 95, 105
utilities: Japanese firms 74, 77, 81, 85

Venezuela 29
Vernon, R. 46, 47, 62, 92
Vietnam 20, 21
Vogel, E. 14

Volkswagen 20, 58, 63
Volvo 17, 47, 66

Wakasugi, R. 91, 96, 111
Wang Tao 29
Wei, Y. 92, 106
Wells, L.T., Jr 96
Westney, D.E. 15
Wheeler, D. 96
wind power 32
Witt, M. 49
Womack, J.P. 16
Woodward, D.P. 94, 96, 97, 105
Wu, W.J. 18

Yahama Corporation 77
Yamashita, N. 62
Yamawaki, H. 92, 95, 97, 99
Yang, X. 13, 49
Yin, R. 19
Yoshida, Y. 90
Yusuf, S. 90

Zeng, Y. 50
Zhang, H. 63
Zhang, M. 17, 18
Zhejiang Geely Holding Group 66
Zhou, C. 93, 95, 96, 98, 105, 111
ZTE 29, 38